PRAISE

# Spirited: Taking Paganism Beyond the Circle

"An exciting new voice from a step beyond generation hex. In an account both practical and personal, Gede shares his experience and advice with young Witches and Pagans on the path, looking at the issues that the next generation faces. An excellent guide not only for those in that generation, but for those of us seeking to understand and deepen our relationship with them."

—Christopher Penczak, author of
*Sons of the Goddess* and *The Temple of High Witchcraft*

"A timely guide for young Pagans, Wiccans, and magicians! This is the real deal. Only a handful of 'teen' Craft books are written by teenagers themselves; luckily, this is one of them. *Spirited* is written in a realistic, intelligent, and spiritually inspired light, and will no doubt influence young seekers who wish to claim their power and self-awareness in this crazy paradigm we call 'reality.' Going beyond the glitz and glam of Witchcraft, and certainly beyond the '101,' Gede Parma compassionately approaches key issues for the growing number of young Witches and magicians. A noble and successful work that will undoubtedly help seekers for generations to come!"

—Raven Digitalis, author of
*Shadow Magick Compendium* and *Goth Craft*

"[A] thought-provoking exploration into the world of Magick and Paganism from a modern young adult's perspective. Impressive and insightful."

—Ellen Dugan, author of
*Natural Witchery* and *Elements of Witchcraft*

"[This] is one of those guides that will inspire an entire generation of young Pagans. *Spirited* covers a wide range of topics, but readers will most appreciate the delicate and humorous approach to social issues concerning young Pagans ... Parma writes with skillful compassion and recognizes the beautiful diversity of young Pagans living today. Ultimately, *Spirited* shines like a bright star in the sky with helpful new advice and practical how-to information."

—Gwinevere Rain, owner and editor of *Copper Moon* E-zine
and author of *SpellCraft for Teens, Moonbeams and Shooting Stars,*
and *Confessions of a Teenage Witch*

# SPIRITED

## About the Author

My name is Gede Parma. My craft name is Eilan (an Anglicised Scots-Gaelic word meaning "island"), and I am an initiated priest, Witch, and co-founder of the Mother Coven of the WildWood Tradition of Witchcraft in Brisbane, Australia: www.members.optusnet.com.au/wildwoodcoven. I have been consciously practicing Witchcraft for eight years but was raised in a highly spiritual and psychic home coloured by my father's Balinese Hindu tradition and my mother's deep understanding of life. I am of Balinese/Irish descent. I am a vegan. I am a member and seeker of the Church of All Worlds Australia, and I have presented workshops and lectures and facilitated rituals along with my coven at several Australian Pagan gatherings (Pagan Summer Gatherings and Ritual Experience Weekends). I am also a cartomancer and a palmist, and I read privately and at functions. I have been consulted several times for interviews regarding Pagan spirituality and Witchcraft (books, newspapers, and magazines, such as *Feelin' Witchy* by Mitchell Coombes and Dennis Ganchingco; *Confessions of a Teenage Witch* by Gwinevere Rain; *Toowoomba Mail*; and *Bizoo*), and I am keenly active in the southeast Queensland Pagan community. I am a feature writer for the Australian Pagan magazine *Spellcraft* (www.spellcraft.com.au) and am currently working on a guide about deepening one's Pagan spirituality through the ancient Celtic trinity of land, sky, and sea.

GEDE PARMA

# SPIRITED

TAKING PAGANISM
BEYOND THE CIRCLE

LLEWELLYN PUBLICATIONS
Woodbury, Minnesota

FIRST EDITION
First Printing, 2009

Book design by Donna Burch
Cover art © Paul Nichols/Digital Vision/PunchStock
Cover design by Ellen Dahl

Llewellyn is a registered trademark of Llewellyn Worldwide, Ltd.

Library of Congress Cataloging-in-Publication Data
Parma, Gede.
 Spirited : taking paganism beyond the circle / Gede Parma.—1st ed.
  p.  cm.
 Includes bibliographical references and index.
 ISBN 978-0-7387-1507-0
 1. Neopaganism. I. Title.
 BP605.N46P37 2009
 299′.94—dc22
                          2008048778

Llewellyn Worldwide does not participate in, endorse, or have any authority or responsibility concerning private business transactions between our authors and the public.

All mail addressed to the author is forwarded but the publisher cannot, unless specifically instructed by the author, give out an address or phone number.

Any Internet references contained in this work are current at publication time, but the publisher cannot guarantee that a specific location will continue to be maintained. Please refer to the publisher's website for links to authors' websites and other sources.

Llewellyn Publications
A Division of Llewellyn Worldwide, Ltd.
2143 Wooddale Drive, Dept. 978-0-7387-1507-0
Woodbury, MN 55125-2989, U.S.A.
www.llewellyn.com

Printed in the United States of America

*To Persephone~*
*you who are the light of the world's youth*
*and the depth of shadow that underlies our conviction.*
*This is for you, goddess of my heart and soul.*

## EDITOR'S NOTE

Readers may note that this book contains word spellings and phrasing unique to British English. These have been retained in order to honor the author's individual voice and spirit.

# CONTENTS

PART TWO

# BEYOND THE CIRCLE

## 8: Ritualising . . . 127

## 9: Divinity . . . 165

# Acknowledgments

First of all, I would like to thank the small but active Pagan community of Toowoomba, whose open arms and caring smiles helped me become the person I am today.

To Debbie for being a great friend. Our paths are truly blessed by one another.

To Aedan for inspiring the spellcraft chapter. Your late-night questions helped develop the foundation of what I believe is a very helpful chapter of this book.

To Jess for supporting me, taking time to chat, offering advice, and sharing experiences.

To all the *Bizoo* folk for giving me a place to sort out my thoughts and express my spirituality. And to *Spellcraft* magazine, who welcomed me with open arms.

To Kim, whose light burns brightly! And to James for your incisive grammatical endeavours and friendship.

To Mitchell for being a strong and kind, down-to-earth guy! And Dennis, who guided me in the right direction.

To Tala for listening and responding to my incessant questions. And De for your gentle courage.

To Brent and Jarrah, wonderful editors and great friends.

To Mum—you gave me space when I needed it most and trusted in my greater judgement with gracious patience. Thank you for being you!

To the Old Ones for your eternal love, understanding, wisdom, and inspiration—you helped me by showing me how to help myself.

To the Witches of Earthwyrm Coven, your example has inspired me to become more a part of the whole.

To my tribe of the Church of All Worlds Australia (one of my beloved families) for seeing the shine in youth and revelling in it.

To the gods and Coven of the WildWood, my heart and home. Blessings to Talaria, Anaseidr, Sabrem, Luna, Damionos, Awen, Moverin, Namanga, Arione, Amy, Ratna Devi, Nina Pixie, Millie, Joel, Harley, and to the countless other Witches who have graced our circles. May the WildWood flourish in our hearts and minds forever.

To Elysia, who urged me to succeed, and to Becky—you are an editorial goddess!

Last but not least, to all the young Pagans out there who live their spirituality and celebrate life. This book is for you.

# PREFACE

I will begin by highlighting that many sections of this book refer exclusively to the practice of Witchcraft, and thus the word *Witch* is used to address the subject matter. The majority of this book, however, refers to the "Generic Pagan," including all Pagans regardless of their tradition or beliefs. I have capitalised various words throughout this book (e.g., Magick and Nature) to indicate their importance in Pagan practice. I have also used the word *spirituality* wherever possible instead of *religion*, as I do not feel comfortable with the institutional and dogmatic connotations of the latter. The bonds (from the Latin *religare*) of the orthodox faiths constrict the free spirit that is the essence of the Pagan revolution. Spirituality serves the interests of those who seek to evolve and progress along their journey without adhering to erroneous precepts.

This book is a product of my experiences within the Pagan community,[1] my understanding and personal contemplation of the world around me (and the world within), and my interaction and relationships with others, both Pagan and non-Pagan, and how they have affected me along my journey. It also arises from my service to the gods and what I call the Great Mystery of Life.

I began creating the basic structure of this book several years ago, and the finished product that is before you now has undertaken numerous evolutions and transformations, which is a testimony to the power of Paganism in itself. We, as Pagans, are free to become anew, to transmute our energies and to actualise potential. We embody the law of change, which is universal. We are infused with the very spirit of the WildWood, the green, wild heart within all things and the namesake of and inspiration for my coven; may it flourish.

I began the journey with this book after having visited one of my favourite occult bookstores and leaving empty-handed because each book I looked at was the same repetitive drivel repackaged. This was further fired by the injustices I felt as a young Pagan within the wider community.

There is a tendency among the Pagan community when defining "fluffy bunny" to refer specifically to young people who develop an interest in Witchcraft and Paganism after having watched *The Craft* or *Charmed*. I know countless Pagans, young and old, who grew into Paganism after having seen such films and perhaps even experiencing a period of immature delusion; in fact, I was one of them. Am I a fluffy bunny because of it? Not that I know of. It is often these encounters with media representations that simply cause us to remember old patterns and rhythms we buried long ago. Regardless of the medium, it is an awakening to truth.

---

1 I consciously began practising Witchcraft in 2001; I self-dedicated and self-initiated to begin. In 2002, I received initiation into a teen Wicca coven, which disbanded that same year. From late 2002 onwards, I lived and celebrated as a solitary Witch until early 2006, when I co-founded the Coven of the WildWood, and a year and a day later, I was initiated as a priest of the coven. I am also consecrated to the goddess Persephone and to Lady Aphrodite.

Throughout the whole of this book, it has been my aim to provide a philosophical work for you to relate to and question, for it is when we question that we confront the triviality of habit and ultimately gain the courage to dispel it. It is assumed that you, the reader, are well versed in the intricacies of Pagan living and desire a mature presentation of the realities of Paganism in the modern world. For this reason, this book is divided into two parts.

Part One, *The Fountain of Youth,* deals with the intimacies of Pagan youth and the rainbow of experiences that they will encounter along the path. Part Two, *Beyond the Circle,* is about digging deeper into the realms of philosophy, gnosis, and elements of Pagan practice. It is about weaving a spiritual path of beauty that resonates true for you.

I sincerely hope that after you have read this book, you will have formed an opinion based on honesty, objectivity, and conviction, not only concerning the contents of this book but about your sense of the sacred itself. It has been my goal throughout the entirety of the writing process to connect with you and to provide food for thought. In no way is this book the "be all and end all." The book before you now is a compilation of notes, a reflection on experience and spiritual celebration. With that in mind, read on—and know that my words are simply the manifest form of a singular entity in a universal web of creative diversity. I am proud to be spirited.

—Khaire[2], *sláinte* & blessed be,

*Eilan/Gede*

---

2 *Khaire* is ancient Attic Greek for "hail" and is the root for our modern-day *charity*.

## Paganism in the Modern World

*Paganism*: the word is widely misunderstood in Western culture today. Once heard, it conjures images of animal sacrifice, orgiastic rites, infanticide, fire, and other hellish imagery. Yet can these perpetual themes be trusted as true representations of the Pagan traditions?

NeoPaganism, meaning "new Paganism," is an umbrella term defining many faiths, traditions, sects, and religions in the world today. Though not all traditions categorised as Pagan will feel kindly towards the term, the word has evolved and arisen from the historical implications attached to it during the rise of Christianity in Europe and has become a term of personalised spiritual endearment for hundreds upon thousands of modern-day seekers.

For Pagans today, the word is a symbol of freedom, individuality, ancestral reverence, and ancient lore. It no longer implies a rustic or country-dwelling farmer, nor does it hint at Godless heathens. Paganism is a growing, vibrant, and living group of traditions. It often falls short of the acceptance extended to other world religions; however, much has happened recently in the way of educating the public on our practices and beliefs.

Historians and scholars often scrutinise the NeoPagan faiths (especially modern Wicca and Witchcraft) as loose traditions with no link to the past and no relevance to the present. Countless articles and essays written on the subject highlight the opinions that Witchcraft as it is today is a sham, a poor attempt at revival, though a common underlying theme for these arguments is the definition of Witchcraft given by modern Witches themselves and its implied synonymity with Wicca. Despite the cultural importance of things such as linearity and authenticity in Western society, NeoPaganism is a revolutionary spiritual philosophy that seeks to create, adapt, and develop by the law of change—*"Panta rhei, ouden menei"*[1]—*Everything flows, nothing is static.*

Wicca is by no means synonymous with the practice of Witchcraft as it is and as it was; it is a Pagan religious tradition. The longer people persist with this idea, the more scrutiny Wicca and Witchcraft will be subjected to. Wicca in its traditional form is a religion built on what is known of Celtic-Pagan lore, Egyptian and Qabalistic systems, Eastern spiritual ethics, and the ceremonial and hermetic rituals of the late nineteenth- and twentieth-century occult fraternities. Witchcraft belongs to no particular culture or religion, neither in a historical nor modern perspective. Witchcraft is essentially the practice of sorcery and magick.[2] Often this can fall into religious and cultural contexts, but at its base level it is working with the natural energies of life and of the self to achieve certain goals and desires whilst maintaining a strong relationship with the cosmos.

Many Wiccans of various traditions have made the unfortunate mistake of claiming that the form of Wicca practiced today is an exact revival (or "survival") of pre-Christian British Paganism. Though

---

1 Heraclitus of Ephesus.

2 I spell magick with a *k* simply out of habit, though I also find it useful in differentiating between stage-show sleight-of-hand and the magick that Pagans and Witches talk of.

aspects of Wicca reflect the philosophies and concepts experienced in Celtic spirituality, Wicca is not a complete revival of the ancient British traditions, as it draws on a number of cultural and spiritual wellsprings simultaneously, as discussed above.

Witchcraft is a universal concept that surpasses all cultural boundaries and limitations. It is the shamanic journey experienced by the Inuit medicine man. It is the spiritual healing of the Balinese *balian*.[3] It is the craft and life path of the modern Pagan Witch. Witchcraft is not a static, unchanging, rigid tradition; it is forever growing, evolving, and moulding to suit the practitioners of today. Witchcraft is as valid as it ever was, and obviously it has made a lasting impression.

Paganism is a rapidly growing spirituality in the Western world. The United Kingdom, the United States of America, and Australia have all experienced a swelling growth of Pagan adherents among their populations. More and more people are reclaiming their right of individuality and seeking a spiritual identity that will allow for the nurturing and fostering of the Self as a progressive being of power. The environmental damage inflicted upon this earth has stirred many people's minds and has encouraged more eco-friendly attitudes. The sometimes rigid, hierarchical, and controlling aspects of the orthodox faiths (i.e., Christianity and Islam) have led many seekers to the ancient traditions of both the East and the West. The discrimination against indigenous peoples and women has exposed the flaws and injustices of our societies and has caused many people to reconsider their attitudes towards conservative policies.

In such a time of change, unrest, and revolution, many of us have returned to Nature in order to experience the wisdom, beauty, and honesty that is so raw and explicit in the natural world. Pagans honour and value the seasonal shifts, the lunar phases, and the transformations from seed to tree as pure acts of Life. These processes and rhythms have remained unchanged since the dawn of existence. Our reverence for these cycles and for the earth that supports them is ancient in and

---

3 A balian is a village priest, or medicine man, working within the Balinese Hindu tradition. His work is decidedly magickal.

of itself. Every moment we breathe, we are breathing the air of the ancients. As we look towards the full moon in all her glory, we feel the same awe as people did millennia ago. As our bodies change and grow from child to adult, we experience the same fears, anxieties, and hopes as those who have gone before us. And as we understand that time is not the linear construct we have been pressured to live by, our spirits marvel as the earth continues her movements, passages, and cycles in intricate grace.

Paganism in the world today is not built on the relevance and consistence of belief but rather on the depth and humanity of our growth and life on earth. Though our civilisations have changed, our communications have improved, and our day-to-day survival is easier, we are still human and still spiritual beings with the need to express ourselves emotionally and creatively.

Paganism is not a spirituality founded on the preaching of commandments. It is the spiritual living and understanding of the natural, essential, and raw energies within this world. As Pagans today, we have a responsibility towards the earth, our mother and teacher. We have a charge to defend justice and equality. We are inspired to bring the ancient lore into a modern world.

Modern Pagans have come to understand that though our experiences on this earth vary incredibly from those of the ancients, our vision and inner energy remains a common blueprint coursing along an unhindered cycle. As globalisation, political greed, war, and famine slowly destroy the earth, who has so willingly provided for us, our positive relationship with the natural world has never been more urgent. As we push our trolleys along the orderly rows of mass-produced, genetically engineered foods and products, we are subjected almost unwillingly to the undeniable and harsh truths of today's industry.

The way of our ancestors—the hunters and gatherers, the nomads and herders—are now faint memories held within dog-eared textbooks. As our societies have changed and we have become more and more accustomed to the luxuries so plain in our lives, it may seem more than a little impossible to resurrect the archaic tribal traditions of the past. But this is not necessarily the aim of the modern Pagan.

Each of us is born into this world with the gift of free will and the seed of Magick sewn into the very fabric of our being. The potential and ability to effect change, to stimulate growth, and to create art is innate within each of us. These gifts are the cornerstones of Magick— the threads of a divine tapestry. As Pagans, our ultimate goal is to strive for balance and wholeness. To achieve these things, we cannot simply believe that all in existence is inherently "good" and "right"—we must also honour the dark in life.

As Pagans, we reject the dualistic view of the world; therefore, the belief in absolute sources of power for "good" and "evil" are alien to us. The black-and-white philosophy is far too simplistic for the intricacies and complexities of life. To give specific colour to something that is by nature a rainbow is to diminish the opportunity to experience all that life has to show us.

To Pagans, life is eternal. It is an ongoing cycle tied to the passages of birth and death. We are urged to speculate and to question the mysteries of this universe so that in turn we may learn, grow, and evolve. Life is a journey—an active path of choice and challenge. To live passively and to hand over the reins of power to Fate is to turn your back on all that the future has to offer you.

Life is a two-part system. It is an empty vessel with the strength and construct to deliver you across the wide and never-ending ocean. Without you to steer, to direct, and to intend the course of the vessel, life will be an inevitably unchanging, repetitive, and meaningless existence. As Pagans, we need to acknowledge and harness the inner power we all have. We need to assure ourselves of our ability to change, to make life, and to destroy what no longer serves us. We are beings that are fuelled by primal emotion and passion. Our lives are blank canvasses, and our intent is the brush. Seize your potential, give it life, and bring it into the world. For a Pagan in the twenty-first century, there is much to know and much to do ...

## Youth and Paganism

*We do not inherit the earth from our parents,*
*We borrow it from our children.*

—Antoine de Saint-Exupéry

The word *Paganism* has already been discussed above, but what of its relation to youth? Is there a place for the young in the Paganism of today?

Paganism has never been more accessible to the young people of the modern world. Amidst passing trends and superficial phases, there is something real stirring in the youth of today. More and more of us are beginning to realise that *we* are the future—that our opinions will help shape the world of tomorrow. It is our legacy that we are born with the free will to do so.

Look around you now. What do you see? Are you in your room, your living room, by your computer, or maybe even outside? Now try to get out of your own head. Strip yourself of your preconceived notions. From an outsider's view, can you tell what is important to you simply by noting where you are or what surrounds you? How do you know what is important to you? Now return your attention back to this book. What are you reading? A book on the Paganism of the youth, right? A book written by a youth not unlike yourself who just so happens to live a life that respects the individual and the wider concepts of Nature and the Universe. Now can you guess—by reading what is written before you—what makes me tick? It is this similarity between you and me that I believe can make a difference. It is my sense of spirituality and my coincidental age that just so happened to bring us together. It is this very connection between us now that is both sacred and beautiful.

I am a Pagan youth. I do not deny that soon I shall enter the ranks of adulthood, at least numerically, and be expected to take full charge of my own destiny. However, I started a tad ahead of my time. Writing this book is, in fact, a piece of the destiny that awaits me in the future— a step further to what lies ahead. I believe that you too have the power and potential to discover your own destiny and to consciously walk your path. As Mahatma Gandhi once said, "Be the change you want to see in the world." What he meant by that is that we cannot simply stand aside in the face of adversity. We do not have to submit to the harsh realities of this day. If you see something wrong with the world, do not complain about it: change it! You might argue that no one will listen to you because you are young, and that is just one of the many injustices that we have the chance to object to. Change must start within. In order to truly affect the world around us, we must first begin with ourselves. Understanding that we are the catalysts for change itself is one of the most essential lessons.

"Pagan" is not a label that we wear but a name we give to our very essence. Calling oneself Pagan does not narrow your experiences, it breaks down the outworn barriers that keep your emotions pent up inside. It helps to confront the inner anxieties and fears we all have and releases frustration and anger. Paganism is a spirituality based on respect, action, and energy.

The active principle of the Pagan traditions is one of the key attributes that separates us from most organised religions. Pagans are encouraged to experience, to learn, to evolve, and to speculate within our own belief system in order to stimulate a personal rapport with the divine. Our faith is not built on clergy and priests who deliver sermons and preach the word of a transcendent God; Paganism is connected to the raw, essential, and intuitive faculties of humanity. It is not blind or submissive faith; our faith is instinctual and evolving. Pagan faith does not lie in false hope or submission to a higher power but in community and in Nature. Paganism is forever changing and adapting to suit the practitioners of today.

Time is a concept that we have shackled and constrained into the mere forms of wristwatches. In truth, Time is unruly, ravenous, and militant. Like Death, it waits patiently, forever weaving upon a spinning loom. Age is Time's daughter, and she comes to all those who live and die. Youth is revered and relished. It is the fresh, effervescent spirit of Time—the kind generosity served to all. Yet society encourages Youth to grow older, faster. Yes, we must all grow older, gracefully and honestly; there is no denying that fact. And there is no denying that responsibility helps young people mature and develop into respectable beings.

But Youth is not a physical passage; it does not disappear when we hit thirty. Youth is eternal. Youth is in thought, in action, in sound, and in spirit. Youth is not naïvety, childishness, or immaturity. Youth is inspirational, flowing, experiential, and cultivated. Youth is here and now; it is in these words before you, in the sacrificing of my humility to record my thoughts, philosophy, and spirituality on paper. Youth is forever embedded in the depths of Life's essence.

Gerald Brousseau Gardner (1884–1964) is believed to be the father of modern Wicca and one of the instigators of the renaissance of European Paganism. Part of what he believed as his inherent duty to the Craft was to secure its place in the future as an accessible spirituality and for its traditions to be embraced by the new generation, the youth, so that Witchcraft and its ancient lore would not perish into obscurity. It seems many contemporary Pagans forget or minimise Gardner's great deed to us and are content to think that younger people who approach Pagan spirituality are fluffy morons seeking fantastical powers. This is an unfortunate situation, as the youth are those who will herald the Craft into the future and who will continue to practise the old ways and customs in a modern world of technology and globalisation. The future remains unclear, forever lingering on the horizon where dreams and desires are born into reality.

Like most things in Paganism, the young Pagan is an eternal paradox built into the very matrix of Pagan culture. Being a young Pagan in this world does not imply we are less versed in our lore and practices than older Pagans, nor does it suggest we are less experienced or of lesser value. A young Pagan is devoted, innovative, unique, and spirited, and it is the latter quality that this book is named for.

PART ONE

# THE FOUNTAIN OF YOUTH

# 1: THE INNER WITCH

## A WITCH'S BECOMING

A commonly asked question from the curious towards many Witches today is "Can you become a Witch or do you have to be born one?"

My response to this is unconventional in that I have built up support from various esoteric philosophies and personal revelations to conclude that, to some degree, magickal ability must be a natural predisposition for someone to practice Witchcraft. However, I also acknowledge that all humans have the potential to wield power within them.

Every culture in the world originally sympathised with a form of shamanic worship, or spirituality, in which the spirit worlds and the human planes could be connected through the concentration of the mind and the use of special plants and aromas to obtain occult, or "secret," information, usually for the betterment of the community. So therefore, in truth, each and every one of us has a family history of some version of Witchcraft. Thus, this ties into the Voudoun belief that every human is born of Magick. This means that each soul brought forth on this earth bears the ability to harness the energies within and without them for their own use. Whether we choose to honour this advantage or not is something of a personal decision. To have the potential and therefore the ability to "become" a Witch is to simply be born with a creative energy. In essence, the life path of Witchcraft is cultivated by all who seek to express, not through overt logic or reasoning, but through those actions and suggestions that are so vividly human we often mistake them for primitive activities. Dance, song, poetry, and music are all creative self-expressions. These crafts form the nature of Witchcraft and are often employed in ritual to raise energy.

It is said that we each have an individual gift. The so-called gifts that are apparent in almost every human today are, in my belief, forms of Witchcraft and Magick—and in fact, one of the more obscure definitions of Witchcraft implies expertise in a certain area, supernatural or not.

Witchcraft is a system of working with and understanding Magick, and Magick is the essential flow of life's energy. When we are creative, we are honing in on the flow of life's energy and using it to fashion, form, and express our innermost desires and needs. With this skill, we are able to evoke a plethora of emotions and change an entire perspective simply through rhythmic breathing. This is true and genuine Witchcraft: the ability to make ourselves feel what we wish ourselves to feel. The ability to seemingly create life from nothing. The ability to invoke the spirit through the simplest of gestures.

Today, after centuries of oppression and a gradual growth in favouritism towards conventional science and matters of "logic," the fields of creative expression and artistry have faded into childish recreations and hobbies. Western society has sought to emulate this in matters of family and community values, raising their children to outgrow games of visualisation and imagination at a young age and forcing them to grow up faster. However, our society's belief in nurturing and protecting a child's innocence has balanced this factor out, and so the belief in such characters as the Tooth Fairy and Santa Claus has become widespread.

However, the children of today and past generations have grown into a conformist world where we must belong to the alpha group or be ridiculed and ostracised because of differences of opinion and unconventional traits. In a way, this has often destroyed the morale of the spirit of individualism to such an extent that those who do, in truth, have varied beliefs and philosophies shy away and adopt the guise of the social sheep, simultaneously ignoring the validity and political right to express themselves freely.

The Witch embraces social diversity and is the very archetype of secrecy, anarchy, and emotive extremity. The Witch questions what is evidently backward and suppressive while upholding change and transformation as successful pathways leading to genuine self-discovery. It is the Witch who rejects fear in the name of curiosity and thus opens the door to the world of Magick, which is the underlying resonance residing in all things.

Witches are the inheritors of an ancient skill that unites the wilful force of the conscious mind with the subliminal realities of the unconscious. Witches are the weavers of fate itself, and for this reason our knowledge is eternally bound to humanity's prevalence on earth.

## THE NATURAL WITCH

"Witches are born, not made" is a statement that bears some attention. The philosophy and reasoning behind this statement are as follows: being born a Witch does not mean you must have come from a family of Witches. Its basic meaning is that those who will "become" Witches were Witches all along. The process of becoming a Witch is actually one of realisation and revelation. At the end of the road, you will have come to realise you have just walked a circle and come to the same place you had initially begun. However, the time in which it took to walk that circle has evidently changed the face and feeling of the beginning cycle, and now an entirely new experience is unfolded.

Our existence as Witches is a paradox in this globalised and industrialised world. We are the nonconforming cogs of the social automaton and therefore spin off to create our own personal validations for our existence. As Witches, we fight for our independence and right to freely express publicly or otherwise who we are without having to live in shame or remorse. We should not have to fear losing our friends or being cast away from our homes because of who we are. This is our home just as much as it is anyone else's, and we demand our right to live here, in equal standing with all life forms. As Witches and Pagans, we seek to highlight this system of cooperation and living. We are living beings, as are all things that breathe, consume, excrete, adapt, and so on. There are no standards of living apart from those introduced by the feudal systems of caste imposition.

In a world that has gradually fallen to political shouting games, war and destruction are imminent, and because of this there is a kind of destiny that seems to work its way into the potential lives of humanity, the voices of the earth. There will always be those who wish only to live and let live and to be the force that will allow for true democracy to continue. Consider the greatest and most renowned historical and spiritual figures—Gandhi, the Dalai Lama, Jesus Christ. These individuals are celebrated and even deified by their respective followers because of their nonviolent teachings, their peaceful stature, and their infinite compassion towards others. It was the Dalai Lama of Tibet who said "my religion is kindness" and Christ who instructed his followers to "love thy neighbour." And not unlike Gandhi, Pagans and Witches also actively incorporate the principles of peace and love into their spiritual paths in order to cultivate a positive reality.

Witches are born into families of any description, but from an early age we will all bear a keen curiosity for those things termed *supernatural*. We will often hold on to our childlike longings and dreams, ignoring the constant nagging to grow into "maturity." Whether those who are born to be Witches and Pagans are born into families that preach extremist views on religion or not, there will always be that persistent hole inside of us that yearns for attention and desires fulfilment. Fate then brings us to realisation and, as they say, we come home.

## MY MAGICKAL GENEALOGY

It has only been quite recently that I have fully accepted the concept of "Witch blood," or the inheritance of the power/gift from biological ancestors. I have always known that my father's family is deeply reverent, steeped in the animistic mysticism of Bali, where they still live. My late grandmother was noted in her village as a skilled healer and holy woman and consulted as a priestess, for lack of a better term. My mother has told me stories of members of our extended family falling ill after a rather intense possession (this tends to happen a lot in Bali) and then seeking refuge with my grandmother, who would nurse them back to good health. My grandmother had the gift of divination through the oracle of dice and was a spontaneous medium, as spirits would enter her at any given time (a predisposition that is now manifest within me and was evident within my sister when she was younger). My mother relayed to me the time of the blessing of my father's newly built temple. My grandmother had been carrying a tiger's skin to bless it, and as she walked, her behaviour began to change into that of a tiger. She dropped what she was carrying and fell to the ground, clawing and snarling at those gathered around her. Similarly, in the past few years I too have been filled by spirits, presences, and even gods without consciously having anything to do with it. I have found myself thrashing around the circle and channelling power that has nothing to do with my mortal frame. Also, like my late grandmother, I exhibit talents in the area of divination, specifically relating to the Tarot and palm reading.

My father is what I would call a lay priest. He serves no congregation, only his gods and his family. He is a devout Hindu practitioner and speaks of his encounters with extraterrestrials, the fair folk, levitation, and all things mystical. My mother's family is another story altogether.

My mum has six siblings, of which she is the youngest, making her the seventh child (a number steeped in various folkloric associations). Her sisters are involved in professions that relate to either healing (in the form of nursing) or that of teaching—concepts that appear within the traditions of the Craft. My mother, while claiming no special gifts, is quite empathic and perceptive. Her late father despised churchgoing and Sunday school, and in one photograph taken with his class, he is the only one scowling at the camera.

Peter Farquharson, my grandfather, owned a chicken farm, where my mum's family grew up. Peter employed dowsers to search for water on the property and invited the bushmen, called "swaggies," to stay at the house. He also spoke to the gypsies, known to everyone else as vagrants, who confided to him stories of stealing chickens for food from other farms. They never touched his. He was a very Pagan character. I have since learned that his family, despite the prominent Scottish surname, was mostly Irish, whose ancestors, perhaps, resided at Goath Dobhair (Gweedore) in northwest Ireland, County Donegal. His aunt also happened to be the famous Sister Elizabeth Kenny, who is world-renowned for her treatment of polio and her many Kenny Clinics in Australia and the United States. She was a remarkable and strong-willed woman who went against the traditional establishment and who earned many honours in her name, being one of the few to be granted freedom of passage to and from the United States. In her earlier days, she was called a bush nurse and was versed in midwifery and healing various injuries and ailments. She was said to be a tomboy who loved nature and horse riding. She was also seen by many to be a miracle worker, whose healing power was more than just a skill acquired by practical physical means.

I do believe that this rich heritage has endowed within me some special affinity with the forces of the natural world, and I do recognise that genetics can add to and even shape the various qualities of an individual—perhaps even metaphysical qualities.

*Blood Witch*—it's a term that the NeoPagan community has rejected, and spitefully so, although the movement permits the words *otherkin*, *dragon*, *faerie*, and (shock, horror) *Magick*, which any other communal sphere on this planet would deride with a high level of scepticism. What is it that other Witches and Pagans find so blasphemous concerning the concept of genetic Witchcraft? Is it rooted in the fact that Gerald Gardner was attacked by people purporting that his Wicca was nothing like the traditional Craft which flourished in various places in Europe? Or was it that many Pagans found their way to the gentle earth rhythms of the Craft via ceremonial rituals stemming from various occult fraternities who taught that Magick was an art of discipline, and by no other means was it possible to attain mastery over it? Or could it be the simple fact that many believe the Pagan faiths to be open to all and sundry, that all who accept the long-kept wisdom of the Old Ones will feel within an awakening of latent power? It is true that any one individual has the ability to channel universal energy; however, are there not those who are of greater skill and who more naturally apply it in their lives? Why is it such a stretch of the imagination to conceive of these naturally inclined Witches as perhaps being heirs to a magickal lineage of power flowing through the blood? I feel that power comes from both blood and spirit (breath), hence the validity of both the blood and the spiritual Witch. But when both power sources are united and acknowledged as complementary and integral to the other, the true Witch is born—one whose Magick arises from the call of the spirit and is infused by the rushing of the blood.

The following is the true account of how I came to discover the path of Witchcraft and how it imbued my life with meaning.

## Childhood

As a child, I was "different." Although most of my male peers were into rough games and sports, I was never comfortable with such mannerisms, and as such I formed friendships with girls most of the time. I found myself playing softer and gentler games with my friends, involving imagination and visualisation.

On my own, I created worlds in which my *other* friends would dwell. Every day after school, my insides would squirm with excitement as I knew I was about to enter my worlds—worlds where I would go on extravagant adventures and meet amazing people.

I truly felt emotion when I was there. When my lengthy adventures came to their climax and I was just about to defeat the dark creature that had been enslaving my friends, I felt courage storm in my heart, and at times I would cry out in sadness when these adventures ended. Throughout my primary education, these games played a major part in coping with growing up. I clung to my love of imagination and these envisioned places where I was special and important.

With my games in the garden, I grew to appreciate the natural world, and the roots of trees would often provide refuge to sit and ponder. From an early age, I also had a keen interest in wildlife, and early school reports revealed that my artwork often reflected the natural world.

As I look back on these experiences now, I can see these worlds as being real places on some level of existence—places I could find refuge in and fashioned through my will.

Alongside this, I would also do what I would now call inspired singing. I would break out in chains of words that allowed me to sink into a peaceful and receptive state, much like the feeling of introspection and reflection I have nowadays as a Witch. My songs came from inside of me and were not of any particular style. They were words spoken of life, the subtle existence that I had. Often they were tainted with sadness, as though something was missing and I needed it back.

As I grew older, I began to take to books, and the library became a second home. I often sat down to read about other countries, and what interested me the most were the sections on culture and tradition. I loved the diversity and beauty of the world's religions, and with this interest safely contained, I was a step closer to my home.

I was eleven when the onslaught of Witches in the media hit me, and it just so happened that I stumbled upon an early *Charmed* episode. After my first taste of Hollywood Witchcraft, I became utterly absorbed into the fantasy of it all. The influence of the show grew on me, and I began to romanticise the personages of the warlocks within the show, dubbing myself a warlock. Having no idea what the term actually meant, I "outed" myself to everyone at school, and most viewed me as eccentric or just plain weird. While my friends and I played at school, I would chant little rhymes that wrought influence on the mundane, and at home I would mix plants and cleaning liquids in jars by my favourite log and use them for magickal purposes.

Towards the end of the year, a Taiwanese student living with us took my family and me to a Christmas function (she was a newly converted Christian), and by the end of the night I had renounced my ways. After this, I announced to my friends at school that I was no longer a warlock, and so I came to a void again. My interest in Witchcraft never died, though; it simply remained idle deep within me.

By age twelve, I took up a speciality class focused on writing and delivering speeches. By the end of the term, I had completed my planned speech on Witches, based on information I had compiled from a book my mum owned—*Into the Unknown* by Reader's Digest. When it was my turn, I gave a very entertaining performance involving a dead lizard within a jar, plastic frogs I threw at the audience, and a clay cat and broomstick to demonstrate a Witch's flying habits. I managed to obtain the highest mark in the class.

There was one boy in my class who I had talked to whilst writing my speech. He had told me at one stage that he didn't believe in good and evil, and it was because of his religious persuasion. I asked him which religion he followed, and after a while of prying he confessed he was Wiccan. At the time, I had no idea what it was or that it was even connected to Magick and Witchcraft.

In the summer holidays that enjoined the years 2000 and 2001, I met with my destiny. I was at a shopping centre with my mum when I walked idly past a bookstore, and out of the corner of my eye the word *Wicca* became the focus of my entire vision. The word itself seemed to be jumping from the shelf, screaming for my attention. My initial thought at the time was only of affirming that my classmate was telling the truth, and that the word *Wicca* was not of his own invention.

For once in my life, I felt as if all the loose pieces of the puzzle had come together and formed a picture. I felt secure at the same time as feeling anticipation for the path unravelling before me.

There is no turning back along a path that is a circle. The Witch's path is a wild way, and it takes great courage to walk it and to continue to walk even if your mind tells you to turn back. It is the way of the heart and of the instinct. It is the way of Magick.

## The Awakening

Perhaps a Witch's becoming can best be explained through an analogy. In this case, I shall speak of an awakening. There are a series of passages I go through before I am fully alert and awake: stirring, yawning, and stretching. These stages relate to various levels of the awakening to the reality of being a Witch along with various stories I have collected from other young Witches at various stages of their revelations.

### To Stir: The Foundations of Curiosity

By opening this book, you have performed the first step. Curiosity may come from several places. Maybe you were at the public library, innocently surveying the shelves, until you came across the occult section and found an array of books on Witchcraft. Maybe you have always held a taste for fantasy since you were a child and now wish to resurrect those feelings. Curiosity marks the beginning of most journeys. Would Alice ever have gone down the rabbit hole if it weren't for her curiosity for the hurried white rabbit? So with your curiosity, you are stirring from your sleep. You feel something calling you, yet a more logical part of your brain is urging you to continue to sleep. But what are you missing out on in the world? What is happening without you being there? Thus, more and more, this curiosity encourages you to open a sleepy eye.

Hannah (twenty) is a Witch, a dedicant of the WildWood, and a daughter of the Old Ones. Her Craft/spirit name is Arione, which is the name of an ancient Greek winged horse—child of Demeter and Poseidon. She is of Friesian descent[1] and proudly claims her heritage.

> *My name is Hannah and also Arione. It's only in the past six months that I have taken active steps down the path of Paganism; however, I've been aware of and experienced Magick in my life for many years. Having grown up travelling through the Australian outback, I've always had a deep respect for Nature and the undercurrent of life/Magick pres-*

---

1 Also spelled Friesland, Fryslan is a province in the modern-day Netherlands, where the Friesian people are a distinct ethnic group. Frysland—the land of Freya.

ent in everything. I was lucky to have many amazing spiritual people in my life, giving me many glimpses into this undercurrent. Also, the acceptance and love of my parents gave me the freedom to explore this world fully.

I grew up quite wild, roaming the forests around my childhood home on foot and on horseback. As a child, I would sit by the flooded creek, watching how quickly the water rose. I'd stand on the water tank before a storm, feeling the electricity in the air, waiting for the rush of wind before the storm. I tracked the phases of the moon through my bedroom window, and I would wish for Magick on the first star almost every night. It wasn't until a few years later that I realised it had always been there.

When I was about ten years old, I went for a walk with a family friend, an herbalist and healer. We sat by the creek, and she told me about her travels in India. I heard the Magick in her stories, and I began to look for it in the world around me. Eventually I began to read books, some fiction, some not, and I learnt more about Nature, about the season and the patterns of the undercurrent. I also learnt about the ancient traditions that honoured and revered these things.

In 2007, I was in the Netherlands, the homeland of my ancestors. Despite the years of Christian influence, the Pagan traditions of the old people were still present in hundreds of tiny ways. At the end of spring, all of the farmhouses lit their summer fires. The lights could be seen for kilometres around. I realised I had come to a point in my life where I wanted and needed to walk towards the path of my ancestors.

Nearly six months later, back in Australia, I finally sought out a coven to celebrate and share my spirituality with. Since then, I have found immeasurable joy, love, and Magick. My path is well lit around me and soft beneath my feet. It stretches out impossibly far in front of me, and I will follow it as far as it will take me.

## To Yawn: Raw Desire

Desire is one of the most essential emotions there is, and it represents the things in life we are instinctively drawn to. These have come to be classed as sins in some of the major religions, especially the Abrahamic faiths. Desire can often lead to corruption, and thus many spiritual ascetics (e.g., Buddhists and Christian monks) attempt to strip themselves of worldly possessions and earthly desires in order to lead "pure" lives.

Paganism does not share the same perspective on desire. In terms of Magick, desire is a powerful fuel that helps direct and focus our intent and energy. It is said that a spell backed up by desire is the most powerful. To ensure our spells will work, we need to get involved in the Magick; thus, desire is one of the most powerful catalysts in the Craft.

I have often said that to be a Witch, all you need to do is simply to desire it. Once we are certain of our innate interest in the Craft and in Magick, we begin to desire. However, life was never meant to be easy, and although the Craft can help infuse our lives with meaning, it does not mean we are above anyone else. We encounter the same problems, we feel the same heartache, and we experience life's ups and downs, although we may deal with these problems differently than others. Even the highly exaggerated programs like *Charmed* and *Sabrina* reveal that the main characters deal with mundane problems while simultaneously saving the world from oblivion. This sacred limbo is the reality of the Witch: while surrounded with problems of unemployment and school, we are simultaneously in awe of the power of a ritual.

Yawning corresponds to desire. We breathe in the scents and dusts of a new morning in hopes that on some level, this day will change us for the rest of our lives.

James is a nineteen-year-old Witch, a devotee of Rhiannon and Freya, and an initiate, priest, and co-founder of the Coven of the WildWood.

*I have found that the desire to follow the Craft comes from deep within. For many Witches or Pagans, this yearning was always present, perhaps only realised at an age when the notion of spirituality became less ambiguous. For me, there was a sense of "homeyness" in all that I found within the Pagan community.*

*It is difficult now to put words to feelings experienced years ago, almost as hard as pinpointing a specific time when these things occurred. If I were required to consider a general time, I would say that I was eight or nine. While I feel that I have always been a Witch and Pagan (spirit and blood aside, I recently watched a video of me as a toddler chattering about the gods), the time when I felt drawn to naming it was a very significant time for me. Around then I felt a stronger connection to the world around me, suddenly becoming conscious of everything, becoming a vegetarian. My personal connection with the earth and everything deepened and brightened, and I suddenly felt the need to name my path. It was a few years later when I embraced the word "Witch."*

*As could only be expected of a boy of ten or so, I loved to proclaim this loudly to my friends. I wrote spells for them in class and passed them around on little pieces of paper. But I'm quite confident in saying now that this was not a phase, as my grade five teacher would vouch. I remember when my class was playing Secret Santa and one of my clues was "I'm a Witch!" When my teacher found out, she took me aside after class and asked me to never say such a thing again. I agreed but crossed my fingers behind my back. This deep and strong desire to follow my path could never be suppressed by anyone, thank the gods.*

### To Stretch: Connecting to the Web of Life

At this stage, we begin to make our first serious decisions—to learn a little more, to take our first step over the threshold into the world of Magick. We turn to the New Age section of the bookstore, although it can as easily be the Internet. This is the stage when we consider committing ourselves to a period of study and experimentation. We begin to ground ourselves in the philosophies and the ideas inherent in Craft philosophy. We test our mental faculties through divination and spellcraft, learn various ways of casting a circle, and begin to celebrate the Wheel of the Year. As we do, we are further attuned to the cycles of Nature and recognise those subtle yet divine signs that have always been there.

At this level, we begin to make connections. We swap ideas with others of like mind, attend social meetings, and—if the situation permits—seek out or form our own groups to learn about Magick and Pagan spirituality together. This is when we begin to understand the extent and seriousness of the path and at some stage begin to rethink and reevaluate our motives and reasons for walking the path. We know that at any time we are free to leave, respecting and honouring the time we have spent there, taking the experiences and feelings with us to cultivate our progression elsewhere in the future.

It is when we begin to stretch that we truly know our limits. New situations and experiences rival our previous ones and impose new barricades. The challenge of the Pagan path is, of course, leaping these barricades, and if they are too high, having the courage to take the long route all the way around. This heralds new life, and we have emerged from a shrivelled cocoon, frail but full of vitality and energy.

Kim is an eighteen-year-old Pagan currently living in Queensland. In her free time, she enjoys dancing, writing, and pixel-dolling. Kim speaks of the events that changed her perception of life:

*I don't exactly remember the first time I decided I was officially Pagan. Over a period of about eight or nine months, I went from not caring about religion, to Christo-Wiccan, to Wiccan, to Christian, and then to Pagan. I never really understood anything about Wicca; I believed that Charmed was a completely accurate portrayal. Then I was asked to attend a local Christian youth group, and after just three weeks I committed. In retrospect, it was a crazy act, but at the time I felt like I connected with Christianity. I had a very Christian upbringing; my grandparents are strict Catholics and my mother is of a more alternative Catholic persuasion, so I guess I felt like it would be the right choice to follow in their footsteps. The feeling I got knowing that there was someone out there, someone that loved me who could make things happen, was incredible. But then things started to change. Through this amazing faith, I started to look at the world in a different light. I started to disagree with the teachings, wondering why amazing, unexplainable things happened. Then I spoke to two of my friends who were Wiccan. I couldn't give up Christianity entirely, so I became what the girls called "Christo-Wiccan." Meanwhile, I was becoming more and more uncomfortable within my youth group and eventually stopped going. I also started doubting the authenticity of the thing I knew as Wicca. I mean, I couldn't stop time like the girls on* Charmed, *so I started looking into it more deeply and discovered something incredible.*

*The first time I ever met other serious Pagans in my town, I was so scared. It was at a Mabon ritual held by the local teen group, and I didn't know what to expect or how many other people would come. It turned out that only one other turned up, but I still had a great time.*

*I remember that first Mabon ritual well. As a person, I don't ever really get embarrassed, but this was one of those rare occasions. There were several silences with me just standing there wanting to crawl into a hole and never darken anyone's doorstep again. The ritual itself was foreign to me, but it felt so strangely right. I related to what was happening, felt at peace and complete, and I knew that this was the way to go. It's a cliché, but there was something there that day which changed my life forever. I started to see life itself as a radiant existence, and I can honestly say that my whole outlook has changed.*

*Despite all the trial and error I've gone through and the challenges that are certain to come, I'm sure that this is what I'm meant to be, this is who I am—and nothing can ever change that. Finally, I've found my home.*

## Realising the Revelation

It has probably been at least three or four years down the track since you first started practicing Witchcraft. Now, when you look out the window, things appear to you differently or perhaps as they always have, though now you have a deeper, more intimate understanding of why, as if every single thing has a secret it keeps and is vibrating with brilliant energy. You have learnt, perhaps, that the greatest confider is the darkness itself. The earth is sacred to you, and you eat the fruits of the harvest, acknowledging the hard work of farmers and Mother Earth's yield. You feel strong, yet still vulnerable to the petty problems people get their feet stuck in constantly.

When alone in your room in the quiet of the night, you are sometimes hit by a surge of nostalgia. Memories and experiences flow through you and lift you up. You look at your past years and smile secretly. So much has happened to you. You have seen and done things some people may never have the chance to see or do. At moments like this, you know that this has always been your path—your fate. You realise that you have always been a Witch, and this knowledge shakes you like the rogue, crescent waves of the sea.

It can mean a lot for people in this commercialised world to find spiritual meaning and to go so far as to be confident and mature enough within oneself to have the ability to change your own life.

We forever dwell in the present and should do. For it is in the present that we are able to affect the future and to understand the past. Life flows; it is not linear, or static. It changes and evolves according to those who are living. We steer our own lives, we choose which roads to take and which exits to turn off. But we cannot forget the map we are all given at the start of our journeys. This is our destiny. However, it is up to us which way we take. In the end, all roads lead to Rome. Drive well, my friends!

Jarrah is a twenty-two-year-old Witch and an initiate and priest of the Coven of the WildWood. He is a writer who flows with the Awen—the poetic life force—of his ancestors:

*He asks me to speak of awakening; I smile and curl back into dreaming. When did I first awaken to myself as a Witch? I remember the stirring: hearing words like* Wicca, *reading with fascination and recognition the ancient mythologies and seeing the sensationalised representations in popular media. I can remember yawning, drawing deep on the books at the library. I browsed the 'net for information on everything from Ouija boards to Tarot, goddesses, herbs, astral travelling, spellcraft, and Jungian psychology. I stretched into the Nature I lived amongst—from the mountains, forests, fields, and waterways of my rural childhood to* the animals, plants, and the flow of the weather. But I now remember, before then, my unaffected and innate childhood; I can now recall singing as I spiralled deosil around an ancient tree, giving my thanks for its wisdom and guardianship. I remember speaking to animals that I had crafted from the intangible light of a half-dreamed otherness, calling upon their aid; gazing at the moon in a sleepless night and being held in a truth that a child has no need to question. I remember this from my childhood, before I fell asleep.

In awakening as a Witch, we learn to embrace paradox. We tread a path that somehow takes us to the extreme clarity of reason and at the same time immerses us in the dreamed truth of the Mystery. Waking up means we discover ourselves at the beginning of a path, and it also means we discover we were always at the end. This moment of awakening is eternal. We were always here, at the beginning and end of all desire, us, the Seekers of the Mystery. We who turn inwards and in doing so find all that is without; we realise in the rising of the day that we have been here before and will be here again. We accept the paradox of the element of spirit: that it precedes all other elements while it is no more than the consequence of their existence. We accept that we Witches are of this element, the cyclical paradox of transcendence and immanence, the falling and rising and the constantly sustained.

Welcome back, brothers and sisters, may you always stand here at the beginning as you release the preconception of an end.

# 2: LIFE AT 4 PRIVET DRIVE

As a Pagan youth, you are most probably still living at home and with your parents. You may be an only child, and then again you may have siblings. Whatever your situation, it is most likely a unique one owing to a number of varying factors, and just like Harry Potter, 4 Privet Drive is not always that far away.

This is the reality of the Pagan youth, and though we may yearn for the days of our independence and freedom, we have to endure several years of living under our parents' roof. With this comes great limitation to our spiritual practice. You may find it hard to establish and define your boundaries. Your bedroom door may as well not exist as your mum seems to barge in at any given moment, disrupting your rituals and meditations. Your younger siblings may be causing pandemonium right outside your bedroom window. Unfortunately, the above and more are the things we inevitably have to face as young Pagans.

Family is an ever-changing concept. As little as ten years ago, *family* was the word used to describe what is now termed the *nuclear family*—

mother, father, and children. Today, however, there are a multitude of varying situations that encompass the vast concept of family. There are now single-parent families, same-sex partnered families, extended families, and the list goes on. Whatever your situation is, you will undoubtedly come to the crossroads more than once when it comes to expressing your spirituality at home. This chapter can be used to create a better environment for concentration and focus and to work out family disputes on the grounds of your spiritual path. Remember, respect is an essential when it comes to families and living peacefully within them. It all starts with you.

## Sacred Space

Sacred space is an important concept to the Pagan. We all need a secret, personal place to seek refuge and retreat from the routine and structure of daily life. We all need a place where we may be ourselves and unwind and calm down and recuperate from the many problems and obstacles we face in life. This is our sacred space—a place of privacy, silence, peace, and beauty, where our bodies may instantly relax and our heartbeat attune to the natural flow that underpins the chaotic strain of the average existence. Living at home with a family can often inhibit any chances of establishing and defining your own personal territory. Unless you have the house to yourself, it can be fairly difficult to find a refuge where you will be undisturbed for a period of time.

In the past, Pagans have worshipped in groves, temples, and stone circles. Whatever the sacred space, it was generally a natural area of significance in terms of lines of power, local deities, faerie and spirit lore, or sacred geometry. As the deities of the ancient Pagans were generally local spirits known through oral myths and stories, certain places nearby the community were seen as sacred to that particular deity. Many sacred spaces were conceptualised through shapes, especially circles. Stonehenge in Salisbury, England, is just one example.

As Pagans, we understand and honour the earth and all of Nature as sacred and imbued with the universal life force, Magick. All places are therefore sacred. However, through centuries of environmental damage and exploitation, many places on earth now seem empty and devoid of life. Fortunately, not all of Nature has been exploited, and there are many natural places that are dotted evenly between housing and shopping centres in urban settlements. Then again, you may be completely comfortable in the confines of brick or wood, and your bedroom may be adequate enough for your Craft.

Sacred space is defined by the interaction and relationship felt between the place and yourself. If you feel uncomfortable or edgy in a certain park or district, do not seek to forge a friendship with that energy. Use your intuition and be honest with your feelings.

Once you have found your sacred space, you can begin by familiarising yourself with the area and attuning to the energy frequencies. The following is an easy-to-do exercise that requires nothing but yourself and your sacred space.

### Sacred Space Meditation

Begin by finding a position you are comfortable in. The ideal meditative position is to be sitting up, either on a chair or cross-legged. Lying down often confuses your inner vision, and if you draw too far into your meditation, you may even fall asleep. Personally, I find it easier to kneel.

Now focus on your breathing. Breathe deeply though your nose, letting the air move down into your abdomen, and allow your stomach to push out to its extent. Now hold your breath for four counts and release, allowing an even exhalation of the breath.

Feel yourself centred and aligned and open to the energy all around you. Do not hurry yourself or push for something to happen; simply enjoy the peace you have and remain patient. Soon enough you will receive impressions on the energy in your sacred space. It may not be a distinct feeling; it may be something subtle—perhaps it may even remind you of an event or stage in your life. If the energy here is compatible with your own, allow yourself to psychically poke around the space. Extend your consciousness outside of your physical being and explore. Get to know the place well.

Once you feel you understand the energy of your sacred space and have bonded long enough with the area, slowly return your focus to your breathing and gently reawaken your body through physical movement. Wiggle your toes and fingers, roll your neck, stretch your arms, and attune to your worldly senses. Now slowly stand up and explore the area physically. Make sure you are aware of any hidey-holes within the place, or any identifying marks that will help you return to your place if need be. Once this is done, you may leave the area and silently or loudly affirm that you will return.

The rest is up to you. You may desire to formally consecrate the space for the work of Magick, or perhaps you may simply begin to work there and allow a relationship to evolve from scratch. Whatever you decide, make sure you treat your sacred space in a respectful manner. If the time comes when you wish to introduce your sacred space to a fellow Pagan or close friend, make sure you ask your space beforehand. Through the connections formed between the location and yourself, a sentience will build that will respond both negatively and positively to each action, intention, and emotion you bring to it.

Sacred space may not suit your lifestyle. Perhaps you move around a lot and simply cannot expend the time and energy needed to form a relationship with the surrounding area. For other Pagans, it may be that they need variety within their spirituality to keep things fresh. In any case, keep your mind open to new experiences and opportunities.

*Interior Design*

In connection with your sacred space, you may like to decorate the area with greenery and flowers. You can hang ribbons, lanterns, and wreaths about the place, and if circumstance permits, secure votive or pillar candles in various spots around your space.

Physical offerings and devotions are a pleasant additive to your personal sacred space as they help to reconnect your senses with the archaic customs of ancient Pagans who have always honoured their gods through gifts of food and liquid, otherwise known as sacraments or libations. Offerings also help to reaffirm the faith of the individual and to act as symbols of focus for meditation and prayer.

Pagan traditions generally have certain rituals of blessing and conse-cration of food and drink, which is then offered to the gods. Generally after the bulk of the ritual is finished, the rite of cakes and ale takes place, and whatever food and drink is available is consecrated and eaten. In most cases, after the circle is opened, the remaining leftovers are offered to the gods and crumbled or poured onto the ground as a sign of respect for the earth. Beyond this, the act of creating and decorating devotional offerings is often neglected by the average Pagan.

## Making a Wreath

A common offering among Pagans who practice routine devotion today is the wreath, which is simple, beautiful, and easy to make. All you need is a garden vine of some description (e.g., ivy), a sink or portable tub, scissors, and plenty of patience!

Gather enough ivy to make the amount of wreaths you want, and then soak the vines in a sink or tub full of lukewarm water, removing clods of dirt and roots. After the vines have been soaked properly (and not for too long!), find a sunny spot to dry the ivy. After a few minutes, cut the vine to lengths of twice the circumference of your head. Wrap the length of ivy around your head, ensuring the fit is not too tight and not too loose, overlapping the ends. Entwine the overlapping vine firmly around the foundation of the wreath, remembering to bend the final tips of the vine back and over the ivy.

If you want, you can add complementary flowers to the wreath by threading in the stems. You can wear wreaths during rituals and leave them as offerings after you have left your sacred space. Ivy is a versatile plant that you can also use to decorate your Craft tools.

Banners and flags are another evocative way of furnishing your sacred space. Simply take a suitable piece of white or lightly coloured material, and paint the desired symbol/s on it. Depending on the construct of your sacred space, you can use either curtain rods or branches to sus-pend the banners. In an inside space, you can print out images of sym-bols or traditional Pagan litany and verse and laminate them to attach to your walls.

There are a multitude of things you can do to induce the right kind of feel in your sacred space, always keeping in mind your obligation to keep natural places free of litter, foreign toxins, and clutter.

## PAGAN PEACE-BUILDING

People are by nature the most argumentative and emotional beings on this planet. Simple comments, phrases, and words spark passionate and fiery reactions that result in physical or verbal retorts. War is just one of the examples that prove humanity is a species built on the primal desire to feel bigger and better than others. War is an endless entourage of exaggerated and repetitive claims of "I am right, you are wrong! So you can all follow me or else!" Many wars, both past and present, are founded on the eternal disputes experienced between religious groups. Religion happens to be one of the most controversial topics dividing the world. Differences in belief are unnerving for many, and that difference is what Pagans cherish.

Being Pagan in a predominantly Abrahamic world[1] is something that many Pagans have had to struggle with over the last few decades. Our federal laws are founded on the ethical and dogmatic principles of the Christian faith. Whether or not your parents are religious, they live in a community whose generic moral outlook is governed by Christian values. Many young Pagans I encounter live with parents who hold conservative views. This causes much anxiety on the Pagan's part concerning whether to be open about their spirituality. Sometimes the virtue of keeping your trap shut is the most convenient and stress-free choice in the long run.

When the time comes that you have mustered up enough courage to confront your parents about the truth, I suggest you do not worry so much about how they react but about how you convey the truth to them. Take some time to yourself to understand how you feel about Paganism, how it has changed your life and how you have developed and matured alongside your involvement with it. Make sure that you

---

1 *Abrahamic* refers to the three book religions that originally stem from the biblical Abraham—Judaism, Christianity, and Islam.

have the basic blueprint of what you will discuss with your parents, remembering to always be tolerant, understanding, and firm. Backing down and submitting to your parents' every whim and command does not display a sense of independence or confidence. Part of being Pagan is acknowledging that you alone have the right to choose your own path to spiritual fulfilment; no one else should be able to pressure you into believing or experiencing something you do not.

Family friction and disputes are inevitable for many young Pagans who have opened up about their beliefs. Parents may often feel anger, fear, resentment, and disappointment when it comes to their own child choosing the path of Paganism. They may feel that they have failed to uphold their duty to raise you in a safe and stable environment. You may represent all that is wrong and sinful in the world to them. However, if you do experience any of the above, understand that your parents only want what is best for you, and their fear of losing you does not necessarily lie in their animosity towards your spirituality but in the tendency to keep you innocent as long as possible. Parents forget far too often that today's generation of youth is far more cosmopolitan than any before. We are continuously exposed to a world of diversity, war, and individuality. Pondering one's sexuality, identity, and beliefs is a constant struggle for many young people today. Essentially, youth is seen as a period of growth, development, and rebellion. Your family may dismiss your spirituality as a phase you will outgrow; unfortunately, this is where many of the problems begin.

Being treated as delusional is one of the most frustrating things a young Pagan has to deal with. The inevitable cliché that "You're a teenager, you don't know what you want!" is the reality for many Pagans. Often our families see our involvement in Paganism as a hobby. Spirituality is not and never has been a way of spending your free time. There are no collectables, passwords, or club benefits. Paganism, like any spiritual path, is a way to express oneself through a connection with the divine. Paganism deserves the same treatment and recognition afforded to the other world faiths.

Siblings are another story altogether. Generally it is unpredictable as to how your sibling/s will react. As you are closer in age to your siblings, your relationships with them are, in most cases, informal. Disagreements and arguments can result in hot-tempered slurs, insults, and physical fighting.

If you want your siblings to understand Paganism, then it is important to tone down the Pagan-specific terminology and convey your spirituality through analogy and example. Isobel Bird, a Wiccan author, demonstrates this beautifully in Circle of Three, a series focused on three unique teenage girls and their year and a day of Wiccan study. In the twelfth instalment of the series, entitled *Written in the Stars*, Kate, the archetypal seeker struggling with her newfound interest, attempts to explain Wicca to her older brother Kyle after he confronts her about their frosty relationship. Initially Kate falters, afraid that she will not have the competency to convey her feelings and experiences of Wicca verbally. However, Kate is suddenly inspired by a voice in her head to begin with her altar, or rather the statue of Demeter upon it. After the divine inspiration, Kate soon finds the words to help explain Wicca to Kyle, and despite her brother's original response to Kate's interest in the Craft, he learns to accept her for who she is. The scene within the book is a very involved emotional exchange and strikes a nostalgic chord with young Pagans. I highly recommend the series to any Pagan, young or old, as it deals with Pagan spirituality in an authentic, familiar, and vivid way.

If you are ever met with scepticism or disbelief concerning your faith, it's best to keep quiet about your spiritual views until such time that you feel you have achieved a sense of security within yourself to confront your oppressors with maturity and tact.

As youths, we are all at a stage of physical, mental, emotional, and spiritual development. We are beginning to learn the ways of the world and to become familiar with the psychological makeup of humanity, our peers in particular. Despite your understanding of the mentalities of the human species, it is safe to say that as a youth you are also struggling with your emotions and discovering the extent to which your feelings affect your entire being. Earlier on, while I was still living at home, I suffered from spontaneous mental breakdowns, emotional hurt, and torrential self-doubt, each connected with my spiritual identity. In saying this, I must make it clear that it was not Paganism that caused these problems but the extended links with external forces and individuals that have suppressed me at various points alongside my magickal progression.

Family values are important to most of us. We all seek to belong, to fit in, and to feel comfortable with our family. For the sake of convenience, it is important that each of us attempt to relate to our family members in an honest, open, and free-flowing environment. By no means is this a push for you to come out of the broom closet; when you are ready, you are ready. You need to honour the pace of your own development; don't rush things. Ultimately, the family issue is one of expressing how you feel, processing and reacting to your family's feelings, and allowing for mutual compromise. At times, this may require a low profile in terms of your publicity. In the end, it is your decision; whether you take on your family's wishes is up to you. Keep in mind that if you wish to be seen as a mature individual, you need to act in a considerate and reasonable manner. Discuss with your family the reasons you feel so strongly about Paganism and allow them the time and space to come to terms with your spirituality. To them, it may indicate the transitions occurring internally as you develop as an individual.

If you feel that Paganism is more of a progression than a radical transformation, make sure you communicate this to your family. Seize the opportunity to talk about your feelings with your family and make sure you articulate! The guidelines suggested in chapter three are applicable in your family life too, and it may help your case to encourage your family members to find out about the truths of Paganism for themselves. Lend them this book and indicate the chapters and sections of most relevance. Afterwards, discuss with your family how they feel about your involvement with Paganism. Ask in earnest that they be completely honest with you and that they attempt an educated and informed response to the reading material. If the issue is of religious abandonment, make it clear that Pagans do not seek converts but do encourage speculation, questioning, and examination within one's own belief system. If you attend any Pagan social gatherings, ask your family to come along to meet your Pagan friends. Pagan social meets are open ground for curious people who have inquiries about our traditions.

Your family may feel that you are obsessed or restricted by your involvement with Paganism and only wish you the freedom of choice that you are entitled to. If this is the case, I suggest you take this in stride, respond in humour, and explain that it was your choice that led you to examine the Pagan traditions.

The experience of family, youth, and Paganism is a unique passage of coming into being. Many young Pagans who encounter the negative response find they grow a great deal during the period in which the family seems fanatical about the matter, to the point where both parties come to an agreement and acceptance occurs. Whatever happens, know that you are loved by your family, cherished by your gods, and enfolded by your spirit.

## Magick of the Home

When it comes to family, Magick is a vital energy that can help sustain peace in the home, strengthen ties between family members, and protect them. The rituals below are open to family participation, or you can perform them on your own. If you are not satisfied with how the rituals have been written, adapt them to your own purposes and take it from there.

### A Ritual to Banish Negativity from the Home

This ritual can be used to purify your house of any negative energies and to bless it with peace and tranquillity.

You will need:

> A large bowl (preferably ceramic)
> Rose water
> Rain water
> Sea water (you can substitute blessed
>     water with sea or rock salt)

Spring water (the bottled stuff is fine)
A white taper candle
Chalice
Matches or a lighter
Four illuminator candles

It's best to perform this ritual at the new moon and in the room you consider to be the heart of your house (where your family spends most of their time). Place the bowl in the centre of your altar and the vessels holding each type of water around it. The white candle should be positioned behind the bowl and the chalice to the right or left of the bowl depending on your writing hand. Before you begin, set out the four lit illuminator candles at the four directions to form the outer ring of your circle. Allow yourself enough space for the ritual to go on without hindrance. You will also need to ensure that every door in your house is wide open. It is permissible for your front and back doors to be closed for privacy and security reasons.

Begin by focusing and centring your awareness. Kneel or sit cross-legged before your altar, and ground and centre. Once you are focussed, join hands with those around you and cast the circle by envisioning a sphere of white light pulsating around you all. Hold the visualisation for several minutes, empowering and sealing the circle with these words:

*Serene white light, be bound and blessed*
*Flow in beauty, put darkness to rest*
*Seal this space by our intent*
*Sacred circle, these words are sent!*

When you feel that the circle has been cast, light the white candle on the altar and see the flame as a source of peace and serenity. Say:

*This flame is a beacon to love, understanding, warmth, and purity*
*It is the heart of family that beats within us all*
*May it enfold us in its cloak of peace and concord*
*May it dispel all darkness that troubles this home.*

Each family member present, including yourself, should each say one line. The blessing should go deosil[2] (starting with you) and will finish with the last person in the cycle. If there are more than four, you may add new lines to the blessing to accomodate for the extra people. If you are doing the ritual on your own, recite the entire thing.

After a moment of silence, take the chalice and the vessel of rose water and measure out half a cup of the liquid. Pour this into the bowl, and say:

*Water of the rose to court the heart.*

Pass the chalice on deosil and instruct the next person to pour half a cup of rain water into the bowl, saying:

*Water of the rain to cleanse the soul.*

Instruct the next person to pour half a cup of sea water into the bowl, saying:

*Water of the sea to heal our wounds.*

Instruct the next person to pour half a cup of spring water into the bowl, saying:

*Water of the spring to purify.*

Each person should now place the index finger of their power hand into the liquid and stir deosil while envisioning white light filling the mixture. See the light increase in intensity the faster your fingers spin. As you stir, chant:

---

2 The word *deosil* refers to the sun and its passage through the sky. Contrary to popular belief, it does *not* mean "clockwise" but rather "sunwise"—and therefore, in the Southern Hemisphere, *deosil* is anticlockwise as the sun rises in the east and travels through the north to set in the west, whereas in the Northern Hemisphere, the sun travels through the south to set in the west (clockwise).

*By the rose and by the rain*
*Banish from this house our pain*
*By the sea and by the spring*
*Bless our potion in this ring*
*Waters of the soul arise*
*Wash away ill spirits and ties*
*Bless this place and all within*
*No longer shall the darkness win!*

Repeat the chant as many times as you need until you feel the energy reach its peak. When the climax comes, visualise the water reflecting a concentrated beam of white light upward from the bowl and through the ceiling. Imagine the beam spinning outward (deosil) to saturate the house. Feel yourself in the midst of blinding white light. Bask in the glory of pure energy for a few minutes and then signal for everyone to stand. Pick up the bowl and ask someone else to carry the candle. Before you step outside of your circle, see it extend to surround your entire house. Now walk through your house, flicking the potion in each and every corner while visualising the house encompassed by the sphere of white light. Once you have covered every room of your house, including pantries, storage cupboards, and toilets, head to your front yard and organise everyone into a circle. Hand the bowl to the person next to you (going deosil) and ask that they pour a little of it over your hands. Rub your hands together, allowing the potion to soak into your skin, and recite the following:

*Pure by this potion made*
*Blessed by this spell we've laid*
*No more shall negativity reign*
*No more shall darkness feed our pain.*

Each person should do the same, passing on the bowl to the person next to them and reciting the chant. Once everyone has been blessed, pour the remainder of the mixture into the garden or specifically on the roots of a particular tree while silently asking its blessing.

The ritual is complete.

*A Ritual to Promote Understanding*

This ritual is best preceded by the above ritual, which helps to pave the way for new and more peaceful family relationships. This ritual helps to establish a firm foundation of understanding within your family. If you can, get everyone in your immediate family involved.

You will need:

Cauldron or fireproof container
Methylated spirits or rubbing alcohol
Matches
Paper and pen (blue ink)
Six metres of white satin ribbon (or enough to suit the
    circumference of a circle created by your family)
Six metres of blue satin ribbon (as above)
Dried basil leaves

Considering this ritual uses a cauldron and fire, it's best performed outside in the backyard, preferably at night under the light of the waxing moon (or just straight after the above ritual).

Begin by handing a piece of paper and a blue pen to everyone participating and ask them to write down their hidden animosities and anxieties towards the other family members. Ensure that no one else will be reading the papers and that they should each pour out their pent-up emotions onto paper as best they can. Once everyone (including you) has finished writing down their feelings, gather everyone into a circle around the cauldron and pour a considerable amount (but not too much) of either the methylated spirits or rubbing alcohol into the base of the cauldron and throw a lit match carefully into it. Once the fire is going steadily, you can cast the circle as you did before by visualising the sphere of white light. Then, beginning with you, throw the piece of paper into the flames with a handful of basil leaves while chanting:

*I pray release will find its way*
*To this fire on this day*
*May patience and love embrace my soul*
*Animosity be gone as fire burns in the bowl!*

As you watch your paper turn into ash, feel your hidden anxieties, reservations, and dislikes towards your family members evaporate. Replace those old feelings with love, compassion, and kindness for your kin. Going deosil, everyone else should do the same. Now join hands and recite the following chant while envisioning the circle growing bigger and brighter around you:

> *Joined are we by common aim*
> *Flesh and blood; we're of the same*
> *May we see that kinship wins*
> *Peace and love lies within.*

Now take up the two lengths of satin and begin to entwine them so that there is one length of six metres. With the two end pieces in your hands tied together, make sure everyone is holding the circle of ribbon mid-air with both hands. You are now a circle within a circle within a circle. Take a minute or two to visualise the circle of ribbon as a flowing cycle of blue and white light curling around each other. See your family getting along, laughing, and giving time to understand each other. Feel safe, at peace, and honoured as a vital part of your family. Instruct the others to focus on the same images and feelings. Begin to walk deosil while holding the images and feelings, and chant:

> *We are a circle within a circle*
> *With no beginning and never ending.*

If you know the actual tune of this popular Pagan chant, then begin to sing it and the others will catch on.

Increase your speed and begin a slow run while visualising the energy as a cone of power, with its apex protruding through the top of the sphere around you. See it pulse with energy and grow brighter and more concentrated. When you feel that the energy has reached its climax, shout "Understanding!" and fall to the ground to earth the excess energy. Prior to the ritual, you should inform everyone that you will be raising what is known as a cone of power and that the word *understanding* will be the key to release the energy and to fall to the ground to earth the power.

A cone of power is generally restricted to experienced covens; however, anyone can successfully raise a cone of power if they are in a peaceful state of mind and are aware of the operation beforehand. It is also a great way to bond with your family, as it ends in a somewhat dramatic but equally humorous fashion. Laughing and dizziness is to be expected afterwards, and you should lead your family through a grounding exercise by suggesting that they all place their foreheads against the ground and visualise the excess energy draining through them and into the earth beneath.

Once you have recuperated and everyone is standing up again, open the circle by walking widdershins and visualising the sphere of light disappearing into the air. Retire inside and play a board game or just have a nice chat while snacking on food and drink.

From now on, you should make an effort at keeping your emotions in check and opening up to the best of your ability to your family when you feel the need. You can repeat the first phase of the ritual (paper-burning in cauldron) by yourself when you feel that you are in dispute with a family member. If you can find basil essential oil, make use of its inherent qualities by burning it frequently in your house to keep the peace.

## A Note to the Nomad: Moving On

After graduating from high school and enjoying the first few months of having nothing much to do at all, I spontaneously packed up and headed off to Brisbane, the capital city of my state. It was a fairly spur-of-the-moment decision, backed up by years of begrudging my woeful hometown. As we entered Brisbane, I received a text from a friend of mine telling me of a room in the Valley that was available and cheap, in a house with several other alternatively minded people—Witches included! I went to see the place, had an interview, and was asked to join the rest of the housemates. It was definitely a destined event, and I learnt so much from my few short months of living there.

When we take the initiative to move forward and explore the endless possibilities that life has to offer, we commit ourselves to the way of Wyrd, which expresses itself essentially through patterns of growth and transformation. We take the stag leap and cross the abyss of the unknown, flying forth from all that is unreal or illusion to that which is real and wholly present. Some would suggest that we begin the descent and come to realise that effect has cause after all. Our lives are not merely psychological shells but take on the substance that underlies the sacred reality.

I never really made an affirmed decision to move away from my family and my hometown, though it was never really a place that I enjoyed being. I always knew that my destiny awaited me somewhere else, and while time and place cannot fully constitute an unfurling of fate, there is definitely more chance of having a run-in with serendipity in a place that your very soul feels drawn to. It was also in this city that I became a founding member of the Coven of the WildWood and am now surrounded by a group of devout and life-loving Witches who help to bring out the best in me and direct my conscious effort to great things.

Leaving home and loved ones behind is neither hard nor simple. Some thought is necessary to any adventure leading away from those to whom we are related by blood and by spirit. Leaving friends, family, and security for the great unknown is something we all must do eventually if we intend to fully know ourselves. Everything in life has its spiritual dimension, and this realm, this plane of awareness, is the essence that washes over me every moment of every day.

We can never truly settle down, and this is because at the core, each human spirit is endeared to the wild spirit of adventure. Standing where you are today, you are in contact with everything that has ever been, is, and will be. Move forward and keep keen eyes, clear and bright, for while the sun has its day, there is beauty in the wilderness of night.

# 3: SCHOOLING PAGANS

Most of us attend school at some time in our lives. School seems a trivial inconvenience at most times, especially when we are forced to study things like algebra and advertising. But as it is, our futures depend on our education.

As Pagans, our lives at school can often make it harder to define our individuality. Our spiritual path will often conflict with teachers and students. The conscious decision to publicly affirm your spirituality can lead to friction. To make the best of your own school experience, read on.

## PEERING PUPILS:
## COMMUNICATION

School is not so much about what we learn but about who we learn with. Our peers are those who sit beside us during class. They are not necessarily our friends but may simply represent the majority of the student body we are unfamiliar with. These are the people whose opinions "really matter" when it comes to fashion, popularity, and the social ladder. These are the vicious bureaucrats who pass judgement on individual worth. These are the individuals who spread gossip like wildfire through campus and can make or break our appeal and identity. Amongst our peers are also our friends, those whom we have come to love and bicker with.

School is a blur of faces and personalities … a mural of diversity, laughter, depression, and tears. English and history soon disappear into the vague realms of irrelevance when we come to the crossroads in our relationships with others.

Communication is a vital bridge between two or more entities. However, the concept of communication does not suggest positive feedback and can often result in huge, meaningless debates over trivial details. This seems to be the norm, especially in the schoolgrounds, where we are forced to endure lame comments from idiotic students for who we are. Personalities often come under fire because of a social fear of the way someone is acting or how they identify themselves—for instance, guys who tend to make friends with girls and who are more academically inclined than sporty are often accused of being "fags."

As Pagans, we are open to all sorts of insults and jokes from our peers, as Paganism is not wholly understood by the majority of society. It is not unheard of that when a Pagan or Witch comes out to their friends at school, there is a window of approximately forty-eight hours until the rest of the grade knows. I was fairly open about my interest in the occult when I first began high school and would often read Witchcraft books during classes or even bring charms to school. Soon my entire class knew, and then it spread on to the rest of my grade. There was no immediate backlash, and I merely received jokes and curiosity until my best friend at the time learnt that I was a Witch. This did not go down well, as he was a pious Christian, but he at least listened to me explain myself and my newfound spirituality.

It is not always a good idea, no matter how proud you feel, to publicly announce you are Pagan to others. Our relationships suffer and friction happily abounds. People soon realise they can use you as a scapegoat or even as the school joke. Unless you are seeking to experience how this can all feel at such a vulnerable time of adolescence, then I suggest you keep your beliefs private. I'm not saying deny your faith and simply lie about being Pagan but to be mature with the situation and to learn to know when there is a risk factor about being open. Remember to be yourself and to not fall to society's own stereotypes about what a Witch or Pagan is. I'm not saying don't come out of your shell but that you should do it gradually and get used to the idea of being assertive with your peers.

Often it's not just ill-mannered humour we are subjected to but also religious evangelism. Most Australian schools, public and private, have prayer services catering to Christian students. Unfortunately, a majority of these groups are founded on the pretences that non-Christian members of the student body need salvation, and active conversion comes into play.

Some time ago, several Christian students discovered that I was a Witch and so began their long-winded attempts at converting me. Whenever I had class with them, they would constantly prattle on about the glory of God. This elevated into verbal attacks against me. It just so happened that these Christians sat with some of my friends who I occasionally visited during lunch. I remember the fear I had whenever I gained enough courage to venture up to where they sat. Often my visits ended in religious battles, in which both my beliefs and theirs (ashamedly so) were put under scrutiny, though I seemed to be on the receiving end most of the time. The situation grew to the point where their entire church was praying for my soul, which they readily admitted to me. Eventually, the friction wore away and ironically we became friends, and religion is no longer a topic of discussion between us. This is simply one of thousands of similar situations around the world today in which individuals are discriminated against because of spiritual persuasion. Yet, as my experience proves, reconciliation is a possible and valid pathway to solve the problems that arise between people.

At other times, it is not necessarily the fear for the purity of your soul that causes people to feel they have the right to abuse you but also the mocking disbelief in Paganism and Witchcraft in terms of Magick and spells.

Have you ever had an obnoxious moron approach you with a lop-sided grin? You stand there, innocently wondering what all the fuss is about, only to discover you've been on the receiving end of a horrible joke. In many cases, once you have outed yourself, you will be met by harsh laughter, which can break down your internal self-esteem.

"Can you really cast spells?" "If you're a Witch, then where's your broom?" and "Go on, then, curse me. I dare you!" are all examples of the types of questions that are fired constantly from self-absorbed brats who have nothing better to do. It takes a strong-willed person to remain unaffected by comments such as these, and it is your right to feel angry and irritated. However, never allow them to see that you are annoyed or frustrated with them. Fight fire with fire; sarcasm is only ever quelled with sarcasm. Instead of wasting your time educating people who do not matter to you, use some of the following retorts:

> *"Oh gods, I've dropped my wand! Have you seen it?"*
> *"My broom? Oh, we don't use brooms anymore. I took the Hoover to school."*
> *"Curse you? Looks like someone else beat me to it."*

Sarcasm can be taken to the extreme and beyond, and you'll need to know when to drop the act and to don your educator's cap, ready to regurgitate condensed versions of what you have learnt. Never give anyone an excuse to think they are right when they are obviously wrong, unless of course it's at their own expense.

Fighting for the right of fair treatment and equality is an ongoing battle for Pagans, but it is one that has proven successful in many respects. Though there are still those who view our spirituality as superstitious, we are also regarded as genuine spiritual people by many others.

Honour yourself, others, your environment, and the universe with sincerity and humility, and swift comprehension will follow. Remember, it is not how we dress or what jewellery we wear that defines who we are but our thoughts and our words and how we compose them—and even then that leans dangerously close to the realm of egomania.

Be mindful that anger and frustration are all negative emotions that will not only enrage your "opponents" but will also amplify their own feelings and increase stubbornness concerning changing their preconceived notions about you. Be firm with your words while ever remaining gentle and wise. Do not hate others simply because they believe differently than you, but understand and accept that these feelings are also human and entirely valid. Acting on your hatred with violence is weak and ultimately stupid. Know that it is better in the long run for you to choose to back down from religious wars with others and to acknowledge their feelings and background. Many people who preach their word as the absolute truth are brought up in fundamentalist families and are inundated by these ideas from an early age. Opportunities to reassess one's belief system are often futile in relation to these individuals, and hope should not be spent on their willingness to change but on the effect these views will have on you.

Every day in our lives, we are surrounded by people whose personal convictions are so varied that we often lose ourselves in the ocean of opinion. It is wise to always question your decision to open up to others on the subject of your spiritual path. If you do feel like opening up to a friend at school, then you will need to ask yourself a few questions regarding their attitudes towards issues not just of a spiritual or religious nature, such as homosexuality and abortion. Generally, if you have known them to react to the above issues negatively, chances are they will not take to the idea of you following an alternative spirituality. Even so, we cannot always be so readily strategic with our dealings with others, and often the truth finds ways to out itself. In cases such as these, it is best to simply take a straightforward approach and hope that the person in question will accept you. Many Pagans find that they have incorrectly assumed how others will react and rejoice inwardly when friends and peers simply smile and nod.

As Paganism is essentially a decentralised, autonomous, and sometimes anarchistic group of spiritualities, there are no universal organisations or networks that apply to all Pagans. Therefore, it is important to note that everything we say about our spirituality will affect the way outsiders view Paganism. When discussing your spirituality with peers and attempting to reconstruct their misconceptions, it is preferable to start small and use solid examples. For instance, start with the pentagram; bring the person's attention to the construct and design of the symbol. Indicate the five points and how each individual arm interlocks and passes onto the next. Also mention the circle that encompasses the five points, and explain what the symbol means, highlighting common misconceptions and deconstructing them, replacing them with truths.

After you have introduced your peers to something apparent and visible, the next step is to attempt to give words to your thoughts and to allow yourself to make sense. Explain the basic beliefs of Paganism, remembering to use examples wherever possible and to attempt to answer all of their questions kindly and not in contempt.

The following is a list of key points you might like to include in your spiel about Paganism:

- Paganism is a Nature-based set of spiritualities that has its roots in the pre-Abrahamic (or pre-Christian) ancient civilisations of the world.

- The word *Pagan* derives from the Latin word "paganus," which literally means "rustic" or "country-dweller" and was applied to people who retained their native and cultural practices and customs, e.g., agricultural and pastoral communities who continued to worship Nature deities and local spirits. Later on, the word evolved into an insult implying a savage, unintelligent, backward, and hedonistic person.

- Pagans do not worship Satan or demons, as these entities stem from Judeo-Christian and earlier Zoroastrian concepts that developed into complex schools of thought. Nor do Pagans see opposing forces as inherently good or evil, as we have no absolute power recognising either.

- NeoPaganism, a term referring to the current Pagan traditions, abides by the general law of "Do unto others as you would have them do unto you" in its varying forms. Though this is not a central tenet of all Pagan traditions, it is a reasonable assessment of generic NeoPaganism.

- Witchcraft, Wicca, Santería, Voudoun, Asatru, and other reconstructionist traditions are all essentially Pagan.

- Equality, respect, creativity, and individualism are all qualities admired and adhered to by most Pagans.

- Both female and male deities are honoured, though not all adhere to this principle—some prefer to form personalised relationships with individual deities, called patrons.

- Pagans generally fall under a polytheistic, pantheistic, animistic, ditheistic, or archetypal belief in divinity (or a variation of several of these). Several Pagans subscribe to henotheistic monotheism—the worship of one deity whilst simultaneously acknowledging the existence of other deities.

- Most Pagans see science as compatible with their belief systems.

- In general, Pagans believe in and work with Magick, the universal, underlying flow of energy.

- Most Pagans are pro-choice and liberal in attitude towards issues of government, sexuality, birth control, etc.

- Discrimination on the grounds of race, gender, sexuality, appearance, religion, etc., is frowned upon by Pagans.

- Pagans generally seek to attune themselves with the natural cycles of the environment by celebrating festivals based around pastoral and harvest rites and/or the solstices and equinoxes.

• Sin is an alien concept in Pagan belief systems in terms of original sin, the definition of sin, and the guilt based upon sin. Salvation is not a widely recognised concept either.

• Pagans do not seek to convert others or proselytise their faith.

Note that the above statements are generalised and do not necessarily apply to all Pagans. Always remember to link your statements to universal concepts or symbols; for example, when discussing divinity, you might like to make mention of the moon and the sun as embodiments of the feminine and masculine spirits of the universe.

## THE WIZARD'S APPRENTICE: TEACHER AND STUDENT RELATIONS

Teachers are the universal archetype of wisdom, or in this case, government-sanctioned slave labour (i.e., homework). Whatever your attitude towards teachers, they are an ever-present component of school, and we will all deal with them at one stage or another.

Unlike the somewhat informal relationships and language you share with your peers, the relationship forged between teacher and student is more robotic. Personalities are strained and words controlled so as to keep the teachers placated. There are times when it is not just lack of attention or incompetence in class that is our downfall but our spirituality and how it is perceived by the teacher.

During my five years of high school, I encountered only fantastic and open-minded teachers who were all genuinely curious about my beliefs and treated me as an equal despite deep-set animosities or preconceptions concerning what I did. I feel I am very lucky in this regard, as I know several other young Pagans who have had trouble at school concerning their spiritual persuasions.

Most teachers found out that I am Pagan not by word of mouth but by my own personal decision to open up. Generally, if I felt the risk was not too high, I indirectly let them know; however, it rarely came to that point. While at school, I did many of my assignments on Paganism, and through this many teachers began to ask me about my beliefs. In response to these inquiring minds, I usually offered a variety of concise textual sources such as the Pagan Pride pamphlet on Pagan students at school. Ultimately, it allowed my teachers to develop an understanding of who I am. However, it is not a good idea to loudly proclaim to every teacher within earshot that you are Pagan and you have free information to hand out, because that *is* proselytising and is not attractive behaviour.

Generic prerequisites for becoming a teacher are having an open mind, a willingness to educate, and an ability to listen to and cater to students' needs. If you ever feel you are being discriminated against by a teacher, you have the right to inform an authority figure about it. There is discrimination in schools, and some of it does come from teachers and staff. Sometimes I felt that ignorance was being conveyed towards my beliefs, and it was a narrow-mindedness that has no place in schools. I do not wish to persecute anyone for not ever having heard about Paganism, I am simply admitting to feeling a little out of place because of it.

I once brought my Tarot cards to school to read for a friend. A teacher walked past and asked what I was doing. I told her and she walked off, seemingly unaffected. Eventually she returned and told me they were not appropriate for school and to put them away, which I did. However, I felt that my rights had been abused, as the same teacher had exclaimed that it was "cute" for students to bring Bibles to school and to read them during their breaks. Now what is the difference between reading Bibles during a break and reading Tarot cards? Both are channels for the divine to give advice, and both are valid spiritual tools. However, it is quite obvious the teacher in question thought there was a difference between the two and probably associated Tarot cards with something sinister.

The ignorance portrayed above is not based on an intended hatred of Paganism but on the basic ignorance of what it is and a fear of what it can mean.

In general, teachers will strive to be accepting. I have interacted with countless teachers who have treated me and my spirituality fairly and with no problems in doing so. Many of them are Christian; in fact, one was a retired Catholic priest! Understanding is not a one-way street—it involves both parties meeting halfway and encourages acceptance of each other.

The way you present yourself, the way you speak, and the depth of your sincerity are all factors that contribute to your overall persona as understood by teachers. Building bridges between the generations allows for new insights and advice from a source you may never have considered before. Intelligence is one of the most respected attributes in our society, and with it you may achieve what you want to as long as you have the willpower. Many would like to tell you that university degrees are the only assured way of securing your permanent access to opportunities awaiting you. I say go as far as you want with institutionalised education, and as long as you can apply what you know and have the patience and humility to continue learning, you will get where you want to.

### Assignments

This word strikes fear in the hearts of students everywhere. However, homework also tends to drain us of time and energy, and it reminds us of the shackles restraining our freedom while we attend school.

The great thing about subjects such as English and history is that assignments are generally format only, in which we are given choices of what to enter into that format. Instead of writing an essay on the French Revolution, why not try the New Age Revolution? When the prospect of analysing a Shakespearean play is staring you right in the face, read up on *Macbeth* and compare the traditional Elizabethan views on Witches with real Witchcraft. Put a Pagan spin on your assignments, and you'll soon find that you are able to get good grades as well as further your knowledge of Paganism.

Below I have provided a list of assignments I did at school on the topics of Witchcraft and Paganism, to help inspire you and get your own creative juices flowing:

- An oral performance on stereotypical Witchcraft
- A mini-magazine on modern Witchcraft (articles included an examination of the Tarot's Major Arcana, teen Witchcraft, and Wicca and its origins)

- An argumentative essay debating the existence of Magick
- A comparison between two spiritual poems—*Desiderata* by Max Ehrmann and *The Witches' Creed* by Doreen Valiente
- A Shakespearean-styled performance implementing Pagan lore and custom
- A persuasive speech on the validity of Paganism as a modern spirituality
- A portrait of a Mother Goddess
- An essay on the New Age revolution
- A website about Wicca
- An artistic appraisal of Francisco José de Goya's "The Sabbat"
- Creating, marketing, and selling "spell boxes"
- Film treatment and storyboard with Pagan theme
- Oral commentary on Witches in the media
- "Chapter One" writing task—Pagan fiction
- Community feature article on local Paganism
- A series of paintings based on the myth of Persephone

### Regulation Jewellery

Most schools have regulations restricting the wearing of excessive jewellery on the body. At the school I attended, the regulation was female-specific and listed what could be worn. A signed parental note was necessary for the wearing of religious jewellery for both males and females. Though not all teachers actively enforced these rules, there were occasions when students were asked to remove non-regulation jewellery or have it confiscated. On several occasions, I was asked to remove my spiritual jewellery. To ensure you are never bothered about the wearing of Pagan-related imagery, simply follow the standard procedures set down by your school, i.e., retrieve a permission note from your parents, and keep it on you.

There is no discrimination here, simply an unawareness of the implications and meanings of Pagan-related spiritual symbols. While I was hanging out at the front of the school with my friends, my maths teacher noticed my bind-rune pendant and politely asked me to remove it. I simply replied that it was of religious significance. I knew what would come next and told her that it was a Pagan symbol. A sceptical look came over her face, and she quipped, "That's a bit old, isn't it?" Luckily enough, an older student who was fairly respected during her time at school stepped in and explained to my teacher that Paganism was alive and well in the modern world, and after a few short moments she seemed to accept the fact.

I am well aware, however, that there are many cases in which a student may be asked to remove jewellery because it is seen as dangerous, inappropriate, or satanic. This is where it is essential that you step in and inform your teacher that your jewellery is of spiritual relevance to you and that its stereotypical associations are outdated myths. It is important that you also apply the educational techniques you learnt earlier in this chapter when confronting teachers about your right to wear Pagan jewellery. Be kind, patient, and assertive, and respect for your rights should follow.

There are many Pagans who share differing opinions on the matter of jewellery and enforcing the right to be able to wear it. Some say it isn't worth fighting for, and if asked to remove jewellery at school, then you should comply. It is really up to you. You may even feel that wearing Pagan jewellery is more of a fashion statement or attention-seeking method than anything else, and you are entitled to believe so. In cases such as these, it is important to remember Paganism is not rigid and does not require you to believe certain things—or wear them, for that matter.

Wearing spiritual jewellery is an act of devotion and connection to one's traditions. Currently I am wearing the triskele, as it is a symbol of my Celtic ancestors and my gods. It also allows me to feel a part of the Pagan community. The adrenaline rush you get when another Pagan recognises your symbol and approaches you is truly magickal.

Responsibility comes with wearing Pagan jewellery. Whether we ignore it or not, there are certain individuals who wear the pentagram to induce shock and to frighten others. People like that are best left to their own insecure psychological worlds. Wearing overbearingly large pentagrams is not recommended either, as chances are you will be seen to be trivialising Paganism. This doesn't mean you have to hide your jewellery under your shirt, it just means that you need to take into account the fact that society is inclined to categorise and brand people into specific groups or classes, and Pagans are no exception.

Spiritual symbolism is a beautiful thing, and when treated with respect and understood as potent expression, Magick is afoot and the gods are at work.

# 4: THE PAGAN SOCIALITE

Paganism is not a label you throw on when you want to feel spiritual or advocate that you are even the slightest bit mysterious, rebellious, or different. Pagans are human beings who embrace the immanence of divinity in the world and, above all, acknowledge and live the principle of sacred equality. A Pagan is a philosopher, an active participant in life, and a priest/ess of the earth.

Paganism is my life, and I say this in complete honesty. My perception of life, my view of the world, and my very breath is the essence of my spirituality. All things in my life revolve around who I am and how my spirit communicates with the universe. However, this concept is not to be confused with fundamentalism or obsession. *Pagan* is simply the closest word in the English language that defines who I am. It is the foundation of my identity and the primal rhythm of my soul.

Identity and labels are deeply associated with one's social life and how an individual chooses to experience it. Pagans do have social lives; we are not chained to eternal hermitage simply for seeking out wisdom.

There is much to learn from social interaction and the workings of society's institutions of behaviour and speech. When you make your pilgrimage to the shopping centre to hang out or loiter, you bring with you your true personage and your mask—the persona you slip on to confuse and deter unwanted parties or to overshadow the person you are afraid to reveal. Remember that you should never be forced to compromise yourself in order to please others who do not take the time to understand what makes you *you*. This is your life, your time, and your place to experience, grow, and learn. Seize the day and be the person you can truly be proud of.

## Out & About: The Downtown Pagan

If you saw me downtown, would you know that I am Pagan? Pagans are such a varied bunch that any attempt at categorising us all into a singular demographic is futile. Pagans do not all wear the same clothes or like the same music. We are not all gay or straight; we are both! We don't all have the same coloured skin; we are rich, and we are poor. So how can you tell whether someone is Pagan or not? In all honesty, you can't. You might have an intuitive inkling, but based on surface appearances and social and economic background, there is no foolproof way of narrowing down the field.

When you go downtown and out in public, do you put on a mask to keep your true self protected, or do you do it because you are ashamed of who you are? We all spend some time preparing and dressing up before we walk out the door. It's all about how you look and how you act when the general public can view you. But what you are doing, perhaps inadvertently so, is falling into the trap of the social sheep—the conformist who lacks self-confidence and fears persecution.

Every one of us makes up the diversity of society, and we should contribute our unique energy in order to keep things fresh. Just because we're Pagan doesn't mean that we are overtly different; difference is about uniqueness, and we are all unique when we embrace ourselves, the totality of who we are. Rather than hide behind a mask that drains and discolours your inner self, why not laugh it off and show the world what you are truly made of? Don't be tempted to hide and merge in with the crowd; put yourself out there and honour the divine gift of individuality.

In social situations, in places where there are throngs of people constantly weaving in and out of each other, there arises a dilemma. As Pagans, we consciously open ourselves up to life's essence and therefore are left vulnerable to the various levels of that energy travelling about the place all of the time. Humans send out a particular vibration of energy unique to the individual. It can be daunting to feel someone else's vibes so acutely that you end up feeling exactly as they feel. For that reason, this chapter seeks to help you keep yourself to yourself and to enable you to walk through a crowd without feeling walled in and intimidated. There are also various people and situations you may encounter along your way, all of whom will arouse different emotions within you, and there are several spells and rituals provided here that aim to cater to such circumstances. Ultimately, we are all human and do need to venture out in public in order to make purchases and see friends. There's no reason we can't work with Magick to help make sure that experience is a good one!

### Shielding

*Shielding* is the term used to describe the act of working with energy to construct a psychic barrier or shield against impersonal energies. However, rather than the generic medieval version of the shield, the Witch's shield is all-encompassing.

Shielding is a magickal technique that many Pagans perform daily to ensure that they do not contract any "psychic diseases" or fall prey to psychic vampirism, both unintentional and purposeful. The shield can be envisioned as a sphere of white light, a wall of fire, or a network of cobwebs. It is sometimes recommended to use mirrors or brick walls; however, I do not recommend any solid material imagery, as energy follows a blueprint that is modelled through visualisation. If you visualise something that is essentially brittle and vulnerable to constant wear and tear, then the type of shield you will invoke will reflect those qualities and will only negatively affect you.

Shielding is a wise precaution to take when you put yourself into the midst of a crowd. Without shielding, I usually feel drained and irritable whenever I go out because of the barrage of interfering energies and the accidental vampirism that goes on in any public situation.

Each of us has a story of our own, and each story produces its own unique energy or emotional condition. Depressed people may feed from the bubbly and vivacious happiness that is exuded by the lucky ones. Dominant alpha types are on constant surveillance for the weak and vulnerable. The pervasive unawareness of the psychic ramifications of personalised emotional and mental patterns is phenomenal in a society that rejects the effects our astral being has on reality. This is unfortunate, as we could become far more appreciative and considerate if we took the time to respect each other's space and sought only to strengthen the positive, empowering ties and not to take advantage of the draining, negative ones.

Shielding is a practice that takes little time comprehending and utilising. Of course, it is recommended that you take your time to study the various methods of psychic protection and make an educated decision on how you personally will approach the subject. You might like to take on subtle and more elegant shields; pentagram seals, elemental guards, and white-light spheres are among the best. The primary function of any shield should not be to deflect the negative energy (that would just aggravate the sender and increase the possibility of psychic ricochet) but to ground and neutralise it. For more information on shielding, see the appendix.

Below you will find a meditative exercise that can be performed as often as you want to ensure that any negative intent sent your way will find itself firmly lodged in the cooling soil of Mother Earth.

## THE VINEYARD EXERCISE

Do this in a cast circle. Place a bowl of organic grapes in front of you while meditating.

### First Part: Gathering Energy

Sit upright in a comfortable position. Visualise to the right of you a blue or white two-dimensional circle of light shining on the floor. It is coming from below the floor. The floor looks like it has caved in, but the light is sitting comfortably, like a flower, on the floor. It fills you with peace, and in a deosil pattern three other circles of light progressively appear in front, to your left, and behind you. Feel the warmth surrounding you, and then see each circle of light grow into beams of pure and raw energy, stretching infinitely upward and deep into the earth. They begin to move deosil, bathing you in their light. As each light falls across you, a cool breeze breaks over your skin, revitalising you. When you feel at peace and full of energy, the beams of light will stop and shrink back into the earth.

### Second Part: The Inner Journey

Imagine that your skin is breaking away and that it crumbles to dust. Feel the sensation of disappearing as your skeleton breaks away and the residual dust evaporates. You are now left as pure energy, free from any physical attachment. Then the floor shifts beneath you, and you are suddenly surrounded by sunlight as you stand on a hill overlooking a vineyard. As you look out into the ocean of green and brown, you catch sight of a pavilion in the centre of the rows of vines and you fly, run, or instantly appear there.

When you reach the pavilion, slow down and walk through one of its arched entries. The pavilion's foundation is circular in shape and furnished of brick. As you look around, you see four arched entries facing the four directions. Vines are draped gracefully over the wooden framework. As you look up, you see the wooden rafters stretch higher to form an apex in the centre. This too is covered in vines.

In the centre of the pavilion is a beautiful yet simple fountain. The vessel in which the water falls is circular and made of smooth marble. You walk over to the fountain and sit down on the edge. You look into the water and see your physical reflection, though you are still composed completely of energy. It is a calm day, and the gentle light dances playfully around you. Despite all your worries and anxieties, you feel at peace in this place, forgetting the very reason you have come to the vineyard. Let this peace fill you with a sense of safety and security. The vines that provide you with their shade smell of a dew-ridden forest under the rays of the dawn sun. The beauty of this place cannot be destroyed, and negative thoughts and energies sent at you are caught by the hanging vines and directed into the ground to be neutralised.

### Third Part: Returning

Stay for however long you wish, and bask in the peace of mind the pavilion instills in you.

When the time comes to leave, turn your attention to the water in the fountain and jump into the fountain's heart. Open your eyes and take your time to readjust.

To ground, simply sit eating the grapes while retaining your peaceful state. Open the circle and clean up.

Whenever you feel under threat, return to the pavilion and reside within its sanctuary until you feel recharged and ready to deal with the world again.

## ENCHANT THE MASSES!
## SPELLS OF GLAMOUR

### Unseen ... Unnoticed ... Gone!

I'm sure at some point you have wished that you could be invisible—that you could just disappear into the air. The magickal methods inducing periodic invisibility are working realities that are in reach of anyone who has a refined sense of visualisation. All it takes is a couple minutes of intense inner sensation and you will be able to go unnoticed. However, you can't simply stand in the midst of your circle of friends, chatting away, and expect that no one will notice that you are there. Also, if someone close to you is focused on finding you, there is the chance that their clean-cut intent will break through the glamour shield.

This spell is designed to get you out of trouble quickly downtown. If you have caught the attention of someone whose only aim in life is to bully and belittle, then this quick fix will get you out of the sticky situation.

Considering the location and situation, you will most probably have to steal yourself at least five minutes in a store or toilet cubicle so that you can go through the visualisation and then make a clean getaway.

Close your eyes and ground and centre. See yourself in the centre of a brilliant sphere of white light. It laps around you gently, exhilarating your skin and empowering your auric fields. Concentrate on feeling safe, secure, and at peace within yourself. Sustain this visualisation until you feel like an inflated balloon about to burst. At this point, see your physical body disperse into the light and evaporate into nothingness. Allow yourself to feel the sensation of disappearing, and integrate this into your visualisation. Methodically go through each layer of your physical being—outer layer of skin, bones and muscles, blood, and finally molecules and atoms. Then see the white light gradually fade into the air, taking the last of you with it. Focus on your invisibility and silently mouth the following to seal the spell:

> *No human eye shall see my flesh*
> *Or heated blinding hate transgress*
> *And so I'm safe within my skin*
> *My white-light shield comes from within!*

Now head back out into the crowds of people, and keep your mind focused on your state of invisibility. You will now be able to slip by unnoticed and safely escape the attention of your offender.

To become visible again, visualise yourself as solid, present, and composed of flesh, blood, and bone in the here and now. Make sure you eat and drink something, and once you are sure you have returned to your everyday state of being, approach a friend, family member, or stranger and strike up a conversation.

*Note:* Make sure not to approach a friend or family member while still "invisible"—you may frighten them!

### Perfume Is for Scent; Potions Are for Magick

This potion is brewed with the intent of attraction. This tonic will draw to you exactly who you want in terms of qualities (physical, emotional, and mental).

You will need:

Patchouli oil
Rose oil
Lavender oil
A cinnamon stick
A small piece of white paper (a little bigger
   than a Post-It) and a red pen
Red ribbon
One small glass bottle or jar (about the
   height of your middle finger)
A base oil like jojoba, almond, or sunflower

This potion is best made within a cast circle on a Friday night under the waxing moon. Chant the following to bless your evening's work:

*By Freya's night 'neath waxing moon*
*By oils of love I'll conjure soon*
*A partner who shall know me when*
*His/her eyes fall upon me, then*
*Our love shall blossom from that time*
*And on this night he'll/she'll dream me fine.*

Now take your glass bottle or jar and pour in the base oil one third of the way to the top. With the space left, devote one third each of that space to patchouli, rose, and lavender oil respectively (be sure to leave at least two centimetres of space at the top).

Now take the piece of paper and pen and write down at least five qualities you desire in a partner while visualising each one. When finished, hold the paper to your heart and focus on what you have written. Visualise your paper radiating with pink light and sustain the vision for several minutes. Then curl the paper lengthwise and tie it to the cinnamon stick with the red ribbon. Acknowledge in your mind that the cinnamon stick represents you and the piece of paper your desired partner. Try your best to fit these into the bottle. If they just won't fit, you can tie them to the neck of the bottle with a little bit of ribbon (if you use a jar, you won't have this problem).

Now shake the mixture while saying the following words:

> *Brew of oils, thou art made sacred*
> *Cleansed and blessed by my own hand*
> *So that you bring to me a lover*
> *That we'll meet and understand*
> *And thus as ribbon joins us now*
> *We shall become conjoined the same*
> *With love's great arms as guides between us*
> *By my own will, this is my aim.*

Visualise a pink orb of energy around your bottle as it imbues your potion with your intent. You may apply the oil to your body as you would with any perfume whenever you go out (you can follow the line of your chakras or the points of the Fivefold Kiss[1] if you want). If the potion is yet to work, over a period of at least a month simply hold it close to your heart, envision the qualities you want in a partner again, and recite the above chant. You'll soon come across what you are looking for.

---

1 The Fivefold Kiss descends from the rites of British Traditional covens. When honouring the divine within each other, an initiate of one of these covens will kiss (in order) the Witch's feet, knees, sex (phallus or womb), breasts, and lips. There are traditional words that accompany each kiss; however, they vary within traditions.

*The "Something Exciting" Charm*

As young people, we can get particularly restless with a repetitive routine. To avoid the static flow, cast this spell to attract some fun into your life! (This spell was originally published in my first *Pagan Prattle* column in the Australian youth zine *Bizoo*.)

You will need:

Dragon's blood resin (alternatively, you can use flour)
Cauldron or other fireproof container
Fire starters

Focus your mind by clearing it of mundane thought (allowing thoughts to flow in and through your mind). Place the fire starters in the cauldron and light them carefully.

Hold the resin or flour in your power hand above the flames, and chant:

*As chemicals do meld to light*
*And sparks of dust would lift in flight*
*May boring times be sent away*
*Ahead of me exciting days!*

Throw the resin or flour into the flames while concentrating on the limitless opportunity for fun and excitement in your very near future.

Make sure that you respond to any intuitions you may have after the spell that could possibly lead to a night of frivolity and partying.

## ROMANCE & RELATIONSHIPS

*Is my spirituality going to affect my romantic relationships, and to what level?* That's the question a lot of Pagans ask themselves when they meet someone they like and want to date. The answer is—it will as much as you let it! Being Pagan shouldn't stop us from experiencing what others so freely experience in this world—love, happiness, and fulfilment. As human beings, we are entitled to all these things and more, and so there is nothing stopping you from claiming them or seeking them out.

Essentially, your relationships with others, if dictated by your spirituality, will be affected by your decision to make Paganism a big deal. If your partner is making a fuss over your being Pagan and endangering your relationship in doing so, is there anything that can be done to calm the waters of turbulence? Then again, is the relationship worth saving if your partner cannot find it within themselves to hear you out? It's unlikely that your relationship is going to survive if you are harbouring feelings of resentment for a partner who is close-minded. Your involvement in Paganism should not keep you from putting yourself out there. Be strong, wise, and compassionate, and someone will come your way.

I had never gone out with another Pagan until my last partner. Since then, we have parted ways; however, I am content in knowing that we helped each other to appreciate the sacred within the physical. Though two Pagans in a relationship would be nice and spiritually enriching in theory, it is not a sought-out prerequisite for a date. Your spirituality should not be the filter for the religious beliefs of your prospective boy/girlfriend. Move past your differences and involve yourself in the relationship for the romance, the friendship, and the support. You should also be able to freely talk about your spirituality around your partner without feeling scared or worried about what they might think. This is another "broom closet" issue, and it is ultimately up to you whether you want to keep Paganism a secret or open up about it. However, a good and nurturing relationship thrives on perfect love and perfect trust, and if your partner has placed their trust in you to always be truthful and straightforward with them, then you've got to out yourself someday. When that time comes, keep it simple, answer any questions to the best of your ability, and make sure that your partner is aware that you are still you—the person that they fell in love with in the first place.

Okay, so now you're open about your spirituality, and your partner is okay with it. If they are not, then you are probably living through a cycle of bewilderment and confusion as to whether to remain in the relationship or not. If your partner has admitted that they're still in love with you despite the surface tension, then you've caught yourself a winner and you may have to simply keep your spirituality to yourself when your partner is around. However, I am also aware that many Pagans would feel hurt, shocked, and dismayed if their partner did not accept their faith; therefore, it is up to you concerning sustaining or ending the relationship.

If you are currently single and on the lookout for someone to be with, then make sure that you do not make your spirituality the central focus of your dates. It's just plain stupid to sit down opposite a potential candidate and matter-of-factly state "I'm Pagan and you are …?" Names first, Romeo! Do not treat your spirituality as a surface label that constitutes specific laws constraining your relationships with others. If that's the case, then you've become the very opposite of what Pagans aim to be.

Going out with someone is about embracing the opportunity of love, friendship, and beauty. It's about the emotional cultivation of patience and peace and the mindful channelling of the sensual energy of the bedroom. Here is your chance for salvation in the arms of your other half, or twin flame, and by seeking out only Pagan partners, you are clashing with the Fates and tempting the tides of karma.

Once you have found someone whom you have fallen for and vice versa, you can get in depth, serious, friendly, and, yes, erotic! Do things for the fun of it; keep the spontaneity and randomness of life intact within your relationship. Embrace the hilarity of occurrence, and transform the downfalls into learning experiences. Keep things aware, growing, and vibrant, and you've got yourself a world for two.

## SENSE & SENSUALITY

Paganism is one of the few known spiritualities that can openly declare its tolerance and open-mindedness towards sexual minorities. For one, it embraces women as equal and complementary to men and considers the Divine Feminine as an especially significant aspect of the various traditions, and two, it does not pass judgement or discriminate against gays, lesbians, bisexuals, or transgendered (GLBT) individuals. Paganism advocates freedom and diversity in all aspects of life, and sexuality is by no means excluded.

As a gay Pagan myself, I can attest to having experienced discrimination on the grounds of my sexuality. I have been physically chased, taunted, and vilified simply because I love men in an intimate way. For the track record, I would like to say that sexuality is hardly ever a matter of personal choice; it is generally something that is predisposed. Whether this owes to genetics or not, I cannot say; however, there are many interesting studies that experiment with the various theories regarding the origin and derivation of one's sexual nature.

I'd like to think that the Pagan community is one of the safest places to be open about sexuality, and in my experience it has been! However, simply because someone is Pagan does not necessarily mean that the individual will feel kindly towards those who identify as GLBT. There is prejudice everywhere. For this reason, I suggest discretion (not cowardice) and confidence rather than confrontation.

There is ample evidence to suggest that homosexuality and gender illusionism were considered sacred by the ancients. In the classical Hellenic world, homosexual relationships between older men and younger boys were socially acceptable, as this reflected a paradigm within the myth of Zeus and his beloved cupbearer and youth Ganymede and Apollo and his beautiful Hyakinthos, who was transformed into the hyacinth flower after he was killed by a jealous Zephyros (god of the west wind). The Amazonians tolerated a women-only society and refused male infants at birth. These warrior women were said to cut off their right breasts so that accuracy with the bow was heightened. Sappho, one of history's first celebrated female poets, hailed from the isle of Lesbos in the Aegean Sea where the current-day term *lesbian* is derived from. Women were often featured as the intimate subjects of her poetry. Androgyny, or the fusion of both male and female aspects to create an asexual or bisexual being, was a prime alchemical status to aspire to. Many considered Hermaphroditos, the son of Aphrodite and Hermes, the embodiment of the intricacies of the natural world—the complementary co-existence and mutual marriage between the sexes.

The sacred Hieros Gamos (Great Marriage) was not and is not an institution for heterosexuality over any other form of sexual expression but the metaphorical symbol for the union of love between two complementary forces, a dynamic that is marked by projection (traditionally masculine) and reception (traditionally feminine), alternating patterns that stir the creative channels. Remember, we all comprise within our psyches masculine and feminine aspects, and these have nothing to do with physical gender. Our bodies are one thing, but our spirits are another thing completely! It is important to raise consciousness to the level where all life is as it is, and is not impeded by the seductive coercion of the illusory forces at play.

Men may love men as women love men and as women love women in whichever way they choose to do so. The fact that there exist in this world organisations and groups of people that hold deep-set prejudices against GBLT-identified individuals indicates that fear is liable to assume the form of ignorance at the get-go. Conservative Christians, right-wing political parties, and fascist organisations (e.g., the Ku Klux Klan) all claim that their love for the social norm—defined by a narrowly prescribed field of a Western paradigm—is their reason for and behind their hatred for particular groups of people. I say it is hypocrisy to uphold a symbol of universal love and divine truth (e.g., Christ), as so many of these organisations do, whilst also engendering bigotry, intolerance, and discrimination.

It is a scientific fact that without varying and contrasting factors, the evolutionary progression of life would stagnate and deteriorate. At their core, Pagan values reflect the beauty of Cosmos and the necessity of Chaos, two forces that are both, in and of themselves, positive and perfect. Remember that to draw parallels between two things is to reveal the quality of the unifying connection that strengthens the ultimate relationship—both Pagans and GBLT individuals have lived the closeted life once (sometimes twice) before.

Below, you will find two spells to bless your love life and to keep the Magick alive and real in your relationship. You may also brew a tea to promote understanding and acceptance in your relationship, and share it over a romantic dinner.

*Two's Company*

This spell can be used to prepare for a romantic night at home with the DVDs and popcorn.

You will need:

> One handful of dried lavender
> One handful of rose petals
> Plenty of blankets, pillows, and soft things
> A sappy love movie, corny teen flick, or even gory horror film
> Sparkling apple juice for the two of you

There is no need to cast a circle, as you will be constructing a temporary sacred space during the spell.

About half an hour before you are expecting your partner to turn up, get dressed slowly and seductively (it helps to turn on some mood music to help dash the self-conscious qualms), making sure you look your best. In your living room (or wherever you are planning to watch the movies), make sure you have a solid surface to carry out the spell. Before you begin, to exude comfort and warmth you will need to arrange several blankets, pillows, and cushions around the space and on the couch you will share with your partner.

Take the dried lavender in your power hand and the rose petals in your receptive hand, and ground and centre. Incorporate pink light into your visualisation, and see yourself surrounded by an aura of pink that is flowing around you like warm honey. See the energy congregate around your two hands, and feel the pink light seep into the lavender and rose. Once you feel the energy reach its peak, chant the following:

> *Flowing streams of warm romance*
> *Fill my hands and weave your dance*
> *Rose, seduction, loving light*
> *Cast upon this house your might*
> *Lavender, your peaceful dew*
> *Open arms so that we two*
> *May drift upon a sea of love*
> *This spell is cast as flies the dove!*

As you finish the last line, see a white dove burst forth from the pink light and fly three times deosil around the room, blessing the space. Watch as the dove settles itself wherever it chooses, and be sure to keep an eye on it every now and then throughout the night.

The only thing you've got to do now is scatter the rose petals and lavender under the couch and pour two glasses of sparkling apple juice for yourself and your partner. The night should be a splendid one, as you are joined with your lover over the empowered properties of both lavender and rose.

At the end of the night, when your partner has gone home or is out of sight, sweep up the herbs from under the couch and go outside. There, reflect on the night and pay homage to the dove as it settles on your shoulder. When you are ready, chant the following:

> *All is well, the spell is cast*
> *This night as memory shall last*
> *For blessed it's been by purest dove*
> *How sweet the messenger of love*
> *And now about the heavens fly*
> *And take your peace into the sky*
> *Until such time I'll call again*
> *Farewell, good dove, my gentle friend.*

Throw the rose and lavender into the air—hopefully a breeze will catch the remnants and scatter them, spreading loving energies of concord and romance. Feel the dove launch off your shoulder before it disappears into the night.

### Friday Is for Fun!

This spell is designed to enhance the act of sex. If you are under the legal age of consent, I suggest that you simply read over this spell to catch a glimpse of the power and sensuality of sex Magick. This by no means is the collective form of sex Magick and is simply a spell aimed at the joining of two consenting individuals.

This spell will not aid in conception and is focused on energising your sexual experience. It is up to you and your partner whether you will use contraception or not; however, it is recommended here. Use this spell wisely!

You will need:

> Patchouli incense
> Ylang ylang essential oil
> Pine essential oil
> Jasmine essential oil
> Two red candles

For this spell, you will not need to cast a circle. Cast this spell on a Friday evening before a lovemaking session.

Begin by anointing one of the candles with equal parts of ylang ylang and jasmine essence. This will represent feminine power and will be placed in a secure candleholder on the left-hand side of your bed. Use the first two fingers of your power hand to dress the candle. Begin in the middle of your candle and going deosil and up, dress the candle until you reach the top; then do the same, but this time start at the centre and go down until you reach the bottom. As you do, visualise a young maiden with beautiful, flowing hair, a body woven of gossamer threads, and soft, voluptuous skin. Her heart is wild within her chest, and she smiles secretively at you. She is the flirtatious and alluring nymph.

Now, with equal parts of pine and ylang ylang, repeat the procedure as above, but this time focus on a young, virile man whose body is well developed. He is a kind-hearted poet and generous friend while also being the spear carrier and the warrior of his tribe. This candle, once dressed properly, will be placed in a candleholder to the right of your bed.

Now light both candles and stand at the bottom of your bed, facing the bed's head; spread your legs apart and lift your arms into the air, palms open and facing out. Ground and centre, and attune your breathing to the ragged cycles experienced during an impassioned lovemaking session. Feel the passion and sensuality of bodies joining and enveloping each other. Feel the pulsing tides of energy as it moves between the bodies. Experience the waves of heat and energy as they sweep over you and spin you into a world of ecstasy and transcendence. This is the eternal spiral of the shaman's dance.

When the power reaches its peak, chant:

> *Gods of love and passion rise*
> *Upon this night of Freya's ties*
> *Fill this room as your sacred shrine*
> *My flesh is charged by this sign*[2]
> *Five by rite and five by life*
> *Mark me well and cast out strife*
> *Union, joining, merging halves*
> *Imbue the air that shifts 'tween calves*
> *Lip to lip and phallus to womb*
> *Bless the spinning Lady's loom*
> *Flesh to flesh and grail to lance*
> *Sacred is the lover's dance*
> *Upon this night of Freya's ties*
> *Gods of love and passion rise!*

Feel as the energy spirals to a pinpoint and then explodes over you in a shower of warmth, electricity, and passion. Now you may light the patchouli incense and begin, making sure that the candles' flames are safely contained.

*Note:* This spell can also be used for two gay guys or girls. You may like to stick with the original candle-dressing routine invoking both God and Goddess as symbolic forces of co-creation, which are inherent within both you and your partner, or you might like to focus on two specific male or female deities who

---

2 Gesture the shape of the pentagram across your body. Use the first two fingers of your power hand and draw the arms of the pentagram as follows: from head to right breast, from right breast to left shoulder, from left shoulder to right shoulder, from right shoulder to left breast and from left breast back to head.

are associated with homosexuality. If you are male, you could invoke Zeus and his lover Ganymede, the cupbearer of Olympus,
or Apollo and Hyakinthos. For two girls, Artemis and one of her
maidens are valid options. In any case, do your research on your
chosen deities beforehand so you are familiar with their myths,
their energies, and their characteristics.

You may also like to change the wording of the chant from
"Lip to lip and phallus to womb ..." to "Lip to lip and limb to
limb, weaving wonder as we sing. Flesh to flesh and heart to
heart, no longer do our bodies part." You can adapt the words
to suit your own tastes.

Both of the spells above are open to adaptation, and if you like, you can
ask your partner to help cast the spells with you.

# 5: PAGAN COMMUNITY

The word *community* is generally used to define a group of people who share a common historical and cultural background and live together in a specific area, interacting and weaving a complex web of interdependence, responsibility, experience, and power. However, in the case of Paganism, community does not imply that all Pagans must live in the same area—or, for that matter, interact.

Think of J. K. Rowling's Harry Potter series. The "wizarding world" is almost exactly synonymous with the Pagan community in terms of how the phrases are used. *Wizard* in Rowling's interpretation is a word referring to a magickal person. *World* and *community* can also be identified as representing similar circumstances. However, the word *world* implies that wizards live in a separate place with different rules, in contrast to the day-to-day routine of muggles. That world is one of perception given its distinct qualities, because those who live within it accept that Magick is real, whereas muggles are oblivious to its presence or equally defiant that it cannot and will not exist. Likewise, Pagans seek to maintain their connection with the physical world while at the same time experiencing something that is often described as paranormal and supernatural. To Pagans, however, it is very much a part of who we are, and to separate the two is inconceivable.

*Pagan community* is a concept that is flourishing rapidly. Having that sense of connection with people on the opposite side of the world inspires us to communicate our ideas and philosophies and contribute our individual energies to a universal movement. Despite all of our differences, there is a sense of unity among today's Pagans. But in order to consolidate and progress into a brighter future, we Pagans need to reassert the communal values that unite us, despite unwarranted Witch wars and power struggles. Let there be no more ego-tripping and battering of salt-soaked wounds.

## SOMETHING OLD, SOMETHING NEW: BRIDGING THE GAP

NeoPaganism is a decentralised, autonomous, and anarchistic spirituality. Essentially, NeoPaganism is pure democracy. Discrimination on the grounds of race, religion, appearance, sexuality, etc., is frowned upon. Freedom and equality are admired and upheld, and opinion is valued for what it is—opinion. Unfortunately, despite accepted Pagan attitudes, Pagans are human and therefore prone to mistakes. Making mistakes is not necessarily a bad thing—in the long run, they can help us to learn and progress along life's bountiful path. However, despite the discrimination Pagans receive from non-Pagans, there are still those who suffer from ill treatment within the Pagan community. One of these groups is the youth.

There is a gap between the older members of our community and the younger ones. This gap is evident in all aspects of life; Pagans are not the only ones who recognise it. The gap between the younger generation and their parents or the older members of society is there. Things have changed over the past few decades, and that change has given way to a new generation.

My generation lives in a world of shifting attitudes and deteriorating fashions. Sexuality is something that is generally celebrated, although there are still many who revile homosexuality. Multiculturalism is seen as a necessary component of a modern democratic nation, though racial friction still exists. Freedom of speech and expression is guarded and given sanction by the law; however, hypocrisy still reigns.

Youth is change, revelation, and awakening. Youth is the bridge from childhood innocence into adulthood, and the Pagan reveres both. Unlike modern Western society, Paganism does not view time in broken and separate phases but in ongoing cycles and necessary passages. Childhood, adolescence, and adulthood should not be seen as separate and discrete stages but as passages serving the experience of the next. They are all intertwined.

Bridging the gap between us and the "adults"[1] should not have to be a momentous trial but an enjoyable experience full of life's lessons. If we are to succeed, the effort needs to go both ways. Both adults and youths need to cooperate and honour each other as evolving beings in order to create a sense of peace and harmony in our community. Honesty and humility are wise things.

If Paganism is to survive into the future, we need to retain our unique spirit of honour, community, and friendship. Look to Nature, our great teacher, and see how she celebrates the links between every individual being. Nature does what has to be done so that life may continue to flourish. Rather than drown us in eternal torture or shower us in perpetual light (and light does blind!), Mother Nature reinforces the importance of balance. She draws no line between dark and light but sees them as complementary and thus reflects this paradox into our lives.

The wider Pagan community needs to acknowledge the young as a vital strand of existence, and the youth need to honour the older members of the community as a source rich in experience and knowledge. Once both "sides" come to grips with the reality of the situation and

---

1 Though I consider myself both an adult and a youth simultaneously. I think most Pagan adults retain their sense of youth throughout their lives.

seek to promote understanding and cooperation, we will have truly embraced the stuff of peace. Our differences should not separate us but unite us in life's keen diversity. Without change or destruction, life would recede and be rendered extinct.

Working together in reverence, celebration, and understanding should be our main aim in order to bridge the gap. As young Pagans, we need to uphold a positive and dynamic image as well as break down the tendency in the more traditional Pagans to categorise all teens as fluffy bunnies.

A successful community is founded on the principles of compassion, acceptance, and diversity, and Paganism as a spirituality seeks to integrate all of these into practice. Fundamentalism and conservatism are alien and outdated practices that have no place in the Pagan traditions of today. Our home, the earth, is no longer revered as the great mother of all but exploited and disregarded. Rather than allow this pattern to fester, Pagans need to set an example for the rest of the world; the microcosm (in this case, the Pagan community) will work to affect the macrocosm (the global community). Therefore, it is unreasonable and hypocritical to allow discrimination to occur within our own community. In conjunction with "bridging the gap," issues of hidebound tradition and discrimination also require attention. For the most part, Pagans have made it part of their spiritual endeavours to see that the world becomes a better place in both spirit and body.

If you as a young Pagan are ever ostracised or discriminated against because of the circumstance of age, then I suggest you take a good look at the offender and stand your ground. Several years ago, I had to endure a period of feeling uncomfortable and "lesser than" the older Pagans at a local social gathering I attended. I finally voiced my concerns, and I no longer felt small or worthless but empowered and inspired. Positive self-esteem is required for any individual who desires to develop their skills of perception and to evolve spiritually. Never allow yourself to be compromised in the name of social hierarchy.

When you approach the gap, don't anticipate that either side will make the first move. If you internally reject the gap and affirm that it only exists in relation to the community's attitude, then you have successfully begun the bridging process. Over time, the need for a bridge will dissipate, and the gap that once seemed so vast becomes a mere memory. Celebrate unity in diversity, and understand that the path to healing lies in your motivation to become whole. I think when it comes to removing the injustices in our community, we can take a page from the Witch's Pyramid: *Know* who you are, *Dare* to be yourself, *Will* that justice is done, and *Silence* the voice that feeds intolerance.

## The Curse of the Fluffy Bunny: A Social Syndrome

Over the past decade, NeoPaganism, or more specifically Wicca and Witchcraft, have become the fastest-growing spiritualities in the Western world. Teenagers make up a large number of this sudden growth. Television programs such as *Charmed, Buffy,* and *Sabrina, the Teenage Witch* have opened up teens to worlds where Magick is real and where Witches are powerful beings with abilities beyond the norm. *Harry Potter*, renewed interest in *Lord of the Rings*, the *Wicca/Sweep* series, and *The Witches of Eileanan* books cater to the thirst for fantasy and Magick among the younger generations and portray the supernatural as awe-inspiring and accessible in a way that no literature has ever done before. Teens are now presented with what has been an innate fascination spanning centuries—Witchcraft, Magick, and the occult. For those teens who are naturally predisposed to the Magick in this world, a door has opened and Paganism has greeted them. Unfortunately, this portrayal of Witchcraft and Pagan spirituality as trendy, straightforward, and supernatural has also conditioned the generic teen's approach to the subject. Initially, it may be the search for power and popularity that inspires their interest; however, the more they look into the reality of Witchcraft and Paganism, the more they realise they have fallen in love with what it stands for. What has happened is that society has put forth a new myth concerning Witches and Paganism that has diluted its essence in order to focus on the trappings and conquests of Magick. Teens who don't know any better and yet are deeply attracted to the concepts abide by these misconceptions, and these are the fluffy bunnies.

In a nutshell, a fluffy bunny is an individual who is involved in Witchcraft and/or Paganism and appears to lightly skim the surface of Magick and spirituality, living a fantasy of "white light" and "harm none." Unfortunately, an archetype has been born, and many older Pagans (as well as some self-righteous younger ones) see fluffy bunnies everywhere, to the point of paranoia. Gossip, slander, and "holier than thou" attitudes have bred rapidly throughout the community, and many innocent people are being accused of being fluffy. The stereotype of a *Charmed*-obsessed, white-lighting, and naïve teenager has preceded the truth. Yes, there are those individuals who come to the Craft in the hopes that they fulfil an ancient prophecy and are instantly imbued with the power to freeze time; however, many of these individuals soon realise that what they are looking for is a self-induced illusion. For many, this is the turning point of revelation, and from this moment many a true and devoted Pagan is born. I should know, as I too came to the Craft anticipating powers and abilities beyond my wildest dreams. It becomes clear, then, that the fluffy bunny, while being admittedly irritating, is not always a permanent identity but can become a valid doorway to the truths of Pagan spirituality. Therefore, rather than hiss, swear, and preach at the fluffy bunnies who stumble upon your path, attempt to clear up their misconceptions and provide them with accurate information.

The very existence of the term *fluffy bunny* within Paganism is hypocritical in the sense that a word devoted to the use of belittling another is essentially discrimination. Ideally, Pagans—or anyone, for that matter—should not judge before the facts are known, and categorising or stereotyping isn't a trend to be proud of. Despite this, many Pagans do discriminate, and those who do are prone to the many social pitfalls that exist. I, for one, despise the term *fluffy bunny,* and any notion to abolish it from usage in Pagan circles is fine with me! The very idea that Pagans have a word of their own to toss about superficially is terribly off-putting, as I like to think of the Pagan community as an open-minded, honest, and creative bunch. I also understand that there are times when, for the sake of convenience, "fluffy bunny" is the only phrase one can think of to use.

The future lies in our hands, and like the generations that came before us, the job of improving on what we see as hampering necessary growth within our community is now ours.

## Teen Pagan Network

Over the last couple of years, support groups and organisations have sprung up across the world specifically focused on the development of teen Pagans. In most cases, these networking groups are run and operated by teens themselves and have no formal connections with each other.

Teen Pagan Network is not an officially recognised or ordained organisation; it is the tip of the iceberg of a quiet and humble revolution occurring globally.[2] Pagan teens and youths in general are beginning to realise that they have the right to be treated in fairness and equality with the older members of our community. This is not a radical attempt at rebellion against the Pagan community but a cry for common sense.

Teens, as minors, are often unintentionally left to their own devices because of legal restrictions preventing them from joining covens, other Pagan organisations, and study groups. I am not implying that the majority of older Pagans in our community reject the new surge of interested youths, and indeed it is only a minority that do. However, I have personally encountered several older Pagans who initially dismissed me as fluffy and superficial based solely on my age. Assumptions based on age and appearances are rooted in discrimination. Generally, Pagans make an effort to remain objective and nonjudgemental when it comes to interacting with other people; however, being Pagan does not instantly make one a saint. We are all human.

Teen Pagan Network is a concept. The various support groups bearing the title are not necessarily interlinked or even aware of each other. Teen Pagan Network is a source of compassion and friendship

---

2 I was first introduced to the concept of Teen Pagan Network when I met the co-founder of the Brisbane Teen Pagan Network at the first Australian Pagan Pride event in Brisbane in 2002.

fostered by peers who are familiar with the trials and tribulations of the modern-day teen and who have likely been affected by the trend of categorising teens as ignorant and childish. Many adult Pagans admit that they do not understand why teens need separate groups and specific focus, and they are quite welcome to that confusion. It has to be made clear that it is not a purposeful rejection of the adults that causes teens to create and organise their own groups, but it is the need to mix with others of the same age. Teen Pagan Network helps teens gain a greater sense of self-esteem and introduces beginners and the curious to Paganism in a comfortable and open environment. Below you will find advice on how to kick-start your own Teen Pagan Network.

### Creating Your Own Teen Pagan Network

Before you jump into the scheduling and running of meets, you need to understand what you are getting yourself into by creating a Teen Pagan Network. First of all, a TPN is a localised concept, meaning you will have no support or connection with the other groups in your state or country, unless of course you arrange for that. You will be on your own, perhaps with a few other key individuals, and expected to have a good foundation of knowledge in Paganism. After all, teens will be contacting you to ask questions, and you'll need to be able to answer them with a certain level of expertise and experience.[3] By organising a TPN, you need to be aware that you are taking on a serious role as teacher, leader, and role model to other teen Pagans. You need to be secure within yourself to take on such a responsibility.

Once you fully understand what you are getting yourself into, the next thing you need to do is to sit down and record your ideas. If you are co-founding your TPN with others, this is a time to showcase your collaborative teamwork skills.

Begin by structuring a framework for your meets. By this, I mean decide where and when you will hold your meets. It might be a good idea to develop a mission statement to formalise your group. When you get to the stage of creating a website or mailing list for your group,

---

3  In fact, I was once contacted by a journalist who got my contact information from a Teen Pagan Network advertisement. I ended up being interviewed for my local paper, and an article on Paganism with a rather large picture of me soon appeared.

you could include your mission statement on the main page. A mission statement is your group's central objectives and convictions—i.e., what you want to achieve through a Teen Pagan Network. Something like:

*Teen Pagan Network seeks to familiarise young Pagans with the workings of the wider Pagan community and to develop a support unit for Pagan teens who may be experiencing hardships and loneliness.*

If you are taking on the organisational role, you also need to consider your own qualities and whether you can cope with the weight of forming and coordinating a TPN. If you decide that you are capable of facilitating the meets, you are also taking on a degree of leadership. If you lend your name and details as the key contact in your advertising, you are the visual beacon to those who come across your advertisement. Therefore, make sure you can prioritise with your other commitments.

If you feel that organising a TPN solely on your own may be a little too much for you, then I suggest that you network with other volunteers and schedule several preliminary meetings to flesh out your group's framework. This includes a working mission statement, meet details, and advertising. With other willing delegates to help shoulder the load, you can delegate specific roles and jobs to each individual to ensure that everything is done within a short period of time.

The next step in kickstarting your TPN is advertising. This is not as hard as it sounds, believe me! The simplest technique of advertising is with posters and flyers. Suss out the whereabouts of local community noticeboards and start there. Libraries, bookstores, university and high-school campuses, youth hang-outs, alternative music stores, health-food stores, and New Age or Pagan specialty retailers are recommended places.

There is the very high possibility that your posters will be removed by narrow-minded individuals (it's happened to me!); unfortunately, there is no sure-fire way around this. You will find that the places I have mentioned above are going to be the most receptive when it comes to having Pagan posters on their premises.

You can also post your meet's details on Pagan websites. Look for sites hosted by local Pagans first and inquire about posting your meet's details. Most Pagan sites have a link to local meets and groups. Witch-Vox (www.witchvox.com) is another great place to advertise!

Once people are aware that your group exists, word-of-mouth becomes a viable method of advertising. When I was running a TPN several years ago, I bumped into a couple of people who found out about it through members. It's certainly satisfying when all that hard work pays off and things happen naturally. Patience and devotion are definite prerequisites for any TPN founder. If no one responds to your advertisements in the first couple of weeks or months, don't give up! It took me several months before I attracted any attention through advertising. If you suspect that someone has been sabotaging your posters, then you need to voice your concerns to the owner of the store and inquire whether you are still welcome to advertise there. If you are given the all clear, then put up another poster, and check up on it every now and then to make sure it's still up.

When people begin to inquire about the meets, you need to make sure you deal with each and every person individually and with equal conviction. Basically, it's a good idea to personally reply to each person's e-mail or message and to tell them a bit about yourself and about how the group runs. Once you feel you have attracted a good number of willing attendees, it's time to schedule your first meet.

The first meet is certainly an adrenaline-rushing event. All your preliminary organising has paid off, and you can revel in the utter pleasure of being with others of like mind to share experiences, issues, and questions. Make sure that everyone is clear on the location and time of the meet and what to bring, etc. I usually recommend that people bring along a friend, Pagan or otherwise, and a snack. I also encourage people to bring books, magazines, and other interesting odds and ends. For some time, I brought along an activity box, which was filled to the brim with glitter, pens, paper, incense, candles, ribbon, herbs, and an array of other stuff so that we always had something to do.

To ensure that the other teens can find you when the day of the meet comes, organise that the group each wear a specific colour or carry a flower. I've had people turn up to the correct park but not the correct side. To ensure that you are not missed, it is sometimes essential to be "obvious." I am not suggesting you need to do cartwheels, shouting "Hail and welcome!" but that you need to stand out in some way. I've been known to dress up the old oak tree in red ribbon!

Once everyone has congregated, you need to be able to dismiss any awkwardness by making sure you do not convey the same energy. After all, a TPN is useless unless you've got everyone participating in the event. Greet everyone collectively, introduce yourself, and then get down to it; make sure it's not too formal or you'll scare people off! Organise everyone into a comfortable circle and then get the ball rolling on introductions. Give everyone their own time and space to formulate what they are going to say. You need to make sure that you are not too overwhelming or fake when it comes to talking and sharing. Keep things real. A laid-back, energising meet is preferable to an overly structured one.

After the introductions, the fun stuff begins. Things lead where they must naturally, so don't push too hard. When I ran a TPN in my hometown, I usually let people do what they wanted to do while I simultaneously kept the peace. I brought along specific activities attuned to the seasons to reinforce the spiritual element of the meets. For example, during an autumn meet, I brought along a large piece of yellow paper and a bag full of autumn leaves to make a collage. At that meet, there were ten people, and while I had two girls enraptured in gluing leaves in various patterns over the paper, the others were having an in-depth discussion about how each individual perceives Paganism.

There's also the chance that there will be beginners and newbies attending your meets, and you may have to answer several questions concerning Pagan spirituality, which may lead to further discussions among the more experienced members of the group. Make sure you've got everyone involved and clarify that anyone can voice their opinion at any time.

If you feel that you are capable of it, holding rituals in connection with the month's season can help reinforce the spiritual element of the meets. It's also a great way of introducing some of the beginners to Pagan ritual and how it works (See Open Circle, next page). I've held several rituals in conjunction with a TPN at the sabbats and esbats, and I have also led the group through various energy and meditation exercises to encourage people to follow up on them on their own.

When it comes to saying goodbye, announce the date of the next meet and encourage people to get active in terms of spreading the word. I suggest that you hand out a list of the upcoming meets and dates to everyone and include your contact details so that if there are any queries, you are able to help out.

Once your group has developed into a successful support network, it's time to upgrade your services. Constructing a website for your group to access online is not simple; it requires computer know-how and Internet expertise, of which I have none! However, when I ran a TPN, I did have a website, and since I moved elsewhere, the managerial role has been passed on, and the membership is over a hundred! I used MSN Groups to assist in creating an online haven for Pagan teens in my area. If you are a member of MySpace or Facebook, then you've got all you need to construct your site, as the method is simple and stress-free.

So now you're online and your group is up and going. From there, it's just a question of getting old and graduating from teenhood. When the time comes, pass on the reins to a younger member of the group so that the TPN does not end with you. You can remain an honorary member and perhaps give advice from afar, but technically you aren't supposed to attend the meets. I'm sure it's permissible from time to time; however, in your absence, you are reinforcing the very reason for a TPN—to allow teen Pagans to experience the realities of a working community in a comfortable surrounding with people of the same age.

## OPEN CIRCLE

An open circle is one of the most exciting events you can attend. They offer the chance to experience the beauty and power of group work. It takes a lot of devotion to organise and lead an open circle, as the individual is expected to act as the priest/ess and direct the group's energy toward the goal. If you are interested in organising an open circle in your area, then this section is essential reading material.

If you are thinking of holding your own open circle then you need to consider whether you have the experience to lead others through ritual. You need to understand the intricacies of Pagan ritual. If you feel you have what it takes, the next thing you need to consider is the ritual's form and the end it will serve. It's recommended that your first open circle take place on a sabbat or esbat. Once you have decided on the timing of your open circle, you will need to do some study of your own. Search through books and the Internet for the specific sabbat or esbat ritual you are going to perform. Look over several variations and compare. You can use one of the rituals you've found, adapt it, or script an original.

When I organise open circles, I write the rituals from scratch or simply follow mental guidelines instilled in me from my training. If you opt to write your own ritual, then you need to take into account that it will need to be comprehensible and appropriate. The key point to remember is that ultimately all ritual serves the purpose of connecting us with the divine.

If you are celebrating a sabbat, make sure you involve something of seasonal significance instead of falling prey to the pomp and ceremony of dramatic tones. I once attended a Mabon circle in which a Druid priestess officiated. We cast the circle and called the quarters following the Wiccan style. Once it got to the bulk of the ritual, though, I was left at a loss for words, as the ritual seemed devoid of vitality and "meat." In essence, we had taken half an hour to cast the circle, five minutes to acknowledge Mabon, and another half an hour to open the circle. I've always made a point of including seasonally relevant activities and symbolism to honour the sabbat and to attune to the cycle.

You also need to decide where to hold your open circle. I'm sure that you don't want total strangers wandering around your backyard. My coven usually holds open circles in a public park. If you are in contact with any local Pagan organisations, perhaps you could give them a call and ask if you could hold the ritual on their property.

Remember that going public may not be received well in your area, and you might have to consider a private place away from the masses.

If your congregation is a private gathering, then you should be fine; however, you need to consider what ritual tools you will be using and whether they could potentially be viewed as a threat. Avoid using athames, swords, or anything an innocent bystander would find threatening or dangerous. Wands, cauldrons, flower wreaths, and the more natural items are preferable. If you intend to use candles, make sure they are safely contained or within a fireproof container. On that note, rather than lighting a fire within the cauldron, light a few pillar candles and place them inside the cauldron.

Once you have thought things through, it's time to spread the word, advertise, and ultimately pray that people attend your open circle. For your first time, you need to be aware that several adult Pagans will also see the advertisements, and that if you are uncomfortable with an adult presence you need to make it clear that the open circle is for teens only. Obviously it's not a good idea to have **OPEN CIRCLE—TEENS ONLY** in bold capitals across the top of the poster, as that is directly exclusive, whereas something like **OPEN CIRCLE FOR TEENS** would not be.

Advertising is a matter of time and attention. Unlike with a Teen Pagan Network, it is not possible to patiently wait until you attract attention, as the sabbats only come once a year and it's bad organising to post-pone one event after the other.

When the day of your open circle arrives, mentally and spiritually prepare yourself by relaxing, focusing, and keeping it real. You need to have fun and at the same time remember your duty to provide a safe and enjoyable day to open, interested, and curious people who may never have experienced Pagan ritual before.

Arrive half an hour early to set everything up. Don't worry about how many people will turn up, just make sure that you are relaxed and that you keep a positive frame of mind. When people start turning up, greet them and initiate conversation. When the time comes to start the ritual, you can begin to explain how the ritual will run and what the significance of the specific day is. If anyone has any questions, make sure that you answer them to the inquirer's satisfaction. After the preliminary stuff, you can begin the ritual. Remember to keep things running smoothly and to concentrate. Ask for volunteers to help call the quarters and cast the circle.

If you have opted for a simple circle, then simply join hands, ground and centre, and visualise a brilliant sphere of white light around you as you walk deosil. Chant something to affirm the circle's boundaries:

> *Casting circle as we run*
> *Powers of the moon and sun*
> *Hear our voices one by one*
> *This circle's cast and be it done!*

When you reach the climax of the ritual and the energy is peaking, open your intuitive faculties and hand over your mind to divine inspiration. When the time comes to release the energy, you will feel it, and you should shout "Release!" or something to that effect. At the shouting of the keyword, everyone should fall to the ground in dramatic fervour. Allow everyone time to recuperate.

Once everyone is composed, pass around food and drink. Here, you can either choose to discuss the ritual within the circle or open the circle and chat afterwards. Ask how everyone felt during the ritual and make sure to share some of your own thoughts. Accept constructive criticism and take in everyone's comments. Stay as long as you want. Talk, laugh, and swap contact details. Who knows, this may be the start of a new study group or coven!

## PAGAN MEETS:
## A NOTE ON CAT HERDING

We Pagans have a famous saying: "Getting Pagans together is like herding cats." It's true! Unfortunately, the implications of this proverb are that there are times when our attempts at meets, study groups, gatherings, and networks result in hopeless flops. Never give up, though! It takes perseverance, devotion, and patience to organise Pagan gatherings. I've turned up to meets where there's only been me, and I go home angry, disappointed, and sweaty.

Ultimately, it is up to the individual to add to the numbers attending Pagan gatherings. If you feel frightened, anxious, or nervous about putting yourself out there, remember that, above all, a Pagan is an advocate for freedom and diversity. Don't feel as if you should close yourself in simply because you haven't had the training or feel you will appear incompetent and foolish before the older Pagans. You are at your own point and pace of growth, and you need to accept and embrace the path you are on. Remember, you are one more person, and you have the power and presence to radiate your personal energy.

We Pagans are a highly individualistic bunch, and for that reason it's hard to understand how events such as Pagan Pride are such a success! However, Pagan gatherings are the future of our community. They provide friendly and open environments where Pagans can get together, discuss issues of importance, have fun, and get to know each other without feeling an obligation to commit to anything. You can be a part of our vibrant community if you take a chance and visit a local Pagan group or form your own. Pagan meets and gatherings are what you make of them!

PART TWO

# BEYOND THE CIRCLE

# 6: ETHICAL QUESTIONS

Pagan traditions are generally ethically sound belief systems. For instance, Wiccans adhere to the Wiccan Rede, which advises them to act as they will as long as no harm is done. As a Pagan who is not Wiccan, I do not abide by the Wiccan Rede; however, I do seek to live by a code of conduct. I also live by my spiritual creeds, which highlight the importance of treating others fairly and embracing diversity as a primary strength within humans and all of Nature. There are certain ethical codes intertwined with most Pagan traditions.

The current revived Pagan traditions all have their roots in ancient practices and beliefs but adapt these for the modern practitioner. Many scholars view the NeoPagan movement as an extension of the occult revolution that flourished in Victorian England. While Paganism may have benefited from the leverage of interest in occult philosophies during the early 1900s, Paganism in and of itself is a unique blend of ancient and modern spiritual philosophies.

To survive in the modern world, Paganism has had to adapt to current lifestyles and attitudes while at the same time retaining its magickal identity. To do this, notions of sacrifice, drug use, and other ancient Pagan customs have disappeared, and Paganism in general has developed a sound ethical foundation.

Society has changed radically since ancient times, and what is considered the norm nowadays may have been perceived as revolutionary in the ancient cultures. Therefore, there is the slightest chance that historians, raised within highly organised democratic societies, interpret evidence of ethical practice noncontextually because of cultural unfamiliarity.

Hypocrisy runs rife when organised religion abuses its imposed regulations. The Catholic Church has suffered considerably from the controversy surrounding priests committing pedophilic acts. The media's frenzy with fundamentalist Islam has done a great deal of damage to the faith itself. Religion in its orthodox sense is based on a constrained relationship with the divine, facilitated by specific moral institutes. If this is so, Paganism is not a religion but a spiritual expression of connection with the divine through a love of Nature and all that is within it. This love and compassion is the foundation of Pagan ethics.

## Harm None: Ancient Pagan Creed or Modern Public Insurance?

*Eight words the Wiccan Rede fulfil:*
*An' ye harm none, do what ye will.*
—The Wiccan Rede

As Wicca gained popularity in the Western world, several individuals and groups came out, claiming lineage to centuries-old traditions that had secretly kept the Old Religion alive and well. The Anti-Witchcraft legislation in Britain had been repealed, and Witches were free to "go public" and spread the news that Witchcraft was a Nature-loving religion that had remained intact since the medieval Witchcraft hysteria. Unfortunately, those early years of empty claims have affected how the educated public view Wicca and the other NeoPagan traditions. We are only now climbing out of those self-imposed pits to actively promote our community's understanding that we are a new people looking to the past for inspiration.

The Wiccan Rede is testimony to the awareness that the public is a cynical critic who wishes to destroy any notion of alternative revolution and avoid change as best it can. Unfortunately for it, the Wiccan religion—and more broadly the NeoPagan movement—is one of the first "alternative" groups to succeed in gaining rapid support in today's culture. How does Paganism manage to stay afoot in the modern world when it has been described as a "non-prophet disorganisation"? The reason, of course, is the adherence to our ethics.

The Wiccan Rede, in its essential form, was first quoted as a concrete fragment of wisdom during the inaugural Witches' dinner on October 3, 1964, by Doreen Valiente in promotion of benevolent relationships between covens and, of course, between Witches and non-Witches. However, the general inclination to accept such an attitude as a Witch's basic morality was propounded much earlier by Gerald Gardner himself in his book *The Meaning of Witchcraft* (1959). The context in which this suggestion is made does not appear to be overly stressed; in fact, the second point Gardner makes in the text concerns the usage of Magick in terms of "harm none" and is given more emphasis (from page 108 of Gardner's *The Meaning of Witchcraft*, 2004 edition):

*"[Witches] are inclined to the morality of the legendary Good King Pausol,[1] 'Do what you like so long as you harm no one.' But they believe a certain law to be important, 'You must not use magic for anything which will cause harm to anyone, and if, to prevent a greater wrong being done, you must discommode someone, you must do it only in a way which will abate the harm.'"*

---

1 Good King Pausol is, in fact, the bohemian King Pausole featured in the French novel *The Adventures of King Pausole* (1901) by Pierre Louÿs. The literary king himself is the lord of edicts embracing sexual freedom and simplistic moral codes of behaviour, which, apart from Francois Rabelais' novel *Gargantua* of 1534 (Aleister Crowley was known to have been familiar with this work), is the earliest-known literary suggestion of a morality that parallels the implications of the Wiccan Rede. Specifically, these laws would be (as translated from French): one, do no wrong to thy neighbour; and two, observing this, do as thou please.

The Craft Laws believed to have been written by Gerald Gardner and put forth to his coven in 1957 also contain fragments of prose that concern the "harm none" creed. It is evident, however, upon reading through these laws, that wherever this creed is mentioned, it is always in reference to the usage of Magick—though there is also a sense of spiritual morality that is implied by such phrases as "But, they may, after great consultations with all, use the Art to prevent or restrain Christians from harming us and others. But only to let or constrain them and never to punish." Then again, it seems that if any of the "Brotherhood of Wica" happened to place fellow Witches under suspicion, then may the curse of the Goddess be upon them. Willing the curse of the Goddess on your fellow Witches doesn't make for an amiable sense of morality, does it? In fact, there is also mention of a time when the Wica held "power" (assumedly political, within the context) and magick could be used against any who interfered with the Brotherhood. This sounds nothing like the peaceful nature of many Wiccans today who would prefer to shield rather than directly curse or bind. So while these laws may hint at an early form of Wiccan ethics, they have no consistency and do not denote any form of a cohesive "harm none" creed.

After the publication of the aforementioned sources, the Rede appeared in several publications both in Britain and the United States, and it grew to become a significant tenet of the Wiccan faith, as illustrated by both Alex Sanders' and Doreen Valiente's summation of Wicca.

The "Rede of the Wiccae," a twenty-six-line poem that first appeared in the 1975 edition of *Green Egg* magazine, is probably the first instance of a fully fleshed, esoteric litany that made mention of the Wiccan Rede. This poem was submitted by Lady Gwen Thompson (1928–1986), a hereditary Witch who resided in New Haven, Connecticut, USA. Thompson claimed that the poem was originally written by her paternal grandmother, Adriana Porter, who she said had died in 1946. The truth and accuracy of Thompson's account of the history of the Rede is still under scrutiny.

Over time, other versions of the Rede found their way into the community through various publications and individuals who either embellished or embraced the original wording of the Rede, or who, like Doreen Valiente in her book *Witchcraft for Tomorrow* (1978), scripted entirely new pieces that contained the quintessential meaning of the previously quoted Rede (i.e., "The Witches' Creed").

This fascination with such a pure spiritual law reveals the sincerity and conviction of the early Wiccans to establish a firm ethical ground. The popularity of the Rede was fostered by the influx of keen students who were unable to make contact with covens and who practiced the Craft alone. Therefore, the personalised and structured training involved in covencraft was left to those who took time to seek out groups, and the passing on of ethical advice and guidance by experienced Witches to the newly initiated manifested within the pages of the increasing number of published Wiccan manuals.

However, the Rede has its roots in the philosophy of the ancients, as claimed by Doreen Valiente. Saint Augustine decreed, "Love and do what you will," and the Pagans of both ancient Egypt and Greece were adamant in their belief that all things are pure and holy to those who have risen to such a state. Therefore, it is the refined instinct of such spiritual people to commit to the will of love, or that which is sacred. This parallels nicely with the infamous Aleister Crowley's own philosophies. In his *Book of the Law,* Crowley channelled the following from the being who made himself known as Aiwass: "Do what thou wilt shall be the whole of the Law ... Love is the Law; Love under Will."

The Rede offered a sense of community and cohesion to an otherwise autonomous and decentralised religious group. It paved the way for acceptance of self-initiation as a valid entry to the Craft and introduced solitary practitioners who couldn't or had no desire to join covens to a straightforward ethical precept.

The word *rede* is said to mean "advice," and therefore it is immediately apparent that the things outlined in the Rede are merely expressions of guidance and common sense. It is, of course, impossible to live in this technological age without harming *something*. The massive use of electricity is polluting the atmosphere and destroying our resources. Leather products are part of a slaughtering industry that expends no sliver of respect to the lives taken in the process. This unconscious destruction of life has reached such a point that it is unavoidable.

"Harm none" is not a commandment that we must live by or die, so to speak; it is a mantra of peace and life in a world where both are forgotten in favour of a robotic existence. Wiccan or not, "harm none" is a tenet that honours the path of the individual and celebrates a love of life. It gives us room to live freely, without fear of abusing an ancient law, and allows us to imbue our philosophies with that inner, divine spark.

## BLACK AND WHITE: A MYTH

*True magic is neither black nor white.*
*It's both because nature is both*
*loving and cruel all at the same time.*
*The only good or bad is in the heart of the Witch.*
*Life keeps a balance on its own.*
*—Lirio, The Craft*

Magick *is*. It is not a collection of various colours. So where did all this "black Witch / white Witch" stuff come from?

In the past, many Wiccans chose to identify themselves as "white Witches" when being interviewed by the media. Their choice to label themselves as such wasn't seen as fluffy back then, but as a necessary step to indicate to the public that the majority of modern Witches were benevolent. There was also a spiritual need to categorise themselves as such, as the belief that there were "black" covens in existence was common among the Wiccan community. The integration of the Wiccan Rede and the Threefold Law into Wiccan tradition was also seen as an attempt at reinforcing the central pillars of Wicca and to defend against public criticism.

We could go even further back in time and look to the European wise woman or cunning man. It has been said that the village cunning folk helped inspire the European Witch hysteria through their avid promotion of the realities of both black and white Magick and the need to protect oneself against the malice of the "black" Witch. The cunning folk, whose own magickal systems had become influenced by Christian prayer and icons, allegedly identified themselves as white Witches and were trained in counter-cursing and the reversal of "black" Magick. Of course, without solid evidence to back up these theories, this is all merely speculation.

In the twenty-first century, is there any plausible motive to specify the colour of Magick? What is the difference between white and black Magick? Do they even exist as discrete sources of energy?

Pagans actively reject the tendency to define life through strict opposition (dualism). The monotheistic faiths believe that because God exists, an adversary (an embodiment of evil) must also exist. In this way, dualism can often become a tool of control (religious insurance). Good and evil become psychologically instilled in the mind and are constantly reinforced by social dichotomies. This has influenced the way people treat each other in our society.

As Pagans, we have abandoned what we see as an outdated form of expression. Black and white are overgeneralised delusions in a world where nothing is absolute. Life is not an embodiment of social perception but of truth.

"Black and white" is also affected by socio-economic and cultural conditions. For example, if a relatively educated, well-off American Witch sought to self-advertise as a "white Witch," I would be instantly wary. However, if a poor, widowed Italian woman defined her practice as "white," the cultural context would support it. It has nothing to do with how well-off either is that determines their right to the label, it is their motives in applying it. The American Witch has access to bookstores overflowing with modern Witchcraft texts; therefore, the idea that Magick is not black or white should be apparent to him. Also, there is no imminent threat of isolation or physical harm. However, for the Italian Witch whose only income comes from providing the villagers with herbal medicine, divination, charms, and spells, there is motive enough. The reasoning behind this would be that the majority of her clients are Roman Catholic (at least nominally) and need assurance that her magickal knowledge does not come from Satan. What motive does the American Witch have? If he is visible to the media as a representative of the Craft, then he should be honest and accurate in his portrayal of the spirituality.

If you ever meet someone who claims to be a white/black Witch, ask them why they use the label. If you receive a flustered retort, then I suggest you finish the conversation quickly. If someone gives you a straightforward and informed answer, then continue your conversation and delve into the deeper meanings behind the reasons. It's always nice to see how other people live their spirituality.

Today, if someone calls themselves a white Witch, the Pagan community is generally sceptical toward the individual. There is no need for anyone to actively reinforce stereotypes that merely confuse the public. White and black are unnecessary subtitles that disappeared with the belief that a Witch must be coven-bound to be a Witch at all.

There are some organisations that use these labels. White Magick has been defined as a system of communicating with the divine in selflessness and for the ultimate purpose of purifying the soul and rising through the spheres to the divine (theurgy). Adversely, black Magick is defined as selfish acts that consciously result in harm being done, at least by those who profess to practice white Magick. The modern attempt at blending these two forces has birthed a new colour-specific practice: grey Magick. All these labels and terms are unnecessary, as many ethical Witches practice Magick for personal gain!

Colouring Magick is an insult to the universe; Magick is a proverbial rainbow. It is not divided into subcategories in order to allow an individual to feel self-righteous. It is the individual who works with Magick, imbues it with their intent, and releases it into the universe. It is through intent that magickal energy becomes specified. If the results of a particular spell are intentionally harmful, the fault is not on Magick but on the individual who cast that spell.

Ethics must be kept intact and whole, untainted by religious convention and allied with reason and intuition. When you feel you are doing something wrong, don't do it. Trust and know yourself. Placing the blame on something or someone else is weak and disempowering.

Below is an excerpt from an article that I wrote for *Bizoo* (issue #19), an Australian youth/music zine. It is a poetic commentary on the black and white issue within the Craft.

## The Black and White Doors

She stood nervously in the hallway, her agitated eyes flicking back and forth over the smooth panelled walls. The watch wrapped lovingly around her wrist now loomed up at her, hissing menacingly. The honey-like light of the crescent moon played gingerly across the tarnished floorboards. Despite the peace, the stillness of this place, there was still a choice to be made.

The inward chatter of her mind slowly dissipated, and a dim focus ignited within her. *Hurry up*, she thought anxiously, *make the choice!* She stepped forward, but hesitated and withdrew again. A soft rattle droned across the rusting metal sheets of the roof. Determined, she lifted her gaze and looked ahead.

Two doors. On the left, finely crafted ebony painted black. On the right, well-sanded pine painted white. Which one to go through? Her two offered paths lay before her, both imposing and frightening. But her mind remained jarred, static, and uncompromising. It sang for her to relent to the precious gift of free will, though as she stood awkwardly by the thresholds to her future, her free will became the spitting serpent of her nightmares.

Black. White. Left. Right. Her inner voice flailed anxiously. *Choose*, it screeched incessantly. *Why?* Her word hung in the limbo of silence, impressively carved into the currents of air. The eternal question: which way is right? Though does this automatically identify the opposite and other path as wrong? Like vengeful harpies, each question sprouted wings and circled the young woman ravenously.

Then, as if a flame had ignited upon the crest of her beating heart, she began to understand. She had been imprisoned within the house for longer than memory could comprehend, and for just as long she had stood expectantly before the black and the white doors, forcing herself to choose between them. Her only comfort was the consistent, vague drumming coming from deep within the house, travelling to her ready ears through the corridor stretching a stunning length.

Yet in her primal state she had seen the doors and clung to them needily, hoping that one day Fate would chance upon her and turn the knob of the *right* door. Glancing to her left, the dark expanse of the corridor lay before her. The nervous shift of her feet rocked her gently forward, an invisible string pulling firmly from her navel. *Within is the secret. Within is the mystery.* Turning from the doors, she shivered at the void, gaping and plain before her. It is on this path her feet must travel ...

The muffled sound of her feet timidly shuffling over the floorboards came like a breath of moist air to her ears. Her heart fluttered nervously, exhilarated by the foreign shadows weaving shapes and figures across her chest. There was something sacred and ancient about the way her resolute hands hung gracefully by her sides ... something nostalgic about the curves and turns of the labyrinth-like path she was walking ... something familiar about the walls nursing her body.

Deeper and deeper her feet took her as her spirit rushed excitedly forth, bursting from the walls of flesh and bone encasing it. A velvet voice singing a sweet song of faith, beauty, love, betrayal, and loss soared elegantly alongside her. She was free, pure, raw, and unafraid. This was truth. This was simplicity. This was the path she had longed for.

Far behind her, a young man covered in sweat and dressed in dust came upon two doors—one black and another white ... *Which one?* he thought.

## Karmic Confusion

The philosophy of karma as it is expressed by current Pagan traditions is filtered directly from Eastern traditions. Hindus view karma as the universal law of action; it is the sum of all that the individual has done in all their lives. Generally, karma is believed to be repaid in the next incarnation and is seen to take the form of severe retribution or reward. In saying this, it must be said that Hindus specifically work within a caste system and see life as made up of lesser and greater forms according to spiritual evolution. Therefore, if you have been particularly wicked in your current life, it is possible you will incarnate again—as a catfish. However, Pagans actively acknowledge that all life is sacred and equal, and that reincarnation is not a system of hierarchy but a spiritual journey of learning and growth.

Pagans see karma as being repaid in the current life, teaching the individual about the good or bad in their day-to-day activities. However, who's to say what is good and bad? Does the universe truly run on an ethical system as conceived by humanity or is it far more simplistic/ complex than this? I personally believe that karma is not so much "Oh, I missed a sabbat! The gods will strike me down!" but a spiritual reality that teaches how actions affect ourselves and others.

If we violate another's free will, then karma comes knocking. Leading a negative life is bound to activate the metaphysical principle of "like attracts like." If you choose to concentrate on the positive aspects of life, then you will consequently meet with them in your future. However, we must remember that Paganism is not a deluded spirituality. Bad things do happen to good people, and good things happen to bad people. However, it's your attitude as an individual that will colour your perception and discern how fast and how well you deal with the natural problems you encounter.

Wicca's Threefold Law teaches that all actions incur a threefold response. Whether Gardner truly adhered to the Threefold Law as a central Wiccan tenet is debatable. It is believed that Raymond Buckland and the other early Wiccan practitioners who actively taught after Gardner's death took the prevalent threefold symbolism in the initiation rites literally and, focusing on Gardner's promotion of karma, established the Threefold Law as a major operative tenet.

Three has always been a magickal number, representing the balancing and neutralising factor between two forces. It is also a mystically significant number within Celtic spirituality, and many deities appear in triplicities. This traditional interpretation of the number may also hold some clues to the origins of the Threefold Law.

It is clear that Wiccans today have embraced the Threefold Law as a major part of their religion. I have heard that the Threefold Law works within the individual's world, or microcosm. It is said that when a person acts, they send out psychic ripples, or waves, and because of the boundaries that paint one's identity, the waves return three times as strong.

Threefold should not be taken literally. It is simply an expression of "greater" or "more"; it does not necessarily mean that you will be subject to three instances of bad/good luck. In science, we are taught that all actions receive an equal and opposite reaction. Ironically, after being particularly horrid towards my sister one day, I walked into a door, squashed my foot under a chair, and broke a glass jug full of water over my feet. Three strokes of bad luck! Who's to say whether this was a sign of threefold return or simply the universe having me on? Personally, I see being compassionate in life as more of a priority than constantly assessing how the threefold machine will dole out my fate.

Many Wiccans tend to view karma or the Threefold Law as directly influencing their magickal work rather than life in general. Before a spell is cast, several precautions are taken to honour the spiritual significance of the Threefold Law. Phrases such as "for the good of all" and "with harm to none" are included in the wording of many chants to ensure that no backlash occurs.

Pagans in general accept karma as a valid spiritual tenet that promotes acts of kindness. Take an active role in your spiritual life and determine what makes sense and feels right to you and what doesn't. Keep in mind the blessings of upholding the positive aspects of humanity as well as the peace of mind that comes with the right to the negative ones as well.

## SITUATIONAL MAGICK

It's not always possible to consider ethics in times of desperation and disaster. Often the obligation to do what needs to be done precedes thoughts of karmic backlash. So what's an ethical Witch to do when they come to the crossroads concerning what needs to be done and ethics? Sometimes a choice needs to be made between the two.

If you are being continuously harassed by someone and you have tried every possible method (mundane and magickal) of deflecting their attention, then the time comes to consider more drastic options. Things like binding and cursing fall into this category, and while many would be horrified that I have even mentioned it, sometimes cursing is the only option left.

## Binding

Binding is the act of magickally restricting the movement and thoughts of another. When it comes to troublesome people, binding usually comes as a last resort. To bind someone is to impose walls of constraint and force on another to encourage them to reconsider their actions. This is an infringement on another's free will and is ultimately unethical.

If the problem gets to the point where you cannot tolerate any more mistreatment, binding is a possible solution. I have bound three times in my life, and it has always been successful. Binding is a very precise form of spellcraft because of the intense emotion involved.

The first time I used a binding was during my first year of high school. A girl at school was being particularly awful to me; the difficult thing was she sat with my group of friends. I returned home from school one day with everything I needed to bind her and cast the spell. A week later, the rest of the group began to talk about the girl behind her back. By the end of the term, she had been officially kicked out and had gone to sit with another group. From there, she became absorbed into a world of depression. For two years she remained bound, and I had no idea that the pain she was living through was an extension of my spell. I had completely forgotten about the spell and had left the girl to her own devices. I recounted this to a Pagan friend of mine over the phone one night, and he advised me to lift the binding from her straightaway. I reversed the spell immediately.

Knowing that I was involved in causing her depression really impacted me. I had no idea that what I had done all that time ago had affected her so deeply. Removing the binding really helped to release a lot of the tension I had built up over the years as well. It allowed me to confront some of my own issues and helped to restore some of my self-esteem. In retrospect, I wish I hadn't done the binding and that the girl could've developed independently, but at the same time I can see that in a way, the binding helped her to take a look at herself, reevaluate who she thought she was, and grow.

Don't take binding lightly. You need to do a lot of thinking before you decide to encage someone "for the good of all." You may find that binding goes against all your ethics. However, you also need to consider yourself in the grand scheme of things. Downtrodden and compromised is not a respectable state of being. You are entitled to a life, just as your persecutor is, and both of you need to learn that kindness and compassion are empowering. For more information on binding, see the recommended resources appendix (particularly Christopher Penczak's *The Witch's Shield*).

## CURSING

*A Witch cannot heal if a Witch cannot harm.*
—Traditional Saying

Curses disappeared when the stereotypical image of the Witch was thrown out with the bathwater. Unfortunately, many people still consider a Witch to be a diabolical, warty-nosed hag; therefore, many people still believe that a Witch has the propensity to curse. In all honesty, Witches can curse just as they can heal; however, considering modern ethics, it's simply not thought of.

"A Witch cannot heal if a Witch cannot harm" is a saying that merely shows that Magick is not all strawberries and cream. Now, before I am attacked and beaten to a pulp by the Pagan paparazzi, I am going to make my intentions clear: by including a section on cursing in this chapter, I am by no means advocating its use for minor problems but reaffirming what Witchcraft is.

When it comes down to it, cursing is ultimately a self-destructive and draining procedure that requires you to constantly reinforce the energy. If you truly despise a person, are you going to devote the entirety of your free time to seeing that they are scarred forever?

Hatred is a valid emotion when it is felt within the context. When you hate something, you are expressing your negative feelings in order to deteriorate the link between yourself and the subject. Once hatred has done its job, it is put away, and you can continue on your way again.

Hedge Witchery is perhaps the most historically accurate in terms of its approach to spellcraft and ethics. A Hedge Witch does what has to be done in order to keep herself and her family safe from harm. Therefore, if the need arises for a curse, then that need is deeply considered. A Hedge Witch looks at ethics as a thing of necessary adaptation. If the harm factor is not high, then the Hedge Witch will generally exercise compassion towards others. However, when the harm factor is high, the Hedge Witch knows it's time to forget what everyone else would think, and act!

On that note, perhaps the best thing you could do if you are considering cursing someone is talk to the gods. Ask for their counsel and wisdom. Put forth your problem and see if they can't do anything about it. It's important that we stand by our principles as Pagans through and through.

## Love Makes the World Go 'Round

If a situation does arise in which someone is deliberately causing you to feel horrible simply to serve some egocentric problem, you could opt for the alternative route. This option is based on the philosophy of love and fear.

A Druid priestess once told me that there are two extreme forces at work in our world: the two are love and fear, and they go full circle. In fact, all emotions contained within our human experience can be traced back to either one. Hatred comes from ignorance, which comes from fear. Obsession comes from admiration, which comes from love. Often these patterns develop into complex chains of feelings that become irrevocably entangled. Sounds very *Donnie Darko*, eh?

My Druid friend went on to give me an example of how embracing love could create positivity even in the most dismal of situations. My friend relayed the story of how a woman she knew was raped and how her fellow Witches rushed to her aid immediately. They bathed her battered body, and then in unison they turned their attention to the rapist. They sent loving tides of energy to the man responsible.

As my friend's message was particularly relevant to the hell I was living through at school because of someone's wilful desire to destroy my morale, I decided to make use of it. One night I cast a circle and focused my entire being on love. I didn't think about how much I resented him for what he was doing to me; I gave myself entirely to love and let it flow from me to him. That week, several people told me that they thought he had turned over a new leaf. From that day onward, instances of his rumour mongering were far and few between, and I barely let it get to me.

If you are ever faced with the vindictiveness of the human spirit and cursing just doesn't cut it with you, then perhaps my story will provide you with the necessary leverage to act in love.

## RESPECT

*Hold Life dear, for without held*
*Who would know the verge of peak?*
*Take us to your heart again,*
*And our wonders you may seek.* [2]

Respect is an important part of Pagan spirituality. Respect for yourself, others, Nature, and the gods is what empowers a Pagan. Respect is the foundation of Pagan ethics. When it comes to magickal work, respect for the subject of your spell is what gives you perspective. It takes maturity to discern whether or not you are being fully cognizant of the results of your magickal work.

Often there comes a time when someone close is in need of your magickal help. Somewhere along the track, the belief that asking someone's permission before helping their situation was introduced as mandatory. This has more to do with ethical common sense than metaphysical law.

---

2  A stanza from my poem "We Who Are Beneath You" (2003).

You need to decide whether or not it's practical to inform someone that you are going to be working for them. In most cases, you will be met with bemused scepticism. If that is the type of reaction you are expecting, it's best to keep your work to yourself. If you are still anxious about the "ask permission" rule, then instead of being so outright with your words, you can still obtain permission by suggesting prayer. If you are secure in your decision to magickally help a friend or family member, simply stating that you will pray for them should work.

It's also important to trust in the bigger picture. If someone you know has recently experienced the loss of someone close, it's best to allow them some time before you attempt to alleviate their grief with Magick. Then again, you may simply want to offer your support. A good friend weaves a Magick of their own.

Ultimately, respect entails a healthy understanding and relationship with Magick as well as with your loved ones. Strengthen these bonds through reverence, and your ability to wisely guide others will develop.

Respect should be actively expressed in all aspects of your life. Magickal work, environmental activism, and relationships all require your compassionate attention.

As Pagans, we need to pause and consider what makes us who we are—what gives us reason to identify ourselves as Pagans. Do you participate actively in energy work? Do you celebrate the Wheel of the Year? Do you revere ancient gods? If you answered no to all of those questions and still consider yourself Pagan, then who's to say you're not? You might feel that your trust in Spirit and your love of Nature is reason enough to call yourself Pagan, and I completely agree!

Always honour your charge to respect life and foster diversity. If you are locked up inside all day for lack of anything worth doing, then why don't you grab a few plastic bags and scout your neighbourhood for litter? I can assure you that picking up rubbish is one of the most spiritually enriching things you can participate in. Whenever I see rubbish, I take time to pick it up, and it always leaves me feeling peaceful; after all, this is our earth, and we need to give her a hand.

Pagan ethics are rooted in respect. The next time you are asked to assess your personal spiritual ethics, simply reply "Respect" and you will have successfully conveyed the core meaning of Paganism.

## A Note on Will

*Do what thou wilt shall be the whole of the Law.*
—From Aleister Crowley's channelled *Book of the Law*

Generally, when discussing Pagan ethics, two quotes come to mind—the Wiccan Rede and "Do what thou wilt." It has been suggested that the former is simply a varying expression of the latter, though others maintain they arose separately, as they belong to differing traditions with independent histories. I am not here to argue the possibility of Thelemic material in Wiccan liturgy; however, I do agree that there is a similarity between the two. This similarity lies within the will.

Firstly, the will is innately pure; it is at the soul's highest vibration. It is the divine within the inner being. We are predisposed to what benefits the cosmic balance. We are heirs to the purity of will. Therefore, if we abstain from what is corrupt (i.e., what deters from the cosmic balance), we align with our will, and the great work of Magick may begin. Therefore, when Crowley heard the words "Do what thou wilt shall be the whole of the Law," he knew intuitively that this was not a free-for-all but a clue to the secret nature of Being itself. We are as we are because we are meant to be. We are as much Nature as the sky and the earth. We are responsible because of our free will.

"An ye harm none, do what ye will" now comes forth in a new light. Your highest will is destined to complete its orbit, and all other orbits are in rhythm with each other. This is the dance of life itself, exquisitely performed for the sake of itself. To dance is to be wild and free; there is no prerequisite except the rhythm that is self-initiating, self-collapsing, self-aware, and self-expressing. You are your Self that yearns to align with the pure will to dance the dance of life. No harm is done. Be at peace with the rhythm and its flow. Fight against it, and only violence and destruction will ensue.

# 7: THE SPELL OF WITCHCRAFT

The most well-known and yet misconceived aspect of Witchcraft is spellcraft. The casting of spells by Witches and Pagans is not something that is taken lightly. Spellcraft is a method of evoking particular powers by working with spiritual allies (herbs, colours, etc.) to achieve a premeditated desire. However, it must be made clear that the trappings of spellcraft are not necessary.

Like many other things specific to the practice of Witchcraft, the primeval power of spellcraft has suffered from the claim that spells are synonymous with prayers. There are many similarities between the two, but the difference that distinguishes them must be grasped to fully understand spellcraft.

Prayer makes use of the inner voice. The inner voice also helps to formulate moments of raw human emotion into comprehensible cries for help. Prayer is a focused thoughtform that is offered to the divine. It is essentially up to the deity to answer a prayer, and perhaps something is to be learnt from no answer.

Prayer is not a refined or sequential procedure. It is founded in the emotive language of humanity; therefore, it is not necessarily an effective system. Crying out to a noncorporeal spirit or deity in a moment of vulnerability will not necessarily result in a clear answer or divine miracle. However, the power of prayer is a real thing. The success of prayer lies in your connection with the divine. For prayer to work, you need to be reverent to the respective deity and you must acknowledge the living link between yourself and that energy which is indwelling. If you are patient with your thoughts, prayer becomes a powerful force of intent.

Spellcraft stems from the same human desire—to affect and manipulate the guise of reality. However, spellcraft honours a controlled environment, which is further manipulated through specific imagery, words, and physical actions. Spellcraft does not always require the aid of the gods as external transmuters or catalysts. It applies the divine spark within all of us combined with the power of the materials, actions, and words we are using. As such, casting a spell is a procedure that gives form and purpose to our intent. Spellcraft can be empowered through cooperation with deities; however, ultimately it is what you do with the energy at hand that defines the spell.

Both spellcraft and prayer originate from the emotional and spiritual faculties but can be accessed through the mental and psychological facets. Becoming aware and enhancing your own links with each level of consciousness will help to restore the flow of personal energy, which is the basis of all spellcraft.

## THE SKILL OF SPELLCRAFT

*Spellcraft is an art. So many people take it to be
an aspect of Witchcraft one should immediately pick up
and have the ability to do, but I've learnt that it is a skill
developed over time. It takes effort, desire,
understanding, and wisdom.* [1]

---

1 A response I gave to a Pagan friend online who made an inquiry about spellcraft.

We all have something we can do particularly well. It may be something that is not recognised as a valid talent, but essentially it is a skill you have mastered through determination and patience. For the skill to flourish, there must be a degree of personal enjoyment in carrying out the processes that pertain to the skill. You must like what you do for there to be any success in the matter. Like most things in life, spellcraft is a skill, and like all things, it must be practised to enhance its success.

The further development of a skill lies in the desire to pick up the guitar and pluck a string, so to speak. There must be a desire to learn the skill before anything else can happen. For instance, during high school it was compulsory to study maths. My hatred for maths had grown to such an extent that I began to purposefully fail the subject. Set your sights on your goals, work hard, devote some time to the cause, and you'll get there. A skill is fostered by the strength of your will and reinforced by your desire to achieve it.

Think about a spell you have cast. I want you to reflect on every aspect of that spell, recalling the feelings you had during the procedure. Think about what you were wearing while you cast the spell, why you decided to cast it, what materials you were using, what day it was and what moon phase. Could you feel the energy around you? Did you notice the movement of power? Did you cast a circle beforehand? Did you effectively release the power at the climax of the spell? And finally, was your spell effective, and to what degree?

As Witches, it is important to be able to reflect on our past work and to evaluate and deconstruct both the processes and the effects.

## SUCCESSFUL SPELLCRAFT

Remember that it takes time and effort to become a competent spell-caster. You need to become aware of the contributing factors to the success of your spells. There is no shame in returning to the basics to gain a better understanding of how spells work and how energy flows. I believe that the opportunity to advance in any field of occult study lies in the foundation of its basic principles: the ability to focus, meditate, visualise, raise energy, and release it are all basic abilities that can be attained by anyone. Like an artist, a Witch is his or her only critic.

The following is a summary of the factors that contribute to the success of spellcraft. Each will be dealt with individually below.

- Psychological and metaphysical understanding of spellcraft
- Ethical considerations
- Correspondence: Witches' code
- The power of belief
- Need over trivial desire
- Clear intent and energy input
- The active principle

## PSYCHOLOGICAL AND METAPHYSICAL UNDERSTANDING OF SPELLCRAFT

*Magic is the art of changing consciousness at will.*
—Dion Fortune

The first key to successful spellcraft is your comprehension of the psychological and metaphysical processes that a spell utilises. The other factors are extensions of the individual's understanding. Dion Fortune's definition of Magick and Carl Jung's research into consciousness are indicators for both the psychology and metaphysics of spellcraft.

By dictionary definition both the subconscious and unconscious are the underling mentalities working outside the mundane perception. The unconscious is merely an extension or vaster level of the subconscious.

Dion Fortune's definition makes an interesting point, though seemingly incomplete. Changing consciousness at will is part of Magick but not the be all and end all. It could be said that our mental perception of the physicality of life is merely a product of our consciousness. The world is a multitude of experiences and concepts pooled together. Energy vibrates at varying frequencies, and thus each of us encounters life differently. Therefore, the ability to shape consciousness to perceive specific elements of life and aspects of personality is magickal.

To illustrate this concept, I'll use the example of the infamous love spell. I cast the spell, taking into account each factor of successful spell-craft and therefore effectively contact the part of my psyche that is love. My level of consciousness has aligned to my loving aspect, and therefore in my interaction with others this aspect is prevalent. This could manifest as a tendency to involve complete strangers in intimate conversations, which may attract a partner. Or perhaps my loving persona makes contact with another's (someone who is also channelling that aspect). This is indeed part of the mystery of Magick; however, it is not always so neatly explained.

Metaphysically, spellcraft is composed of acts concerning the movement of energy, which are ultimately linked. These acts are as follows:

- **Deliberation:** You need to take into consideration the outcome of the spell and how this will affect the people or situation involved. Reflect on the need to cast the spell. Working for you is permissible as long as you are realistic and balanced. See "Ethical Consideration" and "Need over Trivial Desire."

- **Preliminary Energy Raising:** In Ceremonial Magick, this is achieved through abstaining from mundane and routine activities, e.g., eating. However, it's as simple as thinking about the spell and building excitement for the task ahead.

- **Purification of the Self and Space:** This may include circle castings. Simply allow yourself to focus on the energy residing within and it will begin to flow. You may wish to shower or bathe beforehand to focus your energies and to cleanse.

- **Energy Alignment:** Take in the materials before you, and focus on your goal. In the case of a prosperity spell, you may have gold coins, peppermint oil, patchouli incense, and cinnamon sticks. See "Correspondence: Witch's Code."

- **Raising Energy:** Chanting, rhythmic breathing, music, dancing, etc. are all methods of raising energy. You are moving the energy and increasing its flow. See "Clear Intent and Energy Input."

- **Directing Energy:** You specify the purpose of your energy, and its aim is reinforced. You do this through physical gestures, symbolism, and visualisation. See "Visualisation: Magick Incarnate."

- **Releasing Energy:** This is the stage of the spell where the energy is sent off to do its work. Many Witches release energy by standing straight, legs spread and arms held skyward. The Witch becomes the Rod of Power.

- **Physical and Mental Recuperation:** This involves grounding and returning to mundane awareness. Often, the Witch eats something or participates in a habitual activity that relaxes the mind and body. Often the magickal space is "deconstructed" (psychically and physically) and everything is cleaned up. It is recommended that you do not think about the spell after it is cast, as your speculation is ultimately destructive. If you find yourself thinking about the spell, do not snap yourself out of doing so but acknowledge the thought and put it away. Have faith that the energy is doing its work. See "The Power of Belief."

- **Reinforcing the Spell:** The spell may be repeated a set number of times. Meditation can help to raise positive thoughts and focus them on the purpose. Acting on the material plane in cooperation with the spell's purpose is recommended. See "The Active Principle."

## ETHICAL CONSIDERATIONS

*Do unto others as you would have them do unto you.*
—Matthew 7:12, The New Testament

Abiding by an ethical consideration of others is wise for any spellcaster. You need to ensure you have taken into account another's feelings when working with Magick.

For example, the use of love spells in the modern Pagan community is only seen as ethical if the spell does not specify an individual. A love spell aimed at a specific person without their knowledge or input is perceived as dangerous and harmful, as it disregards the individual's gift of free will and literally imprisons the person.

As Witchcraft has no governing body, there are no law enforcers in regards to the use of spells. It is up to the individual to determine the possible outcomes of their actions and thus take full responsibility for the consequences. Before the spell is cast, the Witch needs to put him/ herself into the shoes of the subject and discern whether or not he/she would feel comfortable with the spell's effects.

Ethical ground rules are not wholly reserved for negative spellcasting and should be referred to in times of stress and inexperience. If, for instance, your grandmother falls violently ill at the age of ninety-five and you want to help heal her through spellcraft, you would have to consider her age, the inevitably of human mortality, and the likely chance it is her time to go. If you decide to go ahead with the working, and your grandmother recovers, only to live in fear of the disease returning, how would you feel?

Before embarking on any magickal endeavour, it is wise to think things through. Spellcraft is no easy task. It requires attention to detail and respect for oneself and others.

## CORRESPONDENCE: WITCH'S CODE

Correspondence is the unique relationship between a physical object/ organism and its energetic qualities. Beginners' texts are filled with countless tables describing in detail the magickal uses of herbs, planets, days, stones, etc. You will find no such tables here. This discussion on the importance of correspondence is to help strengthen your understanding of how and why correspondence works.

Within the following paragraphs, you will see the term "relative association" repeated often. The term itself was one I coined some time ago to personify the principle of correspondence.[2] Relative association,

---

2 However, I do not claim sole dominion over the term, considering I have no idea if other people have also come upon it or use it regularly as well.

as it is used here, is the mind's connection between both the object (the foci symbol) and its associated qualities (the magickal uses). These connections are based on an individual's ethnic and cultural background, upbringing, and the collective unconscious. However, an individual may make the conscious decision to reject notions and beliefs instilled at an early age and seek to delve into symbolism differently. Relative association is both an active and subliminal mentality.

Witchcraft promotes the advantages of learning and applying new symbolism into one's psyche; this is the Witch's code. Colour and herbal associations are unique to the practice of spellcraft. For example, in Western society, the colour black is considered impure and deathly. The Witch, however, sees black as the colour of binding, banishment, and life-affirming destruction. Metaphysics teaches that black is the absence of colour and therefore represents the primal unconscious, the mystery of life, and the harshness of fate. While society has a generic tradition of symbolism, the Witch's code introduces a unique mindset.

It has been argued that the reason Witches use specific herbs, natural objects, and colours in their Craft is that each individual entity, animate or not, resonates with a specific vibration unique to that object/organism. The vibration is harnessed to affect a specific strand of the Web of Life.

Correspondence is a filter for perception and the mental, emotional, and physical reactions caused by the stimuli. To illustrate this, I shall give an example of a love spell, below.

### The Love Spell

What you will need:

> One long-stemmed red rose
> Cinnamon powder
> Jasmine essential oil (diluted in some sort
>   of base oil, e.g., almond or jojoba)
> A piece of red paper cut in the shape of a heart
> Three pink votive candles

TIMING
Waxing or full moon, preferably on a Friday
Early evening

LOCATION
A place of natural beauty, e.g., a beach.

Using the cinnamon powder, create a circle around you wide enough
to move around comfortably in, and place the three candles at equally
spaced intervals around the circle. Take the jasmine oil and anoint
either your seven chakras or the five parts of the body addressed in the
fivefold kiss. As you do this, repeat the affirmation below each time the
oil touches your skin:

> *Sweet scent of Aphrodite's garden, I coax thee hither*
> *May my skin receive your touch of beauty*
> *May my heart reach out to my awaiting lover.*

Now walk deosil around your circle and light each candle, chanting:

> *Glowing light, flow this night*
> *Enchant herein the powers raised*
> *Glowing night, flowing light*
> *Circle's cast 'neath moonlight's gaze.*

Stand in the centre of the circle and visualise a pulsing concentration of pink light swirling around you. Allow yourself a moment of
peace as you contemplate the working ahead of you.

Take the red rose and hold it in your power hand, and draw a pentagram or other relevant symbol in the air before you. Imagine the sigil
ablaze with light. Now hold the heart in your other hand (the receptive
hand) and ensure your feet are spread apart and your arms held slightly
raised before you. Chant:

*Reddest rose upon my palm*
*Bound to flesh, and flesh is bound*
*Call to me a lover's arm*
*This spell I cast in circle's round.*

Repeat this chant over and over, becoming louder as you do. As you chant, meditate on the qualities you desire in a lover, and remember to remain as general as possible. As you feel the climax of power, quickly turn your attention to the heart, and say:

*By my heart entwined in love*
*This spell is cast as flies the dove.*

The spell is cast. Now ground your energy and dismantle the space.

The method outlined above is a classic love spell. The materials, timing, location, words, and gestures are all inherently sensual and focus the mind on love. Any person unfamiliar with Witch's code could successfully cast the spell above and achieve a degree of success, as the correspondence used was not overly esoteric. It is common knowledge that red and pink inspire thoughts of love and sexuality, and that the full moon is an auspicious time. However, correspondence involves more than the average superficial awareness. You need to fully comprehend why red and pink are the colours of love and why the full moon is considered a magickal time. Why is the writing hand considered to be the preferable channel of assertive energy? What of the spell's wording? Why use words such as flesh, lover's arm, and dove?

It's up to you to formulate your own ideas on relative association, correspondence, and spellcraft. Read up on the folklore and literary references of symbolism, and you will begin to see that symbolism is not always a mindset but a source of sacred power.

Make sure you have a solid understanding of why symbolism is so important in spellcraft, and you will begin to find that through your own perseverance, you are able to imbue objects with specific energies, despite them not having a traditional association with those energies beforehand. You are the catalyst; make use of your mental powers of perception and spellcraft will become a joy.

## The Power of Belief

*A person's probability of success*
*is directionally proportional to the belief*
*and execution of their abilities.*
—Kent Calhoun

"Believe in yourself and you will succeed"—as generic and clichéd as this is, its meaning is rooted in truth. Having confidence in your ability to change things and to make decisions concerning your future are the extensions and elaborations of belief. You must trust that you can and do have an impact on transformation.

Egotism and arrogance are the byproducts of a spoilt world shaped by the "holier than thou" attitude. Individuality has been exploited to the point that egalitarian values have vanished, and perpetual hierarchy has been instated as the social norm. You are an individual, you have unique characteristics and abilities; however, you have no right to profess you are higher or better than another.

I truly came to terms with the impact my personal belief had on my Magick several years ago when I was in Bali. My father, who is one of the most spiritual people I have ever known, is a beacon of belief. My dad is always telling stories about how a certain charm or talisman saved him from certain illness or even death, or about his interactions with the gods. One of his stories concerning a ring of petrified wood highlighted the power of belief. My dad had been wearing the ring when a poisonous blade pierced him. He felt no pain, and the ring kept him strong and whole. You may interpret the story however you wish, but I personally see it as an experience of healing faith and the power of belief.[3]

Spellcraft honours belief. Belief aims to reinforce and secure the energy of a spell; it helps to keep the spell working and eventually offers

---

3 Intuition tells me that these natural beings emanate power and influence events all on their own. This inherent life force is amplified through the power of belief, which allows for the reception of such energies.

ground for the spell to manifest. Faith is not something that one should cast away; it is a valid and personal energy that strengthens spirit and heals wounds.

## NEED OVER TRIVIAL DESIRE

*The Power is used only as need dictates.*
—from Scott Cunningham's "The Law of the Power,"
*Wicca: A Guide for the Solitary Practitioner*

The universe is not an effortless machine. It is an active consciousness that processes our energies and gives them direction. It also has a sense of humour. When it sees someone making a fool of themselves, attempting to give someone warts or pimples, it revels in giving that particular fool a great big whack across the head and ultimately sealing a decidedly greater chain of acne for said fool.

There are times when we must honour the traditional codes of conduct concerning our relationship with the Power. Spells for trivial and petty issues are not recommended, as (1) it's a waste of your time and energy and (2) karma accumulates. Remember that casting a spell is an act of devotion and power. When it comes to "need over trivial desire," give room for your common sense to interject.

On the metaphysical side of things, when you are in dire need of something, you will find raising energy for the task an easier process, as need trumps trivial desires. Don't fall prey to the materialism of this world by casting spells to become popular or the like. Be your own person. You need to assess these things for yourself. Balance is the key.

## CLEAR INTENT AND ENERGY INPUT

*Sling the bow and point the arrow*
*As above and so below*
*God and Goddess, hear your Witches*
*Listen to us, make it so!*[4]

---

4 A chant I originally wrote for a fiction story.

We've all heard stories of Witches ruining their spells because of wording mistakes or wrong ingredients. However, is it that simple when it comes to the reality of intent and energy input in spellcraft?

"Errors" in process only work to diminish the power of the spell if the individual believes that they will. If you get emotionally distraught over missing a few words or blanking out about the rose petals, it is obvious that your spellcraft will suffer from your own anxieties. All that truly matters in effective spellcraft is the precision and sincerity of your intent as well as your devotion to the cause. Your choice to cast a spell is the beginning of your intent. From thereon, the intent needs to be concentrated so that it becomes the major driving force of the spell. Intent raises energy, and thus the vehicle of your Magick is born. You need to make sure that your intent is clarified so that you don't miss the target.

In terms of energy, intent must be focused and felt to achieve any degree of success. Maintaining the steady flow of energy during a spell is vital, as this is the link upon which your intent travels into the universe. It is essential to ground and centre before any magickal work, as this clears both astral and physical bodies of toxins and draws in the vital energy of both sky and earth, charging you with power.

Visualisation is another key factor. You need a mental picture or image of what you are working for so that your intent has visuals to relate to and draw power from.

Honour and acknowledge your innate gifts of intent and energy, and your ability to cast effective spells will be born.

## THE ACTIVE PRINCIPLE

*Energy travels the path of least resistance.*
—Unknown

This is often the most forgotten principle, and for that reason many people wonder why their spells don't work or why they take months to manifest. Energy is naturally inclined to travel the path of least resistance. This means that the fewer barricades the energy has to hurdle, the quicker the spell will manifest. If you are in need of snappy results, you may like to integrate the active principle into your spellcraft.

The active principle is the physical procedures the Witch performs to help bring the spell into fruition. For example, if you cast a spell for employment, how is the spell going to work unless you get up and do something to help it along? You need to work with the energy and help to remove as many blocks as possible so that the energy can work more effectively. If you decide to simply lay back and foolishly wait for someone to call you with a dream job offer, the energy will become weaker with each passing day, as you are doing nothing to reinforce the energy. By the time the energy finds something for you, the impact it has on the situation will be at best a flicker. All the effort is wasted. You need to consciously open yourself to as many opportunities as possible so that the energy can make the leap and influence the situation. It's up to you to see your spell into the world and to strengthen its hold on the physical plane. Work with Magick, not against it.

## VISUALISATION: MAGICK INCARNATE

*Seeing is believing.*
—Italian proverb

Visualisation, like spellcraft, is a skill to be developed. There are those who are naturally predisposed to visualisation, and there are those who struggle.

Visualisation works in that the ability to perceive something in detail, through the five senses within the mind, stimulates the likely chance that one will then come across that envisioned situation, person, or object in the physical plane. Visualisation is a logical step in energetic progression and expression.

Visualisation can be linked to the planes of existence. Think of each plane as a step on a staircase. Now, relate your mind to your higher consciousness or simply put it on one of the higher steps. You, as a physical being residing in the material plane, are represented by one of the lower steps. Now envision that someone has poured a bucket of water onto the step representing your higher consciousness. Gradually, influenced by the gravitational pull and momentum (two natural forces working together), the water will find its way to the step representing your physical being. The water on your step is now imbued with the experience of having passed over each step above your own. Similarly, as you visualise something, that specific visualisation is given astral form in the realm of higher consciousness, and this gradually manifests on the material plane by means of natural progression. It is essential that we remember all planes coexist and are not separate from one another.

The metaphysics of visualisation are centred on the individual's ability to construct a blueprint that is eventually given physicality. To ensure the attainment of the desired outcome, one must create a visualisation of it in specific detail and strengthen it through willpower so that a channel of power is created, running through the planes, which will aid in its manifestation.

Visualisation as a skill is composed of various methods. For example, it is recommended you visualise only the outcome of your spell, as concentrating on the process of manifestation negates the spell itself. If I were to cast a spell to improve my love life, I would visualise my relationship as whole and peaceful, perhaps seeing my partner and myself getting on well and being genuinely happy together. I would also draw on my own experience of how it feels to be in a loving relationship to empower my visualisation.

Visualisation is not fully effective on its own. It needs the conditioning of a spell or ritual to fully exercise its power. Within a spell, visualisation becomes the means of creating a vehicle for the power raised to travel toward manifestation.

Visualisation is more than something books suggest, it is an enjoyable method. Think of this structured perception as a more refined expression of your daydreaming episodes. You are capable of it; it's in your childhood experience. Find it and foster it.

# MAGICK:
## THE ESSENCE OF LIFE

*Magick is the science and art of causing change
to occur in conformity with will.*
—Aleister Crowley

In the last chapter, I used the quote "Magick is neither black nor white ..."—
this quote from the cult classic *The Craft* beautifully sums up the truth of
Magick.

Magick is the child of Nature. The cyclic rhythms of the natural world
are bound only by the law of action and reaction. The tragedy and disaster that is wrought by Mother Nature against humanity is void of intent.
Nature has no bias; what's done is done, and life goes on. Today, many
Pagans see the earth as a living, conscious entity.

Magick is the life force of the natural world, and thus Magick is raw
and neutral. Neutrality does not imply a void of action but honours the
complete spectrum of existence. Good and evil as definitive categories
have no place in Nature, as Nature is devoid of morality.

Both Dion Fortune and Aleister Crowley (and many magicians after
them) defined Magick in terms of its active process and not in relation
to the substance of its force. Within this book, I have defined Magick as
"the universal flow of underlying energy" and "the quintessential radi-
ance of life." What I mean by this is that Magick is a force comprised of
the natural and raw energies in the universe.

In his or her simplest form, a Witch is an individual who forms a
bond with Magick and celebrates the relationship. Magick is not a convenient concept or luxury; it is a power and spiritual vibration that
forms the foundation of conscious manifestation—the form and face
of life itself.

Spellcraft utilises the relationship between the Witch and Magick as
the source of power from which it draws. To improve your spellcraft,
you must make an effort to form a bond with Magick and to enhance
this link. See Magick as your spiritual partner; treat Magick as you
would a close friend. I believe this so implicitly that I refuse to say that I
*do* Magick or *use* Magick; rather, I *work with* Magick.

Be wise in your dealings and safeguard your sacred connection with Magick. Never harass or demand anything of Magick. Know that there is a great responsibility that comes from working with Magick. Have your head amongst the stars, but keep your feet firmly on the ground; your body is the presence and your spirit, the force.

## EVERYDAY MAGICK: THE CHARMS OF LIFE

There are many today who regard Magick as a pure and direct path to the spiritual ascendancy of the soul and who would frown upon the "folly" of charms and the little magicks that abide within the hearts of Witches everywhere. The stuff that was known in older days to have actual practical uses is now snidely cast aside. Disregarding this cynical perspective on Magick, I can say with absolute integrity that this "stuff" still has practical uses, and that it still works.

Spellcraft is something that needs to be practised on a regular basis. Does it not make sense, then, that if one wishes to sharpen this skill, it should be harnessed whenever and wherever possible?

At work, at home, or out at night with my friends, I work with Magick, casting spells and setting charms. I can't help it. It's not an addiction; it is in my nature, for I never started and never stopped. This may be hard to fathom, but getting every green traffic light in a row from the coast into the city, cooling down the temperature of hot drinks, finding parking spaces and lost objects, speeding up time, and finding an obscure book on a library shelf is completely possible. In fact, every example I listed I have accomplished with little effort and little time. I simply centre my awareness, channel the current, and go! It is obvious, then, that no tools are needed—simply the Magick and the Witch.

I don't feel that it is necessary to provide you with a heavy arsenal of charms and spells to aid you in your day-to-day life; however, I urge all Witches who are serious about their Craft and who live it to write down their charms and spells. Many of the ones I use regularly have been learnt from others and found in books and on websites. Others I have written myself as need called for them.

Charms and spells are not isolated instances that simply make use of Magick but are successive points along the continuing cycle that strengthen and enhance one's relationship with the energy. This is essential in becoming a good Witch.

First, see the Magick in life: a Witch sees Magick everywhere. It infuses all things and is the pulse that keeps the cycles beating on. It is the vitality that rises and falls with the seasons and creates mysteries and secrets as it does so. These mysteries are shown forth through symbols because of their nature, and thus we Witches must learn this symbolism.

When I shower, I see the water as a purifying agent that cleanses my body and centres me for the day. When I light incense or a candle, I do so knowing that on some level I have just given light to some hidden-away aspect of myself. When I look out of the window to the suburban street, I see the majesty of green that spasmodically bursts through the tar and sidewalks in joyful defiance. All things strive to continue, keeping their grounding. This is the knowledge and understanding that comes with studying the ways and mysteries of Magick that a good Witch then applies to his/her everyday life. For what I have learnt from the trees and the flowers is that I must stand straight and tall to truly begin my journey along the World Tree that resides within and encompasses all. The sun has taught me that to bring forth a desire into manifestation, I should acknowledge its passage of expanding light, so that just as the rising sun is a certainty the next morning, so too will my spell become fixed. There are many things that occur around us all the time that are, in fact, key secrets alerting us to ways that will help create and transform. Everyday Magick is not a fantasy; it is entirely accessible. There is no need for elaborate circles or copious amounts of frankincense to secure our goals, for this is the greater folly. Simplicity is a virtue. A Witch is not one for pomp and priss and knows that charms and spells cast every day will not lose their power or sanctity from overuse; rather, they become like old friends who hover at the sidelines, simply waiting to be called into action.

# 8: RITUALISING

Ritual is an important aspect of Pagan spirituality. It empowers us and allows for spiritual communion with our deities. Ritual provides the bridge between the spiritual realms and the psyche. It opens doors and reinforces primal connections with the hidden facets of humanity.

Ritual allows the individual to enhance the connection between the universe and the self. It is a practice that aids in spiralling progress and deepening understanding through the spheres of life to the core of oneness.

Ritual is self-prescribed; you choose how complex it is. Paganism embraces creative inspiration and encourages us to experiment with the various techniques and blueprints of ritual that are globally available, ultimately creating an individual experience. Rather than blindly accept what others have done before you, be open to new and different approaches, and cultivate the beauty of diversity.

When defining Paganism, the word *orthopraxy* comes up. Orthopraxy refers to the consistency of practice within a specific spiritual group.

Orthodoxy, implying consistency of belief, does not apply to Pagans as it does to the organised religions.

Our celebration of the natural cycles is a fundamental trait of Paganism, as is the tendency to ritualise what appears a minor event but is, in truth, a spiritual revelation, e.g., watching the sun set.

Paganism is a *doing* spirituality. It asks that you take a look at the world and at yourself, and take action. Experience the world through the profound beauty of ritual. You are the catalyst; you have the power.

## REASONS FOR RITUAL

Pagans today, of any tradition, perform rituals for many reasons. Some do so in order to connect and commune with the divine powers, and others do so to enrich and empower themselves and to pay homage to deities, the spirits of place, the elements, and countless other beings.

It has been said that the dreamscape, the realm of symbolism, offers us the inspiration to respond ritually to signals begun deep within the primordial waters of the soul. The unconscious reality speaks to us, and we speak back by consciously using ritual. It is a sacred interchange of energies that joins all of life.

Ritual, which is believed to derive from the Sanskrit word *rtu* (meaning "menses"), celebrates the ongoing cycles that comprise the divine dance. Many Pagans today celebrate the sabbats because they are naturally derived festivals that mark significant points of transition within the seasonal year.

We perform these rituals to mark the passage of life, because without them, we lack the primal patterns that orient our deep selves toward our divine origins.

In ritual, we become a conduit between the above and the below, reconciling the illusional duality that surrounds us with the unity underlying all that exists.

### To Connect and Commune

When I kneel before my altar and invoke my gods of breath, of spirit, I call upon the love and the light. As I breathe deeply, retaining my centre and expanding my consciousness, I focus on the piece of rose quartz in my left hand and the piece of amethyst in my right hand, as Aphrodite is to my left (the feminine pillar of darkness/contraction/reception) and Hermes is to my right (the masculine pillar of light/expansion/ projection). Aphrodite is the temple in which lovers lie together as the night drifts across the indigo, star-swept skies. Hermes is the boundary between farmed land and the vast wilderness—the spirit of fertility sown into all that submits to the whims of desire, which Aphrodite inspires. As their essences intertwine about me, I feel myself drifting into their temple—that of the cataclysmic union of love and light, that which receives the spear and nurtures, and that which spills the seed. From love and light comes life; life is the source of all. All the gods are of the life-flow; they are nothing without it, as are we.

When I make this initial connection and am supported by the two pillars, I take my first step into the halls of communion. It is then that I make the invocation to my gods of breath. They come forth and surround me, adding their power to my workings, but more importantly, their presence reminds me of an essential fact: as a priest, communion with my gods is the very reason behind my spirituality. It is not simply the high they give me but something deeper that swims in my veins and sings in my soul. I feel that this is my purpose: to connect and commune, to offer forth the sacred oaths, and to anoint myself in oils so that I may be a consecrated child before them.

Wherever I am and whomever I am with, this connection remains. Speaking with the gods and sharing my feelings is not restricted to the circles I have at home or with my coven. The gods are truths that go beyond the superficial realities we feel safely contain our needs and desires. They are the powers and forces that make and change, form and flow, inspire and instigate all that is seen and unseen. From one realm to the other, they weave and whisper and partake in the wellsprings of life that fuel and flood the continuum.

What is it we connect to and commune with when we call upon the gods to be with us and add their power to ours? I say it is life itself. In love and in light, they come. Not like parents who fuss and hover, but like brothers and sisters, friends and lovers. They are forces so incomprehensible and yet wholly integral to our experience on this plane and on all the others that we become immersed in the legacy of their brilliance and power.

To those who offer up their livelihoods, they extend patronage and protection, and to those who celebrate their mysteries, joy. When I kneel before my altar and focus on the divine energies, I am, in fact, focussing on all that is life and am therefore becoming anew.

### To Enrich and Empower

As a Witch, I perform feats of transformation that are brought into effect through my relationship with Magick. This is what Starhawk calls "power-with," and it is the heart of magickal reality. If I am not spiritually prepared to contribute my energy to such workings, then I am incapable of creating change. For instance, if I did not ground and centre, calling on the light of the heavens and that of the earth to marry within before a working, I would ultimately burn myself out, because it would be difficult and dangerous for one person to bear the brunt of anything beyond making a flame waver or sending a message telepathically. Small things can be achieved through sheer effort and willpower; however, spiritual tasks that relate to anything "greater" would require a dependence, and that is to be avoided.

Energy is universal and flows through all things. To those who are predisposed and who work to consciously receive such vitality, the energy is enhanced and one becomes enriched and empowered. There should be no unbalanced dependence, as all things need to be in sync and interdependent.

We depend on a variety of sources for our oxygen; however, what gives out oxygen also requires that we exhale carbon dioxide for its survival. We have an integral system of energy interchange in our universe; thus, it would be foolish to suggest that one could go on casting spells and working rituals without taking in energy from sources other than one's own. Ritual, therefore, is important for not only Witches who consciously work with energy but to all Pagans who revere the life force, because as children of the earth, we are intimately aware of where our life is sourced. With this knowledge comes the basic understanding of interchange and how to manifest realities. This is not greed, this is wisdom. Take too much and give too little, and you will overload your system and pay the price. Take too little and give too much, and you may end up an anxious mess. Balance your input and output with the equilibrium instilled by ritual, and ensure your health.

Witchcraft comprises many customs and practices that speak of the relationship between all living beings. As Pagans who work to attune to the natural rhythms and cycles of life, we begin to invoke a flow of energy that is then imbued with our own desires and needs and transformed into reality. However, it is not spellcraft that enriches and empowers the spirit but the journey through life made in concordance with the rhythms and cycles of energy.

As we discover our life source, we feel the urge to create various rituals so that we may celebrate our relationship with energy in reverence, paying homage to the raw entities that are the various aspects of the substance of immortality.

### To Pay Homage and Revere

Beyond all else, I believe, ritual aims at revering and paying homage to the great forces of Nature, to the balance of cosmos and chaos, the immortals, the gods, the ancestors, the elements, and the Fey. Strip clean tradition and dogma and you have pure, raw Being that has come forth from undifferentiated potential and has become beauty, joy, laughter, music, desire, freedom, power, death, beginnings, and endings; they have many names. We too are a part of this great unfolding, and in our own humility we often forget the true sanctity that dwells within all that share in the life force. We are each unique expressions of the divine.

When we hear of Zeus and Hera, of Brighid and the Dagda, there is always a familiar spark that tickles at the edge of our consciousness, straining to illumine the shadow-swept chambers of the deeply stowed-away Pagan soul. Our myths are, in fact, closer to home than some would care to believe. The stories and legends never die, because they are undying and cannot cease to be, unless life would do the same. They are eternal, and we can relate because the myths are not unlike our own stories. The gods reside within us in such a way that separating the two would prove impossible. Carl Jung and others have explained this phenomenon with words like *archetype* and *collective unconscious*, and though we Pagans feel our experiences are somewhat validated by this stream of psychology, there was never truly any need for it.

Regardless of the textbooks and university courses, and the rising numbers that join us in our ways, there is always one thing we do that will never disappear: this is the laying down of flowers and the kneeling of the supplicant, the fires built for high summer, and the spiral dances. We are a people who continue to revere the sacred and who refuse to acknowledge any separation between what is here and what is there. We not only seek the wisdom of the sky realm but also look to the Earth Mother and her oceans and rivers, never forgetting that we are a part of the Magick.

When we ritualise—when we mark the passages with ceremony— we lay down all pretences in order to present what simply is. Perhaps this is the true origin behind the skyclad nature of the British Traditional Wiccan (BTW) groups and perhaps even the Jains of India. When we revere and honour the deities and spirits that are in this world and universe, we come before them (though they are always there) not as priests and priestesses of garment and gold but as ourselves, glorious and beautiful in the eyes of the gods. We come forth as truth.

Reverence and honour cannot be given when one has no understanding of the relationship between the recipient of the gift and the one who offers it. In a true and meaningful exchange, neither one does exclusively the giving or receiving—both mutually participate in the sacred moment. Balance is maintained.

When I am celebrating with my coven or on my own, I present my blessed offerings to my gods not to placate but as a symbol of the memory and truth that we share secretly together. This secret I am willing to share. Throughout history, the gods have often told us that they do not need the offerings and sacrifices we insist on making. However, I do so because in a world such as this one, there is a need for both my gods and me to acknowledge that we haven't forgotten each other.

## Personal Preparation: Harnessing Self-Awareness

*The more we are awake and conscious, the more life takes on*
*a richness we may never have imagined possible.*
*We may feel more connected to our bodies.*
*The world may seem brighter, more vivid, more real.*
*We will feel emotions more fully, or truly appreciate life.*
—Diana Winston, *Wide Awake: A Buddhist Guide for Teens*

Part of performing a successful ritual lies in how well you prepare yourself. Personal preparation is by nature a process of consciously reaffirming your physical presence and reinforcing your self-awareness. You can achieve this by tapping into your sensual faculties and involving yourself fully in the movement of your body as you wash. Allow yourself to soak in the water around you, and actively focus on the pleasure of water. Gradually you will come to the centre.

Visualisation is also a powerful method of focusing the mind. For instance, when I want to cleanse myself of the day's residual energy, I take a shower, visualising the water as a waterfall breaking across my body that sweeps away negativity.

Often personal preparation links the physical with the magickal. To illustrate this, here is an excerpt from an article I wrote for *Bizoo*:

### The Witch's Spell

Hot water spurts from the many tiny holes in the metal shower spout. As he stands there, he washes the dirt of the day down the drain using the washcloth and the shower gel. Fairly mundane, at first glance; however, the intent behind this shower is planned. Tonight the worlds will merge in his backyard to create a space of purity and containment for the energies raised within.

As he stands under the water, he imagines the cascading droplets merging into beings of raw energy (perhaps mermaids, sometimes called undines) and absorbing into his skin. This will cleanse him of the mental and emotional baggage of the day, to allow for a focused and determined mind—a mind that is of good use in working with Magick.

The above excerpt demonstrates the power and sensuality that is incorporated in such exercises and how it creates the perfect mindset in anticipation for ritual.

Generally speaking, after bathing you dress (or, as the case may be, remain naked). As you dress, become aware of the transition from being naked to having clothes on. Do not overanalyse the experience, just allow yourself to sense, feel, and respond. Always remain calm, allowing thoughts to slip through and out of your mind.

If you are bothered by intruding sounds and movements, allow all of these distractions to meld into one symphony of life—see the rhythm underlying everything, and let it be a part of your experience. The concept of selfishness has become increasingly ominous in Western society; however, we all need to realise that in order to operate as a fully present being, the self needs to be paid close attention to. How else are you going to be able to help your friends and family?

In essence, preparing oneself for ritual is not necessarily about fasting and celibacy; rather, it is embracing the sense of self that is inherent in the moment. Once we have achieved this, we are centred and ready for the work ahead.

## PURIFICATION:
## CASTING THE CIRCLE

*You have noticed that everything an Indian does is in a circle and
that is because the Power of the World always works in circles,
and everything tries to be round ... Everything the
Power of the World does is done in a circle.*
—Black Elk, Oglala Sioux holy man (1863–1950)

The circle is a cultural symbol of Magick and Witchcraft. I was once sitting innocently at work during downtime, reading a book from the series *The Circle* by Melaina Faranda, when a woman came over to inquire about a tarot reading. After talking for a while, she noted the title of my book and asked if it was about Witchcraft. I nodded and asked how she knew, and she replied that the word "circle" had triggered the images. There is no other shape that can so adequately encompass the inner meaning of Paganism and Witchcraft, the cyclic nature of the world, and the never-ending flow of life, death, and rebirth.

The circle embodies a subtle reality; it has no sharp points or straight walls that impose a sense of material space. It is a shape that has no weakest point. Throughout history, the circle has been imbued with the qualities of life, protection, Magick, and wisdom.

Ultimately, the circle is a ritual that alters consciousness. It allows the individual to attune to the primal energies held deep within. Various acts may be integrated into the circle casting—for instance, quarter calling, asperging, and smudging—but the essence of the circle is the acknowledgement of Nature's tendency to move in cycles.

In truth, there are no concrete methods of circle casting, and like most things in Paganism, it is open to preference.

## BIRTHING A UNIVERSE: A PHILOSOPHY

*Before time was, there was The One;*
*The One was all, and all was The One.*
—Scott Cunningham, *Wicca*

Casting a circle and invoking the elements is enacting the very creation of Life's origins. Through gesture, word, and symbolism, you are drawing deeper into the eternal spiral of Spirit within your being. When you invoke the air, the earth, the water, and the fire, you are laying down the foundations of our own fertile planet. Medieval alchemists and Platonic philosophers believed that the world was composed of these four elements and animated by the fifth principle of Spirit. We all know that the pure forms of fire and earth do not literally compose our world; however, they are the generalised terms for the things that do. This concept is more easily understood when we equate water with liquid, earth with mineral and organic material, air with gas, and fire with the fuel (heat) that operates their interaction and movement. Spirit is what underlies all.

Almost all indigenous groups that exist and have existed in our world honour and acknowledge the power emanating from the eternal Spirit.

Australia's Aborigines[1] understand creation as an ongoing process of continuity and rhythm; this concept has been called the Dreamtime and more recently the Dreaming. It is believed that the ancestral spirits created all things in existence—the trees, the animals, the water, the earth, the sun, the moon, and humanity. However, there was no singular moment of conception or creation; rather, it was an unfolding process. These ancestral spirits took their rest in the many sacred sites scattered about Australia (and the world) and still dwell there to this day.

Creation is without time; it is the life we all share, and it is the eternal cycle of existence. The ancestral spirits are concentrated beings of energy, the catalysts that influence material form on the physical plane and imbue all of life with their sacred essence. Ultimately, the Australian Aborigines' conception of life and its origins is one of many that expresses the notion of a collection of spiritual beings coming together and birthing the world.

In the original thinking, there was never truly a moment of time or a singular point of space that forged this expanding sweep of stardust; it is a continuum. This is the fluctuating, undulating serpentine force that gathered in the energy of chaos and birthed the cosmos. Their dance is now an eternity.

Before the physical actions of the circle casting are carried out, it is the mental preparation of aligning oneself with the essential void of origin (the chaos within the cosmos) that is concentrated on, or surrendered to.

Before existence, there was chaos. In Hesiod's *Theogony*, the Greek poet relays the story of creation and the birth of the Olympian gods. It is chaos that bears the origin, the seed of life within the gaping mouth of potential.

Deep within the mind, there is a dark cradle that bears the beginning. Once you have centred and allowed the breath to purify your mind, body, and soul, a peaceful and quiet point of equilibrium is reached. It is darkness; it simply *is*. From that point onward, the process

---

1 Aboriginal Australia is not one homogenous clan but is made up of many ancestral groups. This is the case with most indigenous cultures.

of creation spirals into being, and the pace of an unfurling universe propels the momentum of energy into the natural circular rhythm.

When you visualise your circle and project your energy to infuse the potential barriers with life, you reinforce and strengthen the process of creation. You may then invite the elements to bless and guard your space.

Symbolically, you have fashioned a universe of your own through the metaphysical principle of sympathy. You have met with your inner, divine potential for life and resurrected your ancient power to give birth, regardless of physical gender.

The circle is the legacy of our ancestors; it is our spiritual home. This is the place where the primal forces of the divine are celebrated and embraced. You have become the pillar of the universe, and the circle is the womb that holds you firm.

## WHICH WAY IS WITCH?
### ELEMENTAL ORIENTATION

Incorporating the elements into your circle is a question of correspondence. This is where the distinction between hemispheres hits home.

When Gardner first began writing about Witchcraft, he began to formalise what came to be known as the Gardnerian tradition, which forms the basis for much of Wicca today.

The casting of the circle usually involves the invocation of the elements, directions, guardians, and/or watchtowers. Air was called from the east, as this is the place of the rising sun and therefore the origin of the solar wind at dawn. Fire was placed in the south, as this is the direction of the equator in Britain. The west came to be the home of water, as to the west of the British Isles is the North Atlantic Ocean. North was earth, probably as the Arctic Circle is to Britain's north.

These correspondences have been upheld in Wicca as traditional and therefore favoured over other systems of elemental orientation. However, much as the direction the circle is cast depends on the hemisphere, the elements can also be adapted to individual geographies.

There are five systems of elemental persuasion:[2]

1. Geographical

2. Traditional

3. Symbolical

4. Energetic

5. Intuitive

### 1: Geographical

This system works hand in hand with the acknowledgement of your specific locale. In Britain, the traditional elemental correspondences are valid due to the geography of the region. However, in the Southern Hemisphere, if following traditional forms of elemental positioning, it could be said that you are astrally standing on your head. We need to be upright and focused to work effective Magick, and thus the north (the direction of the equator in the Southern Hemisphere) is said to be the place of fire, and earth is designated to south.

However, if, for instance, you are more inclined to acknowledge your immediate physical surroundings, you might like to seek out representations of the elements around your sacred space. For example, if to the east of you stood a clump of trees, then it can only make sense that you would assign earth to east, or if a telephone box was to the north of you, it would be conceivable to assign air to that direction, as communication is a traditional function of air.

In August 2003, I organised a Witches' meet in the local Japanese gardens. Before we began the ritual, the participants stood around the altar and discussed which directions we should call the elements from. After a while of negotiating (I stood back and let them talk), we arrived at a decision. As to the south of us was a lake, we assigned water to south, and so on and so forth.

---

2 These systems have been formulated through personal observation and practice, and may be called differently by other Pagans.

The geographical system seeks to better attune the microcosm with the macrocosm (the universe) and honours the physical manifestations of the elements.

## 2: Traditional

This is the system assumed by most Northern Hemisphere covens and even many Southern Hemisphere groups, particularly British Traditional Wiccans.

In truth, the traditional system is simply geographical under a new guise, though it has been supplanted from its original environment and superimposed over others. In the Southern Hemisphere, however, where the physical surroundings are of more significance to the individual Witch, this system is invalid unless it is supported by the symbolical system, discussed below.

As the majority of Wiccan traditions use this method, I have named this system traditional, if not Eurocentric. Gardnerian, Alexandrian, and Dianic Wicca were all founded in the Northern Hemisphere, and although in some Southern groups the elemental orientations may be adjusted to the locale, most traditions adhere to the traditional system of designation in order to reflect the practices of their respective traditions and to honour lineage.

## 3: Symbolical

This system is based on the poetic aspects of elemental correspondences and does not seek to displace the traditional system. Symbolists employ the traditional elemental orientations regardless of locale.

For example, an adherent of the symbolical system embraces the fact that east is the direction from which the sun rises, and therefore relates air to east because of air's spiritual association with new beginnings and creative inspiration.

The orientation of the elements in a symbolist's circle owes to the associations garnered from our lore, as below:

*Fire:* Passion, Courage, Will, Power

*Water:* Emotion, Fluidity, Unpredictability, Secrets

*Air:* Intelligence, Inspiration, Communication, Clarity

*Earth:* Strength, Resilience, Practicality, Stability

These associations are generic, and individuals will assign different qualities to the elements.

### 4: Energetic

The energetic system has not, to my knowledge, been covered by any Pagan text I have come across.

This system acknowledges the buildup of specific energies from specific places surrounding a sacred space, e.g., a home altar. It applies to Witches who work in their physical sacred space regularly, as opposed to nomadic Witches. The energetic system, however, relies on adherence to one of the other systems.

If, for example, a Witch follows the symbolical system and thus calls earth from the north, and so on, to also adhere to the energetic system, the Witch would continue to call earth from the north. This is based on the principle that specific energies worked with regularly in the same place will be more receptive if called from that respective place or direction.

### 5: Intuitive

Witches who belong to no particular tradition use this system most often. The intuitive system is a concept favoured within the Eclectic movement. With intuition, you are permitted to pick and choose whatever feels right at the time.

An intuiting Witch will often go through a series of meditative exercises to familiarise themselves with the space they are working in and to also feel for the elements. The Witch generally focuses on a particular element and rotates on the spot, feeling for the direction in which the energy is felt most strongly.

This system is most applicable when there is no way of knowing, astronomically or otherwise, which direction is which. Without this knowledge, both the symbolical and traditional systems are nonapplicable. If you have no compass or knowledge of the constellations and the stars, this system will prove a great ally on those rare occasions when you find yourself lost in the middle of the woods.

## QUICK CIRCLE:
## FOR THE WITCH ON THE RUN!

For those who have very little time and who still wish to cast a circle or simply attune to their surroundings, the following quick, easy alternative will serve well:

You will need:

Yourself

Rock salt or another purifying substance, e.g., rosemary sprigs

Kneel, sit, or stand and hold the rock salt in your power hand. Now visualise white light surrounding your power hand and the salt, and imbue it with energy. Sprinkle a portion of the salt deosil in a small circle in front of you, and say:

*As the microcosm ...*

Now quickly hurl the remaining salt in an outward and deosil direction all around you while saying:

*... is to the macrocosm, so my circle is bound and blessed. So mote it be!*

Visualise the energy held within the small circle suddenly expanding and surrounding your entire being. The circle is cast.

To open the circle, visualise the circle's energy condensing back to the small circle, and then slowly pick up the grains of salt in a widdershins manner, imagining that the energy is becoming dimmer, until on the final grain it completely disappears. You may either reuse the salt or bury it (away from any garden beds or lush grass).

This is a simple exercise that will allow you to experience the wonder and movement of energy when your time is restricted or you may be in danger. If it is the latter, you need to be realistic and understand that the circle will not protect you from your offender if you have openly performed the casting in front of them. If they did not see you cast the circle, though, chances are that they will never find you, as the protection function works to deter attention and cloak you in shadow.

## NOTE FOR THE WAYWARD

I am very much aware that the ritualistic casting of the circle may not provide you with the sustenance that other rites (according to your practice) may do. For example, to purify my working space before a ritual or devotion, I use a reconstructed version of an ancient Greek ritual, as it suits my spirituality and honours my pantheon. In fact, not all traditions of Magick believe that a circle is necessary to achieve success in a working.

It is not within my experience or knowledge to provide a space-cleanse or personal preparation that will deal with all Pagan traditions. It is essentially up to you to gather the information from reputable sources and to engage in exercises and ceremonies that will help to centre the mind and connect you with your personal deities. See the appendix for some literary aid.

## RITUAL GUIDELINES FOR THE PRACTICAL PAGAN

There are some Pagans who just can't fit enough into their circle and there are others who cringe at the thought of burdening their ritual space with unnecessary paraphernalia. The former is the obsessive, twenty-four-degrees-right-of-Capricorn Pagan and the latter, the practical Pagan.

If I had to choose to identify with either group, I would side with the latter, as I just can't get my head around some of the correspondences some people come up with nowadays! It is ludicrous to focus solely on the trappings of ritual, as this negates the very reason for ritual itself.

Ritual opens channels of communication within the self and with the divine. How are the gods going to be able to fit into your circle (figuratively speaking) when your tools have taken all the space? We need to return to our roots, reconnect with Mother Earth, and celebrate life. All you need is yourself and your gods.

Below, you will find guidelines and insight into the stages of ritual. This requires no materials except for the bare minimum.

### Purification of the Self

Sometimes it's not possible to take luxurious baths or fast for days on end; however, to fully experience ritual, you will need to be prepared in some way.

To begin with, give yourself a few minutes to focus inward. Deep breathing and corresponding visualisations (such as coloured breathing[3]) should draw your senses to a pinpoint of cohesion that becomes the void. Exist wholly within that void, and all thoughts will soon evaporate. Embrace the totality and nothingness of the void, and dissolve all boundaries and limitations.

Other than the above, you may wish to simply wash your face with warm water while surrendering the stress and exertion of the day to the intoxication of spiritual enlightenment.

### Honouring the Spirits of the Land

As discussed previously, respect is a fundamental aspect of Paganism, and having respect for the land and its ancestral ties is a given. Whether you are indigenous yourself, a recent migrant to a country, or descended from the latter, you dwell upon a land that has a history and a people who have become, over time, inextricably linked to it.

In Australia, we have a history of racial dispute over land "ownership." Before the First Fleet arrived on the shores of Botany Bay in

---

3 Coloured breathing is any technique of breathing that incorporates visualisations of coloured light or mist entering the body on the inhalation and flowing out on the exhalation.

1788, people were already living in Australia—and had been for at least 60,000 years. They were and are the Australian Aborigines.

When the British arrived in Australia, heated skirmishes broke out between them and the Aboriginal people. The Aborigines were understandably disoriented by the sudden appearance of a white-skinned race.[4] Over time, the Aboriginal people were subdued, and a very high percentage were decimated in an effort to be rid of what was considered to be a distraction to settlement. Later on, various governmental policies were introduced in order to "protect" the Aborigines from being brutalised in the white colonies, and so they were provided with base domestic housing and rations on reserves. "Half-caste" children were forcibly taken from their families and given to white homes in an effort to assimilate them into British society. This has left the land severely traumatised.

In an effort to reconcile the land with its current inhabitants, it is essential that we care for it and honour it as our provider and our nurturer. NeoPagan ritual is inspired predominantly by European traditions, and the connection with the invading British is an obvious one that may make the sensitive practitioner uncomfortable. However, our traditions do not demand the desecration of another's holy place or indigenous culture. There is now a tendency to acknowledge the land's ancestral spirits before we invoke our own deities.

Pagan spirituality is rooted in the earth and is comprised of indigenous traditions. There are many who do not agree that we should have to acknowledge the spirits of the local indigenous people, as Pagans already honour the Great Spirit and Mother Earth in our rites. However, I suggest researching the history of your country and familiarising yourself with the native culture/s. Come to terms with the possibly violent relationships harboured between the invading foreigners and the local people, and seek to bring back the balance.

---

4 It has been suggested that the Aboriginal people first considered the British to be their ancestral spirits or, more generically, ghosts, as spirits are depicted as white in traditional Aboriginal art.

You may use the following as a guideline in writing your own statement of honour:

Stand before your altar, and quietly concentrate on the natural vibration of the land around you. Silently acknowledge the ancestral spirits, and recite the following:

> *I stand, a Pagan of the Path, before my altar adorned in the symbols of my spirit and my gods. In this, I acknowledge my right to practice what is meaningful to me in this place and time. I honour and offer my services to the land upon which I walk, and thus do I decree to the spirits of the native realm that I do so in truth and in respect of you. Great Ones of the land whose soil I now call my own, may you be with me and rejoice in my celebration of the earth. So be it forever. Blessed are my words and my charge. Hail!*

## Casting the Circle/Creating Sacred Space

Not all Pagans cast circles and neither do all Witches. In fact, for a while I rarely ever did so unless I was celebrating a sabbat or esbat. Nowadays, casting the circle is very important to me.

When blessing my space, I begin with cleansing my altar, myself, and the space by invoking the primal fire and calling upon its light and transformation. I then asperge with holy water to send away negativity and to invite in purity. I then trace a circle in the air with my stang and become the world tree. After this, I light incense and circle deosil, calling upon the lines of my ancestry and upon the spirits and gods that know me through blood. At the culmination, I cast the circle, thrice declaring that I am between the worlds. I then invoke the elements and the guardians, deities, and totems I associate with each direction.

Like me, you may not identify as Wiccan (in fact, you may not identify as a Witch), and perhaps it is not within your interests to follow what has become the generic preclude to many NeoPagan workings. For instance, if you are drawn to the reconstructionist ideals, you may wish to resurrect ancient cleansing rituals.

Many ancient Pagan practices draw upon their cosmologies to acknowledge sacred space. The old trinity of land, sky, and sea in the Celtic traditions is seen as encompassing all, and each realm is home to its own special kind of Magick. After calling upon my bloodlines and my ancestral gods, I finish by saying, "By the land, by the sky, by the sea—by the ancient trinity, so mote it be."

### Statement of Purpose

Stating the purpose of your ritual and clarifying your intentions sets the scene for the rest of the play.

The statement of purpose can be performed in a number of ways. For instance, during a sabbat I usually like to write an introduction including the seasonal symbolism, history, and traditional lore and customs of the particular festival. It's a way to familiarise yourself and those around you by giving meaning to your intent. Below is the statement of purpose I wrote for Mabon in 2004:

*Here, between the worlds, where the dark and light are lovers and time and space are but fickle memories, we are free and beautiful. It is here that we honour Mabon and his day. Today, the gods of wine and death shall be revered, for such is their importance in the eternal circle. Without death there may not be life, and without life there may not be pleasure.*

*An ancient mystery is here between us; we Nature-folk know of this day as honouring Mabon, the great son. Others may know this day as the Autumn Equinox, when night and day are in balance, yet from here onward the darkness will wax and the god will remove his mantle of summer and move into the Underworld to meet with his dark self, the Lord of the Dead. It is also the second of three harvest festivals in the Pagan Wheel of the Year, the final completion of summer harvest and the beginning of autumn's.*

*In the ancient Welsh myth, it is said that at three nights of age, Mabon was abducted from his mother, Modron, the Great Mother. Distraught, she wept for him, not knowing the secret that Mabon was safe, peaceful, and alive, renewed in the form of the promised light within her own womb. Then, the five ancient beings stirred to restore Mabon to the glory of life: the majestic eagle, the silent owl, the keen blackbird, the gracious stag, and the wise salmon.*

*This day, we look within ourselves—as you have, Mabon. This day, we reflect on all that is beautiful and all that is harrowing in our lives. May our celebration bring resolve and balance, for this day is for the great son and the second harvest.*

Poetry is another appropriate method of stating the purpose. Set aside a moment of reflection, and write down any words that come to mind when you focus on the celebration. Whether or not they are relevant does not matter, as they may come in handy when you least expect it. After this activity, begin to form the basic structure of your poem. Make use of the words and images you recorded to flesh out the poem.

You should now be well aware of what you want to achieve through the ritual and what it means to you. Speak your statement of purpose with vigour and confidence.

### Invocation

Invocation has two working definitions. The first describes the act of calling to a deity in order to attract their presence and/or to petition a specific need or desire. The second has been called *aspecting* by some, but perhaps *possession* is the more appropriate term.

For both kinds of invocation, you will need to be well prepared. Before invoking any being, you will need to have done a good amount of research. Familiarise yourself with the history, rites, lore, and qualities of the deity or being. If you wanted, you could meditate on the deity for a few minutes each day before the ritual. Aspecting is a serious act that requires a great degree of responsibility on your part. The first time I consciously invited another being to enter my body during ritual was a truly amazing experience. Despite all the Hollywood portrayals of possession and invocation, there is something much more subtle and yet overwhelmingly intense about having the living energy of a spiritual being merge with your own essence.

When you invoke, make sure your words are clear and concentrated, but if you do trip up, know that the gods will not consider it a fatal error. Smile and laugh it off—humour is divine!

Your oral invocation should come from you, either spontaneously and in the moment or previously recorded. In the case of the latter, it's best to memorise the words beforehand so that your awareness is not on reading the text but on the meaning of the words. As you call out to the deity, visualise him/her completely, from head to toe (if that is conceivable). You will find that you will not have to make much of an attempt at creating an image. Now make clear your intentions of uniting with the deity, remembering to respect the energy you are about to receive. The deity may not wish to cooperate, and if you do get the cold shoulder, simply acknowledge the deity and thank her/him. Generally, if you exude sincerity, the deity will want to work with you. Visualise the deity approaching you and entering your physical being.

Once you feel the being is within you, disperse all restrictions and respond to the impulses the deity provokes. Release inhibition, and with the knowledge that you are safe, do as your body feels, and embrace the words, sensations, and visions that are liable to ignite.

*Note:* For those of you who, like me, are naturally open to divine forces and who have experienced untagged or spontaneous possession, it pays to be necessarily cautious of the gods or forces you consciously bring into yourself. Practise exercises that affirm your personal authority over your body, your temple. Periodically perform aura and chakra cleanses to ensure that there are no beings or energies attached to your etheric skin that shouldn't be there. Paying close attention to yourself spiritually, if cultivated appropriately, can ensure that you will remain safe.

# GNOSIS

Gnosis is integral to all methods of transformation. The concept of gnosis in Pagan philosophy is the attaining of pure knowledge of and union with the divine by embracing the Self. The Gnostic sects of Europe perceived this transformation as a means of spiritual alchemy that strips away the outer manifestations of form and unites the individual with their divine spark. The Christian belief that the flesh is inherently sinful is irrelevant to Paganism, however. Gnosis, or complete union with the divine, is achieved by means of invocation, which is then extended through embracing the material personification of spirit, our bodies.

Pagan gnosis is a melding of body, mind, and spirit. Creative expression is central to its efficacy, and ecstasy is its success. Gnosis is heightened through trance. Gnosis is both conscious and unconscious, in that you are the instigator and benefit immediately from its implementation. To achieve such a state, it is important to acknowledge and move through the levels of awareness as one that is simultaneously present in all.

In any case, know that this is a moment of the Self (self to Self) and its divinity. Through invocation and ritual, you have altered consciousness, and gnosis is simply the next step—a spiritual progression or deepening. Perceive no binding, except to yourself and thus to your spiritual seed. Let it unravel, too, when the time comes.

## An Exercise in Gnostic Union

Prepare yourself and your space as usual. Breathe deeply, focusing on the moment, the unlimited expanse of reality. Find that void within your mind and exist there. Call out to the divine (or your god/s) and attune yourself to the energy without visualising anything. Just know that they are there and surrounding you completely. Feel that sense of spiritual immersion within the essence, and embrace the union. Forcing yourself to experience with mental aggression will not result in success; this is the delicate line between the world of consciousness and the hidden planes of the unconscious. Feel the dance of energies as you are inspired to move, chant, or whatever. Gradually you should feel a lifting sensation. When you are in the midst of this sensation, throw yourself into the channel and know that you are completely present, joined eternally with the divine. This is your gnosis, and it is here where the structure of human mentality disappears and communion with the universe / the Self happens.

## CELEBRATION

Now comes the time to let go completely and to rejoice in the freedom of Pagan revelry. Of course, there is no need to resurrect the Bacchanalia; simply loosen your inhibitions and enjoy yourself.

Celebration is possible in both solitary and group environments, as the gods are ever-present within the circle. In fact, the senses are heightened in ritual, intensifying the connection between the Self and Deity. Do everything in fervour and abandon. Do as ye will, an' harm ye none.

## WINDING DOWN

Winding down involves the consumption of the blessed feast. This is a period of peace and mirth as the crackling energy of the ritual recedes. Winding down can often take as much time as the ritual itself. Once you are ready, you may open the circle and clean up.

## OPENING THE CIRCLE

Refer to the Quick Circle described on page 141 or go about returning your consciousness and circumstance to the mundane in whichever way draws you.

## GROUNDING

If you still feel on edge or nauseous after ritual, then you will need to ground.

Crouch down and place your forehead directly on the earth, and focus on sending any excess energy back into the earth. Feel it drain from you as it is reabsorbed into the Mother, who will then neutralise it and make use of it herself.

Spend as much time as you need, as it is vital that your energy rides with the vibrations around you. You will affect others if you haven't properly grounded. Once all is well, eat and drink something.

Ritual usually requires an assortment of materials and a basic understanding in correspondence. To have this knowledge at hand is generally thought of as necessary for the average Pagan. However, it is not essential to dress up or colour ritual in order to experience a successful outcome. If you are able to dispense of the trappings and still effectively raise energy and invoke, then that is a path I would suggest exploring.

Ritual is a joyful experience. It is also serious by nature and requires a mature mentality. Once again, balance is the key. Work with your intuition and acknowledge matters of practicality, and you will go far.

## THE DRAMA OF RITUAL

Drama is an art that inspires and provokes our emotions in order to convey archetypes that resonate with the human experience. It is an ingenious method through which to access the hidden realities of the subconscious.

The ancient Greeks were renowned for their dramatic flair. Their skill at moving large crowds to respond to an emotional evocation expressed through scenario, gesture, and costume was highly refined. In fact, Western theatrical drama is thought to have descended from the wild Dionysian rites held away from the public eye in which alcohol, comedic masquerades, and sexuality pervaded. When Peisistratus, a popular Athenian tyrant, came to power in the sixth century BC, he introduced the Dionysia, a religious festival devoted to the god of wine and revelry, Dionysos. The festival involved the performances of comedies and tragedies, and characters were personified through masks.

Pagan dramatic ritual reflects the Dionysian rites. It is wild, sexual, and flamboyant. Participating in such a ritual stimulates the unconscious and awakens the serpentine flow of energy through the body. Dramatic ritual often involves bright colours and elegant dress against a theatrical background.

Below, you will find the discussion broken into three sections: Scenario, Gesture and Movement, and Costume.

## Scenario

No one can deny that performing rites and casting spells within a hidden forest alcove is alluring. Humans respond on a subconscious level to the evocative language of setting and atmosphere. It thrusts us into ecstatic communion with our surroundings. To enhance ritual through drama, the first thing is to locate a place of natural beauty.

Public parks and gardens are the best places, as they are open to all and require no prior organisation with the councils, unless the ritual is publicly advertised, in which case insurance is needed. Perhaps you know a Pagan temple in your area that may allow you to use their land. If you desired, you could even dress up your backyard or room. For example, you could make your own elemental banners to hang on the wall corresponding to each direction, and mark your circle with the cards from the Major Arcana.

I once held a group Litha ritual in my backyard under a pavilion-like tent that was enclosed by sheets and curtains tied around the poles. The altar was set up in the centre and decorated with various objects that represented summer to the participants. It looked magnificent! Later on, my mum helped me to build a small fire, and after having raised energy by all dancing deosil and singing, we gathered around it and threw symbols of things we wanted gone into the flames. Across from the ritual site was a feast my parents had graciously prepared.

When focusing on scene, begin with the altar. Altars corresponding to seasonal imagery and mythological symbolism help to stir the primal mind. At a Yule open circle I held in 2003, I indulged heavily in altar decoration. On the altar was a cauldron with a star candle in it; a beautiful wooden statue of a deer, which had been covered in cloth since Samhain, as a representation of the Horned One (the cloth was removed later); candles and oil burners; incense; tarot cards; chalices; and a tall sun candleholder. I also wrapped ivy around the table legs. Decorating altars is a lot of fun, but remember not to go overboard!

Decorate the space with ribbons, candles, paint, vegetation/foliage, crystals/stones, and even food, if you like! If you are using a lot of fire in your ritual, remember to always keep a bucket of water or a fire extinguisher close by in case of an emergency.

### Gesture and Movement

Ritual gestures help to express the meaning and significance of each stage of the process. They are physical signs that communicate a particular energy to both the invited gods and spirits and the other participants. They can be elegant and poised or simple movements used to imitate a natural entity or process, e.g., fire.

The traditional Wiccan God and Goddess postures taken by the high priest/ess in the Drawing Down the Moon ceremony are prime examples of Pagan gesture. Generally, the priestess stands in what is commonly referred to as a "power stance" and holds up her arms as if surrendering, palms facing outward (the Goddess pose). This is symbolic of the goddess's receptive and yet firm, powerful nature. The angle at which her legs are spread and the composure of the upper torso communicate a sense of balance and understanding. When she crosses her arms over her chest, imitating an Egyptian mummy, and draws her feet and legs together (the God pose), the priestess seals the invocation. This is personified gesture.

In order to integrate gesture into your rituals, an awareness of the links between ancient symbols and their physical expressions needs to be gained. It is possible to physically represent symbols that personify a particular emotion, power, or characteristic. Think of the pentagram and the famous da Vinci portrait of the Vitruvian Man. The spread-eagle posture taken by the body to imitate the five points of the pentagram is a clear example of an occult symbol taking on a physical form. This can further be developed into group formations performed during coven workings and other group situations.

Physical movement composing the entire body or at least a greater portion of it also adds a beautiful quality to ritual. An example of this would be the cone of power. Calling the quarters can also benefit from theatrical movement.

The whirling dervishes are renowned for their orchestrated rhythms of spinning that allow the dancers to experience the divine. Spinning on the spot while using the feet to pivot the body can be applied in Pagan ritual too. At each direction, after the formal invocation is made to the particular element, the individual can then spin deosil with arms spread and head slightly tilted back while envisioning the buildup of energy. Eventually gnosis with that particular element takes place. Obviously you need to be careful, as spinning could throw you off balance and make you feel ill.

Remember to always maintain the original significance of a symbol if used in ritual. As with sigils of power, the associations work on a subliminal level. Then again, some ancient symbols owe their power to a buildup of energy that courses along hidden lines. These gossamer trails are open to all those who genuinely seek to ally themselves with the power of symbols.

### Costume

To wear a costume does not always require clothing; a costume is simply an outward expression that communicates a specific idea or theme. However, at all times the costume must be "worn" on the body. Paint, robes, garments, masks, and jewellery are all valid options.

Classical Hellenic descriptions of the festivities that occurred at the Dionysian revels paint a picture of drunken humour, sensuality, and the complete release of inhibitions. Costumes allow us as individuals to break free from the molds of society and to embrace the stream of pure unconsciousness.

Often in ritual I paint symbols on my skin to honour the Old Ones. Headdresses and other decorative accessories also help to arouse the intended feelings. Why not go all-out in an avid return to Mother Nature? Have a mud bath, wear a few flowers here and there, and go for it!

## Spontaneous Ritual

*Practice random acts of kindness and senseless beauty.*
—Unknown

Spontaneity is a wonderful thing. Without spontaneity, our lives would be void of substance and our emotional rivers would run dry. Being spontaneous is what separates us from routine. It thrusts us into the arms of chance. When this happens, we are truly tested. Our fears and hopes become one, and we dance to a rhythm that is undecided but pulses on.

When I am feeling depleted, deflated, or generally bored, I will go for a walk and expose my body to the natural world. I visit my favourite spots and sit for a while to simply think and reflect. There is such pleasure and peace in that solitude, and in that moment of calm I am often inspired to perform a devotion—to call upon my gods and talk, laugh, and cry with them. This is the spontaneity of ritual.

Spontaneous ritual gives release when structured ritual cannot. It helps us to key into the primal impulse to imbue every moment of our lives with the sacred. Ours is not a Sunday religion; every moment of the journey is something to be remembered and embraced. Whether it happens to coincide with an auspicious date or not, spontaneous ritual allows us to revel in the brilliance of life.

Spontaneity also opens us up to the eternal spiral of the human spirit. Spontaneous ritual opens the door to such vibrant power that it can often become overwhelming. Your intent becomes the sharp precision of an arrow as it is fired at your goal.

The effects and atmosphere of a spontaneous working are something that can only be experienced. This chapter may have inspired you to drop this book and head for your sacred space. It is not always the desire to obtain or destroy something, but also the spiritual need to connect with the divine that invokes spontaneity. Often, that moment may not have been free for ritual. That hour may have been designated to studying or visiting a friend. However, when you feel that sudden urge to be spontaneous and ritualise, do not ignore it simply because you will feel guilty. It's never wrong to do something for oneself as long as it harms no one.

To fully immerse oneself in the spontaneity of a ritual is to abolish the mediator—the gestures, words, costumes, and tools. This is the core of spontaneous ritual.

Spontaneity is your ability to take hold of your life and work alongside the potential of life to achieve what you wish. With that in mind, promise yourself that when spontaneity kicks in, you will heed its call.

## RITES OF PASSAGE

As youths, we encounter and cross many thresholds of growth and transformation. At times, these changes frighten us and shake our foundations. Exploring sexuality, graduation, relationships, and leaving home are the most common experiences and challenges faced by the youth of today. Below you will find rituals addressing each of these passages.

### Free to Be Me!

This ritual focuses on sexuality and the link between sexual experimentation and youth. You are at your prime, and your curiosity is at its peak. Gay, straight, bi, or whatever, we are all sexual beings with the opportunity to love and be loved.

This ritual is designed to concentrate on and celebrate your sexuality. If you have reached the stage of acceptance concerning your sexuality, then this ritual will celebrate that passage into understanding and freedom. Ideally, this ritual should be performed on a full moon.

You will need:

> Patchouli incense (stick variety)
> Incense holder
> Five red taper candles
> Five candleholders or jars
> A sheet of paper and a red pen
> Cauldron or fireproof container

Before you begin the ritual, bathe, and allow yourself to explore the totality of your physical being. You shouldn't feel shame as your fingers trail across your skin. Clean yourself seductively, feeling the spread of orgasmic fire exhilarate your body. Concentrate on your root and sacral chakras. See them glow and spin brightly, energising your being and moving you into a sexual state of freedom and ecstasy. However, at the same time, you are in complete control of your body and your sexuality.

After bathing, tenderly dry yourself and go to your sacred space. You will need to be inside and in a private area where you will not be disturbed, as you will be performing this ritual skyclad.

Set the five red candles around you, ensuring that there is enough room for you to lie down and spread out. Light the candles, and stand in the centre of the circle, facing the direction of fire, and visualise a red orb growing around you, holding you tightly and warming your body. Feel the magnetic pull of wild sexual energy as it swirls around you and your own energy begins to dance.

Now light the patchouli incense and walk deosil, fanning the smoke with your free hand, drawing deeper into your trance state. Kneel when you have walked around the circle once, and place the stick of incense in the incense holder. Now take the sheet of paper and red pen, and draw the sexual symbol you identify with. For a gay male, it could be the interlinked Mars symbols; for a gay female, the interlinked Venus symbols; and for a straight person, the interlinked Mars and Venus symbols.

As you draw your symbol, understand that this is not an imposition but a unique expression of your freedom and pride. When the image is completed, write the following underneath:

*Free to be me*
*By the power of three*
*Free to be me*
*So that I may see*
*What it is to be*
*Free to be me.*

As you write the affirmation, reflect on your sexuality and how it shapes who you are and vice versa. Draw on your past experiences of sexual liberty and channel those emotions into the words.

Now lie back as if you were making a snow angel, with your arms and legs spread out. Visualise the spinning and pulsating orange and red light at your respective chakras and feel the energy sweep over your body, infusing you with sexual sparks. Allow the energy to take hold of your physical being and respond to it. When the energy reaches its peak, chant or shout the following:

> *Sexual freedom is mine to behold*
> *For I am earth's son/daughter and thus I am told*
> *That all acts of pleasure are sacred and bold*
> *Sexual freedom is mine to behold!*

As you recite the above, draw the power to a point and focus on channelling your desire and sexuality. Become completely involved in this release and allow the energy to affect your body. You may find that your abdomen will lift off the ground and that your body will arch slightly. On the last "behold," release the energy and collapse. Give yourself some time to recuperate before you stand up. When you are ready, take the sheet of paper, offer it to the flame of the fire candle, and drop it into the cauldron while chanting the "free to be me" affirmation. The ritual is done.

### School's Out!

School's out, and you've reached the end of your senior schooling; the prospect of further study or employment lies ahead. It's time to take on the world and make use of the skills you picked up at school. Graduation is not just a rash of parties; it also means leaving your comfort zone. The reality of the world hits home, and it's time to take charge.

This ritual aims to celebrate your passage from high school into the workforce, further study, travel, or whatever. It is a reflection on your friendships and experiences while at school and the endless possibilities of life. This ritual can be performed either before your graduation ceremony or afterwards.

You will need:

Dried rosemary

Yellow ribbon

Sandalwood essential oil

A sheet of paper and blue pen

One blue candle

Cast a circle, and light the blue candle. Reflect on the past five years or so and what you have learnt, life experiences included. Take the dried rosemary and tie the pieces together with the yellow ribbon. Light the end of the bundle using the candle's flame, and fan the smoke around you. Draw deeper into your memories, and allow images and scenarios to be invoked. Chant the following while channelling the energy of your overall experience:

> *The past is the past*
> *And my eyes are on the future*
> *For change is its gift and growth is its seed*
> *Now is my path and now is my hour*
> *This is my charge and this is my power.*

Now, with pen in hand, write down the aspects, or qualities, of your personality that you would like to enhance. For instance, if you are heading off to university, you could write "patience" or "curiosity." If you are planning on travelling the world, you could write "common sense" or "wit." Concentrate on what it means to have the qualities you list, and then roll up the paper lengthwise and seal it with sandalwood oil and blue wax. Set the scroll in front of the blue candle, and stand to invoke the divine. Then pick up the scroll and hold it in both hands in a gesture of offering. See your gods bless the scroll. Then chant the following as you envision your own energy surrounding the scroll:

> *My future path is bound and blessed*
> *By the gods and goddesses*
> *And by the oil of sandalwood*
> *May I know the things I should*

*Sealed by wax of azure blue skies*
*This scroll is imbued as my old year dies*
*For the path ahead is mine to create*
*This spell is cast by our Magick great.*

The ritual is complete. Take the scroll with you wherever you go as a talisman for luck and success.

### First-Time Lovers

This ritual is a celebration of your first relationship and of your commitment to your partner. This ritual is designed to be performed with your partner; however, you can adapt it for solitary use.

Before the day of the ritual, you will need to inform your partner of what you are planning on doing and go through the ritual with them. You also need to ask them to think about how they would like your relationship to grow and to bring a gift for you that embodies those ideas. You also need to bring a gift for your partner. This ritual is best done on a new moon.

You will need:

Two gifts
Rose essential oil
Five pink candles
Lavender incense (stick variety)

Before you cast the circle, set up your sacred space by arranging the five pink candles in a circle and lighting them around you deosil, giving yourself enough room for comfort. Turn to the east and recite the following while envisioning a pink mist gliding over you:

*Place of the dawn, sacred Spirit*
*I call to thee to settle here*
*Loving tides of moist, sweet earth*
*Do I invoke to travel near.*

Hold out your power hand and walk once around the circle deosil, envisioning the pink mist expanding to encapsulate the sphere of your circle. Say:

> *Bound and blessed by circle's run*
> *By Mother Earth and Father Sun*
> *And love shall twine as they do meet*
> *And so do we; our love is sweet.*

Return to the centre of the circle and kneel before your partner, interlinking fingers. Reflect on how the two of you met and the blossoming of your relationship thus far. Concentrate on love and how it makes you feel. Chant the following after a few minutes of quiet reflection:

> *Love is love and by it blessed*
> *Are we whose hearts have courted fair*
> *Between the God and sweet Goddess*
> *We know, keep silent, and will, and dare.*

Retrieve your gifts and turn to your partner. Pour a few drops of oil onto the index finger of your power hand and draw a love heart on the gift. As you hand your gift to your partner, say:

> *With love, from me to you.*

Once both of you have exchanged your gifts, light the lavender incense and weave the smoke between you in an infinity pattern. Affirm the blessings of the divine upon you both as you intone:

> *So mote it be!*

Understand that your words have given life to your intent. Be fully aware that a relationship will not always work out, and if so, vow to part peacefully.

To end the ritual, you can kiss. Open the circle by walking widdershins, imagining the pink mist dissipating into the air. Go out for dinner or a movie, and enjoy the rest of the night.

If you decide to perform this ritual alone, then you can adapt the ritual to specify that the next time you see your partner, you will give them the gift. To strengthen the intent, you may also like to visualise your partner in front of you during the ritual.

### Home and Away: Setting Sail

There comes a time when the idea of independence urges one to leave home. This will initiate a new journey. This ritual helps to make that transition easier and helps to bring resolve. It's time to say goodbye to family and friends, and go out into the world to make a life for yourself.

You will need:

> A river, stream, or creek
> Sage incense
> One green oak leaf

There is no need to cast a circle during this ritual, as the focus is on the flow of the river or stream you have chosen. Find yourself a place beside the river or, if you can, a stone or bridge across the river.

Before you begin, cleanse yourself by empowering your aura, visualising it as a white mist enshrouding your body. It grows in density and brightness as you focus on it. Feel it glide freely through your skin, renewing you.

Once you feel centred and cleansed, light the sage incense and smudge yourself. Now look to the river. Watch how the water moves, spiralling and undulating; it is a peaceful flow. As your meditation deepens, you may begin to see shapes and shadows playing in the water—the nymphs and undines. Their curling fins and scales reflect the effervescent light of the sun as it shines through the water. Become a part of that movement; be absorbed into the essence of the river. You are a free spirit on a journey of evolution and learning. You are on the verge of new and exciting experiences. It's time to let go, and trust in the divine. You will have enough money, you will have a safe and secure home, and you will gain new friendships. Change is inevitable, and you are the path on which it walks.

Now take the oak leaf and gently place it onto the surface of the water, and watch as it glides away. It represents you and your new life. Silently ask the blessing of the spirit of the oak that you are forever blessed and guarded by its holy power.

After a while, slowly return your awareness to the mundane level, and leave the site of your rite of passage with faith in your heart.

# 9: DIVINITY

*I do not feel obliged to believe that the same God
who has endowed us with sense, reason, and intellect
has intended us to forgo their uses.*
—Galileo Galilei

Pagans see the divine as immanent within creation. Transcendence, totalitarianism, almighty gods, and divine commandments are completely irrelevant in Paganism. However, it is impossible to generalise how Pagans see divinity, as every one of us has a different perspective on the matter.

What we can all agree on is that divine energy exists and is actively involved in our lives. The gods are not senile politicians seeking to exert influence over us. They would rather see us live our lives and cope with the challenges as best we can.

The creation, or the manifestation of the divine, forms the structure of physical reality. Our physical reality resonates with the echo of the other planes that coexist with our own. Divinity—the principle, without gender and embodiment—is the quintessential flow that suspends existence and gives balance to all things.

Some religious groups look down on Paganism as a path that places too much emphasis on the material and not enough on the creator. What these detractors miss completely is the fact that Pagans perceive no distinction between the creator and the creation. In our philosophies, there is no need for a creator; it is all a continuity, a rhythm that inspires life to be and to be again.

Galileo's words quoted at the very beginning of this chapter ring true in the Pagan traditions. As Pagans, we reject a cold and detached god. We see the divine as a plane of neutrality and extremity simultaneously—the very matrix of existence and emotion. All thought and feeling is comprised within its totality. The divine is not a force of morality, it simply *is*. Therefore, our gifts of "sense, reason, and intellect" are divine.

There is no hierarchy in relation to divinity. The divine is not above or below our humanity, the divine is the seed of it. The divine is relevant in our lives and offers a personal relationship with the universe and the self. Lastly, the divine is your key to perception, the catalyst of individual expression. The divine is your connection and your consciousness. The divine is not your window to the world, the divine *is* the world. You are divine.

## PAINTING THE GODS: DEFINING DEITY

*Speak of the Gods as they are.*
—Walter Bagehot, *Literary Studies*

The nature of deity is not hidebound in the Pagan traditions. Each individual is expected to approach the subject independently, to communicate with the divine. It all falls on perception, experience, and personality. There is no central authority to direct your questions to. Now comes the time for a little soul-searching, for it is within the self that truth is found.

Below, you will find information on the five major theologies[1] embraced in the Pagan community—pantheism, polytheism, animism, ditheism, and the archetype. Each section deals with the historical, philosophical, and cultural aspects of the theology and provides you with exercises in order to further your understanding.

Theology is an expression of one's feelings and thoughts concerning the divine. Religion is merely the sum of a society's codes and mores and is rarely a personalised thing. Understanding that the divine is one or that each deity is actually a vibrant life force unto itself is a highly definitive moment in one's life. It is the revelation of the divine, and this experience cannot be stolen, bought, or traded.

## PANTHEISM:
## GOD IS ALL AND ALL IS GOD

*What else is Nature but God?*
—Seneca the Younger, Roman Stoic philosopher

Pantheism is the spiritual understanding that the divine is within Nature. *Pan*, the Greek word for "all," forms the subject of the word and refers to the Greek god of the same name. Pan, the lusty satyrlike musician of the wilderness, rules over the pastures and is patron deity of shepherds. His connection with the natural world and the animal kingdom, as indicated by his goatlike appearance, is the quintessential heart of the pantheistic worldview. It is in the primal realm of Nature that divinity flows freely. It is in the beauty of the earth that we may attune with the inner sanctum of spirit and soak in the awe-inspiring resonance of the all.

It was from a Jewish community situated in the meeting-ground of revolutionary philosophy—Amsterdam, Holland—that, at the age of twenty-three, Baruch (Benedict) de Spinoza (1632–77) was excommunicated for espousing radical ideas. These ideas advocated a doctrine adverse to the dualistic notions of the organised faiths Spinoza speculated against. In essence, Spinoza was the first pantheistic monist,

---

1 Or perhaps *theological experience* is a more accurate term of definition.

meaning he regarded Nature as being synonymous with God. In fact, he theorised that God was the one and only substance, and that all things were constituted of it. However, Spinoza did not court the fancies of a transcendent creator-God. After all, God was all, and all that existed was the present. Spinoza believed that God was self-caused and that all in existence relied upon God's substance. God was also, in Spinoza's view, composed of infinite attributes and capable of extension and thought, otherwise considered to be an expansion of consciousness. "Spinoza's God is a self-caused substance ... from whose nature everything possible necessarily flows."[2]

By extension, Spinoza saw God as the creator of humanity and all things but in a remarkably different light than orthodox teachings. Individuation, the process whereby a whole becomes fragmented (the individual gathers substance from the whole), is an inevitable fate for a force of dynamic expansion such as God. The name given to the products of individuation is *modes*. We are all modes of God, the one substance, and are therefore dependent upon that substance's continuance. The implications of this are far-reaching, both in this time and magnanimously more in Spinoza's lifetime. God's cause is itself, and therefore all of reality is simply a manifestation of the divine catalyst. To Spinoza, divine reality was simply a matter of *"Deus sive Nature"*—God or Nature.

Spinoza was ultimately a naturalistic rationalist who considered God to be both perfect and infinite. In his view, all knowledge deriving from the present moment is conceived by the unitive substance, and therefore is knowledge of God. The implications of this are startling, in that "knowledge of God" is to be interpreted as both scientific discovery and knowledge possessed by God. As modes of the one substance, we are able to access God's storehouse of wisdom, and like gnosis, the underlying principle of pantheism is made clear: that as beings of consciousness, we are essentially divine in make-up, and therefore our highest aspiration as a species is to attain the divine, or to realise it.

The World Pantheist Movement has put forward a belief statement that addresses the central tenets of the pantheistic worldview. Primar-

2  D. Garret, *The Cambridge Companion to Spinoza*, 4.

ily, the statement explains the very nature of the pantheist: "We revere and celebrate the universe as the totality of being, past, present, and future." The statement goes on to describe the nature of connection and how living undeniably in the present fulfils the spirit.

Pantheists are also actively involved in the preservation and fostering of the natural world, which they understand themselves to be an integral part of. Respect is the basis of all relationships, and all of life is acknowledged as sacred. Each individual is considered a purposeful "centre of awareness." This returns personal power. The inclination to embrace life as creatively ingenious allows the pantheist to accept energy in all its forms, as an evolving and interweaving interaction.

There is a common understanding that because energy cannot be destroyed, it is simply recycled and absorbed into other forms, in which the originality and perhaps even personality of that energy is retained. Reason and logic are indivisible from the reality and truth of our presence in the universe, and science is often considered a pathway of enlightenment. While freedom is embraced as the means to living a highly individualistic and creative existence, there is also a degree of natural humanism in pantheism, which in most cases rejects any spiritual or emotional relation. However, the essence of Nature is vital to all experience, and the conventional religious urge to bend and worship before an authority is completely inappropriate within pantheism. The notions of salvation, resurrection, and spiritual paradise have nothing to do with the pantheist worldview. Nature and the world are believed to be the only paradise, heaven itself.

There is a great deal of collaboration that goes on in pantheism as well. For instance, their belief statement also details the following: "Our beliefs and values reconcile spirituality and rationality, emotion and values and environmental concern with science and respect for evidence." There is a complete practicality and humility involved within this understanding of divinity. There is a need to strip down the impositions and leap the chasms to unite humanity under a banner of reconciliation and healing.

Pantheism offers humanity a theological definition of life that encourages eco-friendly attitudes and collaborative expressions of human interaction and destroys all egocentric illusions of human beings as higher than other life forms. It is essential to embrace the plurality of Nature as mystery and not as fragments of a greater whole.

It is within the inspired awe of Nature that humanity is humbled and therefore freed. Without the institutions of religion and government, the individual begins to grow towards spiritual understanding. We are all aware of the bigger picture, of the presence of something more, and it is within these moments that we are willing to release and to receive. Nature reveals its life force and blesses the self. For it is in the moment that the revelation of unity and of balance within harmony is found, and all things become one.

### Pantheistic Exercise

Before you begin this exercise, you will need to answer a few questions, the first being which natural phenomenon are you most drawn to? The sunrise, the sunset, a wild storm, a gentle breeze? Once you have established a particular natural scene, phenomenon, or being in your mind, you may now begin the exercise. I will use the example of a sunrise.

Arrange yourself comfortably, and ground and centre. Surrender yourself completely to the rising sun. Open yourself to the profundity of the experience. Embrace the overwhelming tide of seemingly unfounded emotions that are ignited within you as your being becomes absorbed into the natural phenomenon. When you feel ready, you may recite the following affirmation (or one of your own invention):

*Gracious face of the all-encompassing divine, I am humbled by your artistry and skilful glamour, though I acknowledge there is no illusion here. I am healed by you and stand strong in my conviction to live in the moment, for this is the charge Nature has given, and by Nature do I keep it.*

Now concentrate on the energy within you. Feel it pulsing in rhythm with the rising sun. Feel it grow to a peak, and in that moment seize its potential and literally explode the energy. Mentally, emotionally, and physically burst in an infinite array of brilliance. You are now suspended within the whirling resonance of a flowing river of energy. The sun's rays charge it, imbuing it with purpose and direction. Throw away all thoughts of who you are and simply reside within the moment. Ride the power.

When you feel it is time, bring yourself back down to earth and ground. Thank the sun and the Spirit.

## POLYTHEISM:
## LEGACY OF THE PANTHEON

*The idea of polytheism is grounded in the view*
*that reality (divine or otherwise) is multiple and diverse …*
*Polytheism has allowed a multitude of distinct groups*
*to exist more or less in harmony, despite*
*great divergence in beliefs and practices …*
—Margot Adler, *Drawing Down the Moon*

Each flame glistens seductively, ushering forth serenity. Each flame possesses a unique aura amongst the sea of fire that gathers over the smooth surface of the consecrated altar. The chant begins:

*Isis, Astarte, Diana, Hekate, Demeter, Kali, Inanna …*
*Pan, Poseidon, Dionysos, Cernunnos, Mithros, Loki, Apollo.*

Many modern scholars define Paganism as a polytheistic tradition that seeks the divine in plurality, meaning we acknowledge the diversity in Nature and personify the working aspects of life through deities. It is here where opinions divert and polytheism becomes much more than a singularly comprehensive theology.

There are those who commit to the complexity of both the human psychology and that of the divine, and who proclaim that each god is, in fact, a living entity unto itself. This is in contrast with those who view the archetypes as gods (or vice versa)—symbols of the collective unconscious relating to aspects of our humanity. There are also those who are of both schools of thought and who see the gods as immortal energies that present themselves as eternal archetypes.

Throughout our known history, there has existed the pantheon— the full sum of a culture's deities and their myths. The word *pantheon* derives from the Greek *pan*, meaning "all," and *theoi*, meaning "gods." It is also in the ancient Greek world that we find the most well-known example of the pantheon.

Hesiod's *Theogony*, cited later in this chapter, provides us with an insight into the relationships that connect each of the Olympian gods with their kith and kin. It also provides us with a creation myth that, interestingly enough, is comparable to the big bang and the beliefs of many animistic societies. *Theogony*, Homer's many epics, and the vast library of literary references to the gods of ancient Greece are enough to form a clear and concise picture of what the Greeks considered their gods to be.

The gods to the Greeks of the ancient world were powerful, raw beings, not completely detached from the mortals who dwell on earth and not completely of them, either. The gods were like an advanced race who, like most of us, quarrel, bicker, and compete amongst themselves, but who are also heirs to an illustrious power.

The Greek gods embodied the volatile forces of human nature and the cosmos. There is Zeus, who compelled the thunder and lightning and who reigned over the earth and the heavens. There is Hera, the queen, the woman in charge. She brought down bitter vengeance against those who excited Zeus's lust. Then, of course, we have Aphrodite, who is not only love incarnate but the romance of Nature—the sweet caress of the sea and the cooing doves. Thus, it is clear that the gods were not products of an ego-inspired anthropomorphism. They were also representations of the forces of Nature—poetic, rhythmic, vibrant, and alive. The gods provided the means whereby a human could cross the abyss between the external persona and the raw, animalistic yearnings within. They literally became as the gods are—heirs to the myths and stories imprinted on a deeper psychological level.

Many people believe that the old polytheistic traditions have long been dead—but take a moment to reevaluate the world you have grown up in. The names, symbols, and myths of the gods of the ancient world still live on. The days of our week owe their names and planetary associations to the Norse and Roman pantheons. The kerykeion/caduceus (the legendary rod of Hermes/Mercury) is imprinted on the side of ambulances and is often used to denote medical organisations. But is this testament to the continued presence of the gods? Is Zeus's anger responsible for the clash of thunder during storms, or is that Thor's domain? And what of love and sexuality—is it Freya or Venus we should turn to? Are the gods merely the product of social and religious anthropomorphism? Who are the gods? These are all hard questions to answer, and I do not have the authority or the audacity to answer all of them. I can, however, make severe generalisations and hope that they will, in some way, inspire you to continue your exploration.

To delve deeper into the mysteries of polytheism, I will refer back to the young adult series Circle of Three. In book 10, *Making the Saint*, Kate, Annie, and Cooper (the three main characters) are each asked to randomly choose a slip of paper during one of their Tuesday-night Wicca classes. Each slip of paper bears the name of a particular Pagan tradition. Kate just so happens to pick Santería, an Afro-Cuban faith that focuses on the worship of the traditional gods, or *orishas*, of the West-African Yoruba tribes. Kate and her friends visit a local *botánica* (a store that specialises in Santería) and speaks with the resident *santera*, Evelyn, a priestess of Santería. Evelyn describes what the orishas truly are:

> *The orisha Chango is the god of lightning and thunder. The orisha Oshun is the goddess of rivers and of beauty. But they are more than just these things. They each represent a powerful human emotion. Chango represents the driving force within us. Oshun is the personification of the force of love.*[3]

---

3 I. Bird, *Making the Saint* (Circle of Three), 54.

This description is paramount to the reality many polytheists feel. In fact, some would go so far as to say that the gods themselves inspire these emotions within us.

Polytheism is a cultural tradition. It works within a specific framework that relates to a corresponding period of time and a particular people. That is why it is so hard to determine who and what the gods are when, in truth, they are inextricably linked to a people, a time period, and a culture. Can the Celtic Brighid be the goddess of fire when the Hawaiians have Pele? I believe so, yes. I believe that these natural forces that stem from divine principles are, in fact, sentient beings. Fire is a powerful and charismatic force that communicates with the primal subconscious and helps to release our inner desires. How could there not be a spirit that embodies and channels the energy of fire and helps us to connect with its timeless sensuality? Fire does exist; it is a material reality. It cannot be doubted or denied as a false idol when it wavers so candidly before us. Call the fire whatever you want—it won't change the fact that it is fire. And this is the core of polytheism. From here on, it is all a question of culture and of mythic extension. Brighid is not just the goddess of fire; she is also patron to bards and blacksmiths. Neither is Pele's domain restricted to the crimson flame; she is the spirit of the volcano itself.

There are many possibilities concerning the origins of the various world mythologies. Many myths, like the Tuscan tale of a sorceress who instructed the peasants in the arts of Witchcraft (recounted in Leland's *Aradia*), arouse speculation amongst historians who believe that the divine nature of such stories is actually grounded in a historical truth. This leads some to believe that the gods (or at least some of them) were humans who left a lasting impression on the cultures they encountered. Think of the so-called avatars Buddha, Krishna, Jesus, Aradia; they all share something in common. They were all historical and literary figures who are in the present-day regarded as channels of the divine and who all have adherents. So it is in this way that some myths can be explained, but what of the stories that seek to interpret a process, aspect, event, or oddity of life?

Creation myths are present in all ancient societies, and interestingly enough, many of them share explicit commonalities. The general idea is of a preceding wasteland of chaos—undifferentiated potential. Then, in a flurry of light and energy, all comes into being. It is at this point that each culture runs with the concept and introduces their own deities.

Mythology is not a science of explanation; however, it does demonstrate the whys and wherefores to people who love to listen to the poetry. It provides reasons and explanations for why things happen and gives people a sense of the passage of time, of history, and of belonging. The gods, to the old folk, represented the civilisations that revered them, and in this way, they secured an almost nationalistic identity.

One thing we must be wary of in the NeoPagan community is the willingness to subscribe to corrupted versions of mythology and history. Many Wiccan essays on the divine can by typified by something like this:

> As Wiccans, we perceive the divine as both masculine and feminine. We personify this polarity and interplay of energies as God and Goddess. The god of forests and of wild things can be found as the obscure face of Jack in the Green and the Horned Man carved into church stoneworks. He is the virile Lord of the Dance, otherwise known as Cernunnos. The Goddess of Wicca rules the waters and the cycles of earth. She is the most primal form of the divine and can be traced back to the Palaeolithic Era. Initially she had within herself both male and female and encompassed all things, but the birth of the Horned God (her active impregnator/extension of self) altered the way in which ancient societies viewed their Great Mother. She is now honoured as the life force of the crops, and she is placated in the hopes that her blessings may be upon the fields.

Whether or not this documents actual history may be disputed; however, perhaps we are simply creating mythologies that satisfy our own needs and desires.

We must never conceive ourselves to be superior to anything else in the universe. We are all of the same substance, and all of us are divine. We are expressions of the gods, and they play through the tapestries of myth we weave. Ultimately, the nature of the gods will always remain a mystery, and better so.

## Patron Deities

It is sometimes thought that the gods grant favour to particular individuals whom they see as candidates for priesthood or simply worthy followers (like poets to Brighid or thieves to Hermes).

The topic of patron deities in the Pagan community is a heated one. Many people inquire into it and are often left at a loss; others are luckier. Obviously, chances are that each of us will attract the attention of some sort of being through our magickal work and our focus on spiritual realisation. We consciously open ourselves to the realm of spirits. We mould ourselves to be conduits of raw power, and it is for that reason that Pagans today place a great emphasis on relationships with personal deities.

Several years ago, during a full moon ritual, I encountered the goddess that would soon change my life forever. While invoking the (generic) Goddess, as I had always done, I looked up to see the ethereal outline of a radiant being. Without stopping to think, I said, "Persephone…," and an entourage of conflicting emotions filled me. I was on the precipice, a place I had wandered near before, but I had always dreaded to dwell there. For several years, I had felt safe and guarded by the twin forces of God and Goddess as celebrated in Wicca, and yet I craved more. Then Persephone claimed me.

There are no specific rituals or ceremonies that you can perform to gain the favour or patronage of a specific deity. There are prayers and invocations, but they will only grant you attention, and ultimately that is it. If that deity then chooses to invest interest in you, that's great! But when it comes to the gods, it is mostly their pick and not ours.

*Polytheistic Exercise: The Rite of Aspecting*

The ritual provided below is intended as a guideline only and is open to adaptation.

Before working with a deity, research needs to be done on the nature, history, mythology, and significance of the being you wish to commune with. You will need to delve into the attributes, likes/dislikes, and myths of your chosen deity, as well as anything else that you regard as being of particular importance to your working (e.g., symbols and correspondences).

Begin by designing a temporary temple incorporating the deity's favourite things (flowers/plants, colours, foods, etc.). This temple can be an extension of your sacred space, or perhaps you might have a private space in your garden to work with. When you've found adequate space, begin to transform it into something worth the deity's attention.

You will also need to create a wearable talisman, which you will carry on your person for the period of aspecting. It can be a bracelet woven in the coloured threads that are sacred to your deity, a necklace or a ring harbouring a particularly significant symbol in relation to the god, or perhaps, if you are so inclined, a design that you can trace in henna somewhere on your body. You'll need to put a lot of thought into your talisman, and once you've come up with the perfect thing, you will then need to charge and bless it for the purpose.

Cast a circle or affirm your space as sacred in your own way, within the bounds of your newly made temple. Make clear your intent by loudly stating the purpose of your ritual. Breathe deeply, and focus your mind. Within your mind's eye, allow the image of your chosen deity to manifest. Mentally and emotionally open yourself to receiving their energy, stating clearly your wish for the deity to share your life for a period of time (be specific—e.g., for one moon cycle). Emphasise the traits you desire to take on.

In a way, you are committing yourself to a spiritual contract. To express this sense of genuine partnership, you might even want to physically create a type of contract that outlines the nature of the aspecting, the period it will be sustained for, and, of course, a short prayer or poem devoted to the deity. To seal the rite, you could burn the contract. You could also adapt the following chant and repeat it at the culmination of the rite:

*(Name of deity) O Great Divine*
*I sing and dance charged in your sign*
*Together, two have become one*
*And as I say, my will is done.*

Open the circle, and continue to wear the talisman until you feel fine without it.

## Animism:
## The Spirit Within

*Listen to the air. You can hear it, feel it, smell it, taste it.*
*Animals are part of us, part of the Great Spirit. The winged and four-legged*
*are our cousins ... There is power in the buffalo. There is power in the antelope.*
*There was great power in a wolf, even in a coyote. To us, life, all life, is sacred.*
—John Fire Lame Deer, Lakota medicine man

The Native Americans of the current day are one of the most powerful examples of ancestral traditions living on. Though each tribe is distinct, there is a universal animism that lives on in the wider community. It is in the beliefs that all of life is sacred and each being possesses a spirit that the essence of ancient animism lives on.

The word *animism* derives from the Latin word for "breath" and "soul," *anima*.[4] Animism is a spiritual understanding that centres on the nature of our being, and all things possess "being," animate or not.

According to British anthropologist Sir Edward Burnett Tylor's research, the soul stimulates our material existence and animates the very nature of our daily activity. Animism is claimed to be the oldest form of spirituality on this earth and is believed to have its origins in the early Palaeolithic Age.

---

4 A. Hefner and G. Virgilio, "Animism" (http://www.themystica.com/mystica/articles/a/animism/htm).

As each soul belongs to one singular body at a time, be it a plant, creature, or "inanimate" object (e.g., a stone), the primal tribes were also aware of the greater spirit, the originator of each soul and thus where the soul would return to after its physical body had died. Souls were also seen as being able to migrate from body to body, which indicates a belief in reincarnation. However, this early belief was not coloured by structured impositions of caste, it was simply a natural process. Therefore, a soul could inhabit any life form it chose to, in any succession it pleased. In the animistic view, all life is sacred and therefore equally important.

Tylor's theories represented the view that animism was the product of a tribal consciousness that developed from a need to differentiate between alternate states of being, e.g., from sleep to being awake. He reasoned that the early tribes learnt to explain the different states of awareness through the interaction of souls. However, Tylor came under high scrutiny from fellow British anthropologist Robert Ranulph Marett.[5] Marett reduced the apparent complexity of Tylor's arguments by suggesting that early people simply observed the commonalities between themselves and other life forms, and thus imbued varying life forms with souls.

Over time, animism evolved into the totemic and spirit cults we now find among persisting tribes in South America, Southeast Asia, Africa, and Australasia. Trees and plants were and are honoured as great spiritual beings who were always given a plea for forgiveness when felled.[6]

Animism is also highly communal, encouraging each individual to pay tribute to the great Web of Life. Animistic understanding relies on the observation and reverence of the relationships between each life form and how each of us support and enrich the continuity of the community.

In animistic cultures, there is no preconceived notion of spiritual hierarchy; there is merely life and its various expressions. In fact, humanity often finds solace and synchronicity in the appearance of

---

5 Ibid.

6 Ibid.

specific creatures and plants at times of great inner transformation. This correspondence between power spirits and a life lived in honour of the natural forces is key to animism.

Each thing in life has a particular understanding, and the desire to share this wisdom with others is universal. Often, it would be the shaman or other village priest/ess who would enter trance and return with the knowledge to help bring the rain, heal the sick, or pinpoint the whereabouts of a herd of bison. When a skilled walker between the worlds approaches the spirits in need of assistance, the spirits will respond how they wish, and not every journey to the Otherworld results in success. A rapport of trust, honour, and respect must underlie any shamanic journey.

The greatest and most profound lesson of animism is this: that each being on this earth lives in mutual equality with one another. There is no essential difference between us except those that we impose. No being is above another simply for a quality it possesses, for who is to say that having an advanced mental capacity is greater than the ability to adapt one's skin to one's surroundings? The grace and humility that it takes to admit that we as humans are no greater than the smallest ant is phenomenal! This obviously raises questions concerning vegetarianism and whether or not to walk on grass; however, if one thinks this way, they are still caught in humanity's paradigm.

Living in eternal gratitude for the air you breathe, the blood that runs through your veins, and the water that sates your thirst is animism at its simplest. Even if you don't affiliate yourself with its lore, perhaps animism has something to teach each and every one of us. It's time that life was paid attention to, for as I look around I see so many who live detached from the great force at work and who simply exist in the void beyond reality.

Animism has never been an institute for gaining any sort of divine power, though it can and will inspire you to live gracefully and gratefully on this earth. Each tree we pass, each blade of grass our feet touch, and each bird that sings deserve the same treatment we extend to our human kin. It doesn't take that much of an effort to reconsider the brutality of the actions we commit daily and to live in peace and love with all things.

*Animistic Exercise*

Resolve to live a week[7] completely aware of every being you interact with. Silently express your gratitude to the grass that you walk upon, make sure you avoid stepping on the many insects that use the footpath as a highway, pick up rubbish wherever you see it, and leave offerings of food beneath the trees that give you shade. At the end of the week, wake up at dawn; standing in a circle marked by a bowl of soil, water, a candle, and a stick of incense, recite the following:

*No longer do I take life for granted, for I see it in all things: the tow-ering glory of my brother, the eucalyptus (or oak, or whatever) ... the sweet chorus of the feathered symphony ... the mighty gale of the four winds. It is in the realm of earth, in all that surrounds me and in all that flows, that I see this life in all its brilliance. These are my fam-ily, my brothers and my sisters. These are the record keepers, the wise, the watchers of the fleeting passage of time. For now, I am a child of the human race, and I pledge that though my kind has pillaged and scarred, I reject brutality and seek to live among you, my neighbours, in peace and love. Blessed be.*

# DITHEISM:
# GOD AND GODDESS

*For two are the mystical pillars*
*That stand at the gate of the shrine*
*And two are the powers of nature*
*The forms and the forces divine.*
—Doreen Valiente, *The Witches' Creed*

Perhaps the most interesting trait of the Wiccan religion[8] is that it reveres two deities as personifications of the polarity of Nature. These two deities are known generically as God and Goddess, and while

---

7 Just to see how you go; but if you pass with flying colours, why not integrate this kind of awareness into your life for good?

8 You will notice that throughout this section, Wicca is mentioned repeatedly, and that is because it is the perfect example of a modern ditheistic faith.

they are often given particular names which resonate personally with the individual, the underlying principle remains the same. The God and Goddess (Lord and Lady) are the divine expressions of a universal energy that divides itself in order to know itself.

In order to fully comprehend the theology of ditheism, it is essential to first consider the universal Spirit. This boundless Spirit is androgynous and unites both male and female, enacting the ancient powers of desire and cosmic fecundity in a rush of passion and pleasure. The ancient Greeks personified these complementary forces as the primordial Gaia (the receptive earth) and Eros (desire), as documented in Hesiod's *Theogony*. For manifestation to occur in our universe, two opposing and yet complementary forces must contrast and create friction to produce something else entirely.

The polarity of Nature and divinity is made clear in what we observe in the world around us. In most cases, sexual reproduction requires two entities of opposite gender to come together and cause the fusion of cellular organisms (sperm and egg) to stimulate the creation of new life. No-thing comes from no-where.

Wiccans embrace this law of polarity in their conception of deity and thus the God and the Goddess. They are not dependent on one another in any political or social way; they are independently vital, and yet without the other, creation becomes regressive. For that reason, creation is not largely discussed in Wiccan circles; rather, it is mutual co-creation that is focused on.

There has been a tendency among Wiccan and Pagan groups today to place a greater emphasis on the Goddess in an attempt to bring back the balance and to reassert feminine power. I, for one, do not believe that tipping the scales in favour of either power will result in universal concord. The assertion of balance between the sexes needs to be prominent to ensure the Pagan traditions do not fall to the same tyrannies that run rampant within monotheism.

Historically, ditheism was present in several ancient societies in which polytheism was the basic principle. In the past, ditheism was not purely the reverence of a god and a goddess exclusively, it was the reverence of two related deities (generally male and female) within an already established pantheon (Gaia and Ouranos, Isis and Osiris, Inanna and Dumuzi), and in many cases, this ditheism was reinforced through the forming of cults honouring the partnered gods.[9] For instance, we need only look to the Tantric traditions of India and it is clear that in the midst of an extensive pantheon, there is a polarity of male and female within the infinity of being.

In Shivaic Tantrism, there is Shakti and Shiva. Their symbols are the yoni and the lingam, and their divine powers of co-creation are honoured in many villages, often at the site of a stone phallus embedded in a feminine pedestal shaped to resemble the vulva.[10] Interestingly, in this particular Tantric tradition, the Shakti (the feminine power) is often central—"[She] embodies the power; the male, the capacity for wonder."[11] This description is remarkably similar to the Wiccan conception of their God and Goddess.

The Wiccan Wheel of the Year is represented by the Goddess; she is the very nature of its transitions and changes. She is the wheel itself, and as it turns, she reflects the underlying spiritual and physical changes that occur during its journey. At Samhain she is the death Crone, and she rests, as does the harsh winter landscape. At Yule she is the Star Woman and gives birth to the Sun Child, as he himself is a star, and we honour the Sun's rebirth. At Imbolc she is the Maiden, and the signs of winter's passing can be seen; and on it goes with every sabbat. The Goddess represents the eternal power, the cosmic force of unity. This is the Shakti of Shivaic Tantrism, the essential power and the embodiment of the feminine.

The Horned God is the active, impregnating principle that accompanies the turning of the wheel and animates its life force. The God

---

9 Though there were many cults that revered two deities of the same sex (e.g., the Eleusinian Mysteries of Persephone and Demeter), they are not included here because ditheism is generally seen to be two deities of "opposite sex" that express an interplay of energy and embody the polarity of nature. The cult of mother/Demeter and daughter/Persephone falls into what are known as Mystery Traditions.

10 D. Odier, *Tantric Quest: An Encounter with Absolute Love*, 24.

11 Ibid., 21.

of Wicca is the creative force integrating the seasonal patterns into his very being as he commits himself to the cycles of life, death, and rebirth. He is the living sacrifice, wild and unruly. He is the willing student, the complementary figure who impregnates the Goddess with his very soul and lust for life and ensures the continuation of a universal love. Shiva—who shares many, if not all, of the Horned God's qualities—is the destroyer of illusion and the erect phallus that signifies the blossoming of consciousness and the penetration of the universe.[12]

The Shakti and Shiva (the Goddess and the God) are equal. They are indistinguishable from each other when our ego-driven comprehensions fade and we recognise the love that pervades their partnership. In full consciousness they are one—the force of the Spirit resonates between them. Once again, the female and male are simply useful expressions for different sides of the mystery. It is this reality that is beyond our mundane understanding. During times of spiritual ecstasy and celebration, however, we become aware.

Historically, it is interesting to note that the Megalithic people of ancient Avebury may have been "selective"[13] ditheists. Terence Meaden discusses the possibility of Tara as the generic earth goddess of the Megalithic Britons in her article "Elements of Pagan Belief in the Megalithic Age." She argues that the archaeological evidence contained in the stone circles of Avebury indicates an ancient belief in the divine powers of polarity. She also argues that the deities who embodied this energy were acknowledged by several cultures. The deities are commonly known as Tara (earth goddess) and Taran (sky god), and etymological parallels existed throughout Europe and the Near East, including pre-Vedic India. In fact, the similarities are immediately convincing: Tara (Indo-European generic earth goddess; Tibetan; pre-Vedic Indian)— Tari (Dravidian), Turan (Etruscan), Terah (Hebrew), and Terra Mater (Roman). These similarities exist also for her male counterpart Taran

---

12 Ibid., 63.

13 "Selective" meaning they probably revered several other gods; "ditheistic" in that the two deities are emphasised.

(Welsh): Taru (Hattic), Tarai (Andaman), Thor (Scandinavian), Thunaer (Anglo-Saxon), Torann (Irish), and Thur (Phoenician).[14]

The archetypal earth/sky dynamic fosters a natural observation—that Nature is a reflection of the microcosm (and vice versa). The calculated positioning of the standing stones at Avebury is testimony to this. It is not only the direction the light falls at sunrise that empowers the stone circle, but also the hills that emphasis the divine union of earth and sky.

In Celtic Britain, hills were of special importance, as they signified the physical location where the receptive powers of earth combined with the magnificence of the heavens. This was made apparent during storms as the low clouds would pass over the summit, which seemed like a divine conference to the Celts.

Western civilisation is popularly believed to have sprung from the Greek and Roman empires. While these cultures were polytheistic, it is interesting to note that at the head of their pantheons sit Hera/Juno and Zeus/Jupiter—the classical depiction of husband and wife. Hera is the jealous wife who broods over her husband's affairs and always seeks justice. Zeus is the all-loving father who gathers his children in his arms and dotes upon them, while at the same time committing many sexual indiscretions. However, Hesiod hints to an older ditheism in Greek theology that is not unlike the Wiccan version of the birth of the universe. It goes something like this:

> In the beginning, in the Time before Time, there was nothing, a void.
> It was chaos. From this chaos was born Gaia and Eros. In her primal
> state, Gaia received the flow of energy conducted by Eros, and Life was
> birthed. For it was the expression of their magnetic love, the connection
> of a sacred polarity. Gaia and Eros flowed in eternity, and from their
> breath all things come into being, and in the end of time it is to them
> that all things shall return.

---

14 T. Meaden, "Elements of Pagan Belief in the Megalithic Age: Was Tara the Earth Goddess at Avebury?"

Gaia and Eros are alike to Shakti and Shiva, who are in turn alike to the Goddess and God.[15] What is most striking about Hesiod's description of creation is the fact that Eros seems to be disregarded for a time and the focus is on Gaia, and another partnership occurs. The earth/sky resonance appears once more as Gaia gives birth to Ouranos (the sky) as a protective and complementary covering. From their union comes the race of the Titans (the raw forces of Nature), the Olympian gods (by Kronos and Rhea), and eventually humanity.

As the two powers that fashion life (love and light/form and force), there is a clear line where God and Goddess meet, and it is this line, like the horizon where sky meets earth, which defines both. Without the differentiation, there is once again chaos ("undifferentiated potential"), and all reverts; the flow of force from one vessel to the next loses its rhythm and direction. If there was no earth, where would sky stop? How could sky even be called sky, for without the earth in contrast, there can be no sky. The God defines the Goddess, and she the God. She keeps the wheel turning, and he dances the way.

While the facts may be dismissed as spiritually irrelevant, the key point to be aware of is that ditheism is not a modern fancy based on the notion of man and wife. It is the raw and empowering survival of an ancient observation.

Pagan ditheists are not always Wiccan. It is essential when regarding ditheism to look past male and female and to meditate on the spirit. Perhaps ditheism is simply another product of the ego-conscious human mind?

Somehow there is truth at the heart of it all. At the heart of human experience, there lies a truth so subtle that it is only within the moment that we become aware. This truth is a simple one. What it is, I cannot

---

15 I have come to believe that when the Gardnerian covens spoke of their "God and Goddess," they were not referring to generic masculine/feminine forces but to specific deities that shared a dynamic relationship and whose names were oath-bound and therefore could not be revealed to the public. In saying this, there are many shamanic cults that have been unearthed in recent times by historians that share links with Witch and Pagan traditions, and often these cults revere two deities—one male, one female. For more information on the shamanic undertone of Witchcraft, I recommend Kenneth Johnson's *Witchcraft and the Shamanic Journey* (Llewellyn, 1999).

say; I simply *know*, for I have felt it often, and I believe, with the power of my faith and of my mind, that it is the spirit, and that the spirit and I are one.

### Reflections on Monism

*Love is the fifth Element, it is our spirit, the force*
*that brings the other four Elements to each other.*
*For ultimately neither God nor Goddess is Creator.*
*Instead, it is their union that is the Creator, and that union is love.*
—A. J. Drew, *Wicca for Couples: Making Magick Together*

Recently, the term *monism* has been used fairly often. It must be made clear that monism is something very different from monotheism.

At the heart of monism lies the doctrine of unity: all things are one. Monism does not preach gender superiority and is of no particular moral persuasion. There is no difference between what is present and here and what lies beyond and perhaps in another dimension.

Many Wiccans tend to regard all deities as faces of the universal Spirit. This belief system is poetically graceful, in the sense that it is not culturally exclusive whilst also causing friction between hard and soft polytheists.

Behind God and Goddess there is the primal catalyst, the underlying presence that infuses the core of all things. Wicca can be seen to be a monist tradition, though its expressive qualities are ditheistic. In fact, one of Wicca's most prominent authors, A. J. Drew, wrote in his book *Wicca for Couples* (New Page Books, 2002): *"To further our relationship with the Creator, it is neither on the Lord or the Lady that we should focus. Instead, it is on their interactions with each other."*

Scientific research at the quantum level has revealed that our physical existence is nothing more than a subatomic façade. Our material personas do have purpose; however, there is a unity that exists beyond this. For those who dare to defy both conventional science and orthodox religion, this "thing" is often regarded as God—not the God of the Bible, the Koran, or the Torah, but the God that is reality, that *is*. God is one, and as Gerald L. Schroeder so eloquently put it in his book *The Hidden Face of God*, "don't think that this is the kind of *one* after which might come the quantities two, three, and four. Nothing as superficial as a number is being revealed in these statements. Rather, the infinite metaphysical as perceived by the physical is an all-encompassing, universal unity."[16]

### Ditheistic Exercise

Many ditheists often become entrenched in a typified view of female and male. The Goddess is confined to fertility and abundance, and the God is merely a romantic accessory. These things do resonate on an archetypal level; however, there is much more to the masculine and the feminine mysteries, and their sacred union, than agriculture would have us believe.

At your sacred space, ground and centre. Meditate on the balance, polarity, and union of the God and Goddess. Focus on each respectively, and allow yourself to be moved by the traditional symbols associated with them. Now move past this and consider modern examples of male and female. Think of your parents or your grandparents, and focus on the connection between them. Now move past the physical genders and delve further into the masculine and feminine. Focus your energies on two men in love, then two women, and know that there is no end to Love. Open your mind to the infinite, and let images come and go. Feel the energy intensify and rise up above you. When the cone reaches its peak, mentally throw your consciousness outward and behold the All. Suddenly God and Goddess, and their undying love, is everywhere. Flow with the power, and reside completely in the present. If you like, you may chant/sing the following:

> *God and Goddess*
> *Within and without*
> *Male and female*
> *Around and about*
> *Ecstasy, union*
> *Undying love*
> *Lord and Lady*

---

16 Gerald L. Schroeder, *The Hidden Face of God: Science Reveals the Ultimate Truth*, 13.

*Below as above*
*Mother Earth, Father Sky*
*Womb unto phallus*
*Weaving the tapestry*
*The sword and the chalice*
*Two halves and a whole*
*To live and to die*
*With Magick abounding*
*Hail most high!*

Reflect on the exercise, recording your insights in your journal. Leave the God and Goddess an offering in thanks.

## THE ARCHETYPE: A UNIVERSAL MODEL

*What is stirred in us is that faraway background,*
*those immemorial patterns of the human mind,*
*which we have not acquired but have inherited from the dim ages of the past.*
—Carl G. Jung, "The Structure of the Psyche"

The unconscious plays an integral part in our daily lives. It is the underlying motivator that inspires us. Culture is the byproduct of humanity's spiritual exploration; it develops highly symbolic attitudes towards life.

Since as far back as we can know, humanity has perceived the divine. No matter what locale or language, the tribes of earth responded in a similar fashion to the mysteries of life. The primal image of a swollen-breasted, voluptuous woman (e.g., the Venus of Willendorf, 22000 BCE) is believed to personify the very essence of the great goddess cultures of Europe. Many of the unearthed artifacts share distinct commonalities, e.g., the curvaceous representation of the feminine. This is simply one of the many ancient archetypes that unites the great tribe of humanity.

Carl Gustav Jung (1875–1961), the late Swiss psychologist, is probably the most influential figure regarding the archetype. He is responsible for the theorising of concepts such as the collective unconscious, individuation, the psyche, and the archetype. His theories propounded the idea that each of us inherits the primal archetypes and symbols of the human experience by virtue of the collective unconscious.

Jung concluded, after identifying successive commonalities in dreams, myths, and "primitive" beliefs, that recurring images and motifs were far too ubiquitous to ignore. Carol Pearson, in her *Hero Within*, analyses six heroic archetypes that can be applied to the individual's life. Pearson argues that the archetypes are reservoirs of eternal truth and are never "beyond our reach."

In his research concerning dream analysis, Jung discovered that we are each composed of an individual consciousness that mirrors the collective unconscious. The dominant archetypes are conveyed through our dreams in the form of relevant symbols and themes. Carl Jung focussed on what he called "direct association" when working with a patient. Jung was adamant that the greater symbols in dreams equated with the archetypes.

Each of us demonstrates certain traits that relate to universal archetypes. It is here that we come to the theology of the archetype: the innate link that unites us with the collective unconscious. In the preface of *The Hero Within*, Pearson introduces the reader to a working theology in and of itself: "Writing this book, was, in part, an homage to the archetypes that have helped me grow as a person and a scholar."

Pearson, through her work with archetypes, has achieved a highly personal relationship with her inner aspects, the archetypes. Archetypes become deified in the sense that they are deeply celebrated aspects of our humanity. It is from these spiritual encounters that we are empowered through relative symbolism to resurrect the Old Ones from the centre of our being.

Jung's psychotherapy aimed at the "psychic wholeness" of the patient. This was achieved through an intimate understanding of the symbols that appear within the patient's dreams. Jung described nine dominant archetypes that appear again and again. These are termed the *dominants*, infused with *mana* (inspiration for personal growth), and are as follows:[17]

**The Wise Old Man:** A figure of foundation, represented as an influential masculine figure, often relating directly to the world of conscious activity (business, organised religion, and learning). The Wise Old Man is often the imparter of knowledge and an advisor. Popular figures include Merlin (King Arthur and Celtic mythology), Dumbledore (Harry Potter), and Gandalf (*Lord of the Rings*).

**The Trickster:** The classical symbol of anarchy, mockery, and paradoxical truth, the Trickster works to diminish the pretensions of the ego. The appearance of creatures such as foxes and hares in myths is believed to embody the principle of the Trickster. Popular figures include Timon and Pumbaa (*The Lion King*), the White Rabbit (*Alice in Wonderland*), and Dobby (Harry Potter).

**The Hero:** While the Hero is essentially a personification of strength, the appearance of such figures within a dream is suggestive of the individual's familiarity with the character in a more worldly sense. This can often lead to self-deception and a desperate desire to perpetuate the Hero within the self. Popular figures include Aragorn (*Lord of the Rings*), Harry Potter, and Herakles (Greek mythology).

**The Persona:** This is a deeply entrenched trait of humanity: escape from society's scrutiny under a mask. This has become a greater problem in our current society, as we are constantly influenced by propaganda. We also suffer from the construction of perfection in today's media. Many of us feel the need to conform to such standards, which leads to compromising the Self. While the Persona is not always such a problem, it has the potential to develop into much more than a label or mask. It is essential that we retain the connection with our true Self. See chapter 4's section "Out and About: The Downtown Pagan."

---

17 J. Altman, *1001 Dreams: An Illustrated Guide to Dreams and Their Meanings*, 15–17. **Author's Note:** The definitions given here of each "dominant" are my own; the concept of the nine dominants comes from Altman.

**The Shadow:** At the mere mention of the word *shadow*, we immediately think of the darker part of our being. In our world, a shadow is simply the reflection of a physical body blocking the path of light. Metaphorically speaking, this evokes the dual nature of the Self (as society has so generally divided us).

The Shadow generally manifests as one of the same sex as the dreamer and provokes aspects we may see as brutal and uncivilised. The Shadow encourages us to reevaluate and confront the negative traits we repress and to ultimately come to terms with their implications, whilst also appreciating the delicate balance that completes us as human beings. Popular figures include Severus Snape (Harry Potter), Judas (The New Testament), and the ugly stepsisters (*Cinderella*).

**The Divine Child:** This ancient embodiment of purity and innocence forms the basis for many world religions.

The Divine Child is an archetype that precedes transformative journeys and hearkens to the regenerative processes of Nature. Such encounters result in a heightened sense of humility and a greater understanding of the transcendent mode of thought in comparison to the egocentric attitudes of today. Popular figures include Jesus Christ (The New Testament), the Sun Child (Wiccan/Pagan mythos), and Krishna (*Bhagavad-gita*).

**The Anima:** The feminine principle of our unconscious self. She encourages us to look deeper into a situation and to do so with integrity and intuition. The Anima expresses the qualities within us that are mythologically and psychologically preconceived as feminine attributes.

Jungian thought prescribes the Anima to males who are yearning for spiritual fulfilment.

**The Animus:** As above with masculine expressions in place.

**The Great Mother:** Perhaps the most persistent divine expression is that of the Great Mother. Primal, sensual, and cyclic, she is the embodiment of our archaic unconscious, and as indicated by the abundance of goddess figures unearthed in Europe and the Middle East, there is a definite energy that is associated with her symbolism—the rotund and voluptuous torso and legs, the highly defined yoni, and the accentuated breasts.

All cultures know her. She is in the veiled form of the Virgin Mary and in the wild rites of Paganism. She is terrible and all-loving, and she is the circle of life that we walk. Popular figures include the Venus of Willendorf (Palaeolithic limestone sculpture), the Virgin Mary (The New Testament), and Isis (ancient Egyptian mythology).

We are the heirs of a long and elaborate psychic development, and each of us draws from this universal sea of archetypes and symbols. The way in which the archetypes manifest tends to be highly personalised and filtered through history and personality.

Jungian thought relates archetypes to mythology. Each figure in myth personifies a particular aspect of humanity. For example, Venus, Aphrodite, Inanna, and Freya are all goddesses of sensuality and sexual desire. The cultures that honoured these deities also honoured the aspects of life they embodied.

According to some Pagan philosophies, the gods are merely expressions of archetypes. Pagans who subscribe to this ideology have no problem with invoking several deities into a ritual space without thinking how they may react with each other. This is contrary to what the polytheists of our community practice, and there is a certain degree of friction between the two. However, simply because someone sympathises with the Jungian concept of archetypes does not necessarily mean they are disrespectful to the divine. In fact, the great percentage of people who subscribe to this spiritual notion are honest, ingenious people. Perhaps instead of seeing the gods as deriving from archetypes, they see the archetypes as being inspired by the gods.

The archetype is that essential embodiment of human experience that allows us to appreciate our own being in a spiritual manner. Pagans who relate to the divine through psychology are those who either support the hypothesis that the gods are beings who reside solely within the mind and represent reservoirs of power or embrace the Great Spirit as the collective unconscious and understand that it has manifested and expressed itself in many forms. It is good to understand the Self through one's innate patterns and how they relate to that world soul. The mana (Magick) that infuses the archetypes is what heightens our own self-awareness. This swift expansion of consciousness can lead to gnosis. For those of the Archetype, there is one guiding principle: the divine and the Self are one within ultimate consciousness.

*Archetype Exercise*

Choose a grouping of deities to work with for this exercise (the Wiccan threefold Goddess—Maiden, Mother, and Crone—is a perfect example). Now, on a piece of paper, write down each aspect of the triformis group, leaving ample space between each. Think of every deity you have ever heard of, and try to equate them with one of the aspects of your grouping. For example, you may think of Persephone as Maiden, Demeter as Mother, and Hecate as Crone. Remember to explore all pantheons!

As you continue, you may begin to feel a little disrespectful cramming all these ancient deities into neat categories that may not even apply. Reflect on how the exercise made you feel. Read and analyse the myths of each deity you have on your list and decide whether or not they do fit the archetype you have assigned. If you decide that they do not, attempt to see beyond the archetype. For instance, Athena is noble and articulate. Her practical nature affirms her as a warrior, and she is seen as a careful tactician, a wise goddess. Therefore, Athena's archetype seems to be the wise woman. Using this as an example, focus on each deity on your list individually, and discern what archetype connects them with the universal unconscious. Make sure you heed your intuition at all times.

## ULTIMATE CONSCIOUSNESS: GOD AND THE SELF

*In all persons, all creatures, the Self is the innermost essence.*
*And it is identical with Brahman: our real Self is not different*
*from the ultimate Reality called God.*
*—The Upanishads,* as translated by Eknath Easwaran

Consciousness, reality, and the divine form an interesting and philo-sophically explosive combination. Their unifier is the Self.

Hindu philosophy, and more specifically Brahmanism, is the basis for much of what the Eastern traditions have to say concerning an individual's relationship with the divine. In 600 BCE, during the post-Vedic period in India, there was a move to unify the Hindu pantheon and uphold a supreme deity whose infinity would subsume all dei-ties. Unlike the religious traditions of the Middle East, this evolution in theology did not result in a strict monotheism but in a multifaceted being who was neither he nor she and encompassed all. This supreme deity is known as Brahman, or Atman, which can be translated to mean "Universal Spirit."

The tradition espousing the concept of Brahman is commonly known as Brahmanism. The Brahman philosophy emphasises the doctrines of karma and samsara (reincarnation). This has influenced the modern Hindu religion, which is now considered to be a world-rejecting[18] tradition. Essen-tially, Brahmanism is a monistic worldview teaching that self-realisation of one's own atman (soul) brings complete unity with Brahman, who perme-ates all things. This transition in theology occurred during the Upanishadic period, which began in approximately 600 BCE.

According to Brahman thought, the atman (soul) is reflective of the Atman (Universal Spirit); as above, so below. The Atman and Brah-man are synonymous, so this of course makes the Atman identical with

---

18 Anthropology defines the world's religions in terms of world-rejecting and world-embracing. The majority of the Eastern religions' traditions are world-rejecting, as they focus on escaping from the cycle of birth, death, and rebirth, and they identify this world with illusion. The goal is to transcend.

Brahman, "the ultimate Reality called God." Here is a revelatory con-cept that has its parallels in Pagan philosophies.

The Self, beyond human egocentricities, is infused with the unwav-ering presence of the divine and is but an incarnation of a working cre-ator—a continuity. However, this creator is not the cold and detached deity of the Abrahamic (Judeo-Christian) faiths; neither is Brahman male or female, but both and neither. Brahman is truth in every sense. Much like the Islamic God, Brahman has no beginning and no end, and is the natural definition of life.

Pagans regard a belief in the divine as a spiritually empowering and enriching practice. The relationship between the individual and the divine is highly personalised, as it should be. There are those who sub-scribe to polytheism and uphold the individuality of each deity, while others are comfortable seeing the gods as archetypal potencies of the hidden unconscious. Behind this multiplicity of theology, it can be argued that there persists a notion of expressive reality—an awareness of the infinite. The Hindus call this Brahman; the Muslims Allah; the Native Americans Great Spirit; and as Pagans, we have many names for this—the Spirit, the All, the Great Mystery.

The Great Mystery transcends and infuses this world. Spirit is imma-nent and self-aware. Spirit is conscious and unconscious, neutral, bal-ance and power. Spirit is the nature of movement, the quality of life, and the rhythm of one's unfurling growth. Spirit simply is.

Western society has long denied the fulfilment of the self in favour of a homogenous community that inherently disregards the health of the individual. Humanity suffers from a deeply entrenched attitude that imposes limitations on us. Both Freud and Jung discovered that much of the symbolism inherent in our dreams surfaces from the tension we feel by repressing sexual desires. Dreams are our release and help us to work through the issues that plague the periphery of the conscious mind. As part of our crusade against the Self, we have learnt to stifle those things that we know will satisfy our desires. I am speaking of sexuality as sacred, of the ecstasy of joining with another in love. It is a part of the Self that is by no means morally corrupt, but it has been made to appear so because of society's attempt at maligning the senses.

The Self is whole within itself. If fragmented, it becomes disempowered and lost. Spirit is not emotionless or impersonal; Spirit is active and continuous, eternally shifting and transforming—becoming, never ceasing, only becoming.

We often forget our connection with Spirit in this hectic world. We must not allow ourselves to degrade the Self through petty materialism or the vindictiveness of the ego. We should live life through experiencing it—by taking risks and not letting fear overwhelm us. It is okay to fall to materialistic desires occasionally; it is completely natural to indulge. It's not about pleading for forgiveness or absolution. Learning from one's mistakes leads one along the path of knowledge; this generally leads to power and wisdom.

Paganism is not a world-rejecting spirituality, and technological advancement, desire, and pleasure are not immediately cast out as spiritually detrimental. In essence, unity with Spirit is not a matter of transcending the material world; it is celebrating the divine ecstasy of connection that is innate within us all. We are one with Spirit because we *are* Spirit.

The Upanishads speak of the Self as being the innermost essence and identical with Brahman, which is the ultimate reality. I speak of a philosophy that distils the moment into a simple observation—all things living are linked through the breath of Being, who is within my digits as I type these words and who is within your eyes as you read them.

## DEITY AND YOUTH

*Carpe diem ("seize the day").*
—Horace, ancient Roman poet

Youth is a passage of growing awareness and finding oneself. Deity, the spirit of expansive being, underlies this transitional period. Deity draws attention to our own divinity and urges us to nurture it.

As Pagans, we are taught to respect and revere the forces of Nature. We begin to identify the microcosmic patterns of Nature within our own lives. Pagans understand that deity, the infinite and unknown, has nothing to do with recorded word or institutionalised law but resides within the harmonising equilibrium of the self. It is not the harsh judge of our moral integrity or the tyrant who oppresses; it simply is and flows. Deity is a force, like Magick; they are intertwined and forever aware of each other. Deity is the presence, and Magick the force. Deity resides within the awe-inspiring magnificence of what appears incarnate as Nature.

Dancing with deity is not about perfection, it is about accepting oneself as perfect. The Pagan concept of perfection has nothing to do with the standardised delusions of the superficial world. Be yourself and you will go far.

The youth of today are a remarkably independent and vibrant species of individual. For those who hear the whispers of deity, courage, vigour, determination, and intent all become intense and intimate pathways. They aid in claiming one's potential as endless possibility.

We all possess free will, and it is part of the journey to learn to exercise it. Experiment and revel in the beauty of the power that we each have within us. Call upon deity as the All and as a source of personal inspiration, and celebrate the momentum. Draw strength from deity in fortitude and embrace the potency of its universal workings (as above, so below). Know that enthusiasm and the determination to achieve will greatly affect your future and your being.

A Pagan youth dwells in a world that does not represent a physical continuum or an astral resonance. We walk the delicate path in between and are subject to the fluxes of energy that are concealed from the majority. For that reason, we each need to celebrate the life we have been born to. Seize the day, for it is within the seed of action that a spirit of intense curiosity dwells.

## What I Believe

As a Pagan, I speak for myself and must make it clear that this chapter has been a reflective contemplation on the divine. It is based on my experiences and may be utterly meaningless to you. My journey so far has been one of change, transformation, and contrast. Interestingly, every piece of the puzzle along the way fits in beautifully with those already placed. At other times, my worldviews have been turned upside down. It is all sacred.

This chapter has demonstrated that within a single community reside countless views and ways of understanding. Are you a ditheist? A pantheist? An animist? Or perhaps even a monist with an archetypal attitude bordering on moderate polytheism? These are all labels, descriptive terms that are used to define perceptions. They address something that is wholly personal for the individual, intimacies that vibrate within the mind and that spawn divine marvels within the heart and the soul. Personally I can attest to belonging to almost every theology mentioned above. For instance, I am a hard polytheist by nature and experience, but I am also a poetic ditheist and monist. I am also an animist and pantheist in that I experience the divine in Nature and treat all things with reverence.

Service to the divine is very important to me, considering I devote all that I am to my gods. As a polytheist, I see my gods as individuals, each with their own personal forms, symbols, myths, etc. They come to me with hints and whispers, provoking me to look more deeply.

Half of the fun of being Pagan is the seeking that comes hand in hand with restoring the ancient wisdom. I sincerely believe that, as a movement, we are resurrecting a new and vibrant feeling of the cosmos, one in which every single thing is an expression of the numinous that has wisdom to impart. We are re-enchanting the world and invoking the Greening, and the Great Mystery is shaking in its boots, for we are connecting and thriving on that connection.

As a spiritual being, I acknowledge the importance of all levels of awareness, and I strive toward a wholeness that will enhance my own will and the truth that is at the heart of the "I" in me. I know that my destiny is unravelling with each step I take and that my gods watch me as I wander, weaving together the sacred threads of the weaver's loom. I reveal and relate to the sacred in everything I encounter.

We are each born into a world of great uncertainty. Nothing is set in stone; everything is in motion and unsettled. All that we have are the stars above us and the beautiful earth that holds our feet, and now even she is in peril. Destiny is simply a word used to help guide the lost soul—to provide meaning to an unfounded circumstance. We each have our own reasons for being, and we each walk paths of our own making, though it can be seen in a shining star's course that much comes to pass by the hands of the gods.

I have my heartland and the warmth that floods through my spirit; this is the power that is both ancient and new, continuing always. I do not need science to prove what I already know to be true, nor do I fear those whose understanding is limited by ignorance. I dance with the gods, and I serve them in all that I do. This book is a testimony to my love for them. May it make them smile, and may they toast to us all, as we do to them.

# 10: COVENCRAFT

Covens are a topic of heated discussion in our community. It seems that everywhere you go, someone is delving into the social and esoteric differences between solitaries and coven initiates. Is being initiated into a coven the ultimate goal for all Witches? I would suggest that it is different for everyone.

Covencraft is a serious venture. It is not to be taken lightly and must be approached with a balanced perspective. You are solely responsible for what you get yourself into and what oaths you make or break. It can pay to be wary when seeking out covens to join; however, the great percentage of working covens today are groups rich in spirit, Magick, and kinship.

For a greater insight into the ornaments and intricacies of covencraft, refer to Amber K's classic *Covencraft: Witchcraft for Three or More.* Also, I find any of the older texts dealing with British Traditional Wicca both helpful and insightful, as they form clear examples of groups founded on initiatory-mystery principles. This is not to say that deviation from the traditional three degrees or coven hierarchy negates the Witch's spiritual experience; an intuitively crafted system can be just as enriching.

Before you dive in, I will add that I am a co-founding member and initiated priest of the Coven of the WildWood, a dynamic and spirited group of Witches that works with the primal forces of this world to inspire change, beauty, wisdom, and peace. We are allied with the Wild-Wood itself, and it is our place of passion—our heartland as Witches.

## You and a Coven

Being part of a coven is a serious undertaking. A coven is a working group of people who, in harmony with their own intuitions, seek to uphold the familial values of honour, trust, and loyalty so as to intensify the Magick. Working with Magick in a group is an ultimate exercise in determination, courage, and character development. It opens us up to both the dark and the light, and purposely introduces us to a sequence of challenges that test the depth and sincerity of our own spirituality. There's no use in sitting back and idly accepting the tyranny and injustice that can sometimes occur in a group. A healthy coven requires individuals who can rely on a reservoir of personal strength.

Degrees and hierarchy may be irrelevant to many young Witches. While the attainment of a formal degree may provide nominal status, there is nothing more frustrating than someone who has the audacity and ignorance to loudly proclaim their rank. Of course, the degree system can be successfully integrated into a democratic or collaborative coven. However, there needs to be an understanding of why in place before a group adopts a particular system.

In my coven, we have an aspirant, dedicant, and initiate structure, and each merely marks the stages of deepening that the Witch must pass through until they become consecrated as priest/ess before the gods of our coven. The Coven of the WildWood is also organised in an inner and outer court fashion. The inner court symbolises the greater mysteries and is comprised of both dedicants and initiates. The outer court represents the lesser mysteries and is comprised of informal participants and those who are aspirants to our coven. My coven also has guidelines that stipulate when an aspirant can be dedicated. Generally, there is a period of several months that ensues after aspiration, in which the inner court carefully studies the extent of participation and depth of sincerity of the aspirant (absences must have reasonable and valid explanations). After this time, the inner court convenes and discusses their opinion on the aspirant. Divination takes place, and the gods and guardians of our sacred realm are invoked for counsel. Only after all of this can an aspirant become a dedicant. After six months of dedication, the dedicant is then offered priest/ess training (if it is felt that the dedicant is ready); if they accept, the training begins and possible initiation occurs six months later.

Developing the foundations of a coven lies upon those who are natural leaders. I have never once considered myself a leader; however, at many Pagan gatherings, that label has been used to define me. One flashback into my childhood and you would find me alone, sitting in the shade of a tree, pondering the mysteries of Life. I do acknowledge the fact that being involved in Paganism has thrust me into situations in which it was impossible to deny the role of leader, and thus I have often retained that role in the community while steering clear of the associated arrogance. It is essential for anyone considering forming a coven to assess whether they feel prepared to take on the extra workload.

Below, I have answered the most frequently asked questions concerning forming covens, and I have provided a list of things to do if the opportunity to join a coven comes your way.

## FORMING A COVEN

If you are thinking about forming a coven and believe that you are capable of initiating a group while remaining true to your Craft, then this section should help you. The following questions are the ones most likely to be nagging at your mind.

## 1. Why do I feel the need to work in a group?

As Pagans, we belong to a decentralised community. However, because of this, many Pagans often feel alienated and vulnerable as a minority group within a predominantly monotheistic society.

Pagan youth who desire to form a coven usually do so because they yearn for the support of other Pagans. This yearning derives from one of the most common human impulses: the need to be around others of like mind in order to develop close-knit communities.

Primarily, a coven is an expression of this spiritual state of being. Being part of a working group allows the individual to commit to something worthwhile while simultaneously lending their energies to a unity (family) that offers a sense of familiarity, security, and support.

## 2. How would a coven benefit the Pagan youth around me?

Pagan youth are a definitive subculture within an already established spiritual minority; therefore, the need to belong and to relate to others of similar experience is heightened. Belonging to a coven can help the individual develop problem-solving skills while building character and potential in a positive environment.

Belonging to a coven also gives young people a chance to sort through their problems and ask for advice without fearing retribution or critical dismemberment. A coven is more than a group of Pagans working together in their love for the gods; it is also an autonomous and constructive counselling unit, which allows us to dispense of our issues and to work towards healing them. This is the Magick of support and connection.

## 3. How will my parents react to the idea of a coven?

Sadly, this has to be taken into account. The law allows parents to intervene on behalf of their children concerning our involvement in extracurricular groups and activities. While it seems trivial and restrictive, we as mature individuals need to acknowledge their right to actively claim their legal position on what we do with our lives. Simultaneously, however, we should be allowed to make our own choices based on well-informed attitudes and decide for ourselves what we believe to be ulti-mately beneficial for us. A lot of the time, parents are wary of strangers mixing with their children. When you present your idea to your par-ents, make sure you are specific with the details and outline that you will most likely be working exclusively with other young people, and that if there is any possibility of "older" involvement, it will come from respected members of the Pagan community only. If your parents are still reluctant, arrange a meeting between your parents and the adults involved with your coven so that a level of trust can be reached.

If you are still in the broom closet and know that your parents will react negatively to any instance of "abnormal behaviour," then you will either need to dispense of your plans or carry on discreetly. If this inter-feres with your ethics, then you will need to either come clean or main-tain the coven's secrecy.

The fear of covens comes from the popular misconceptions that hold Witchcraft to be a cultlike activity that inducts members through brainwashing and other methods of ill repute. This is a chance to cor-rect their misconceptions.

### 4. How will I deal with coven hierarchies, and what position could/ should I fulfil in the case of a traditionally structured group?

First of all, if you are the brains of the operation for the forming of a potential group, then you should have some say on how it is run and who the leading facilitators will be. The role of high priest/ess is one of guidance and support and passing on information and wisdom. A high priest/ess is generally a well-accomplished individual. You might also wish to run your group democratically and rotate the leadership in both the practical and spiritual arenas.

Within a teen coven, it needs to be reinforced that titles are often conveniences that allow for structure when needed. There are groups who are purely collaborative in that their rituals involve everybody and not just those of sufficient rank. Participation is equal, and all commit themselves to the purpose collectively.

Generally, young Pagans should steer well away from hierarchies in groups, as it heightens the chance of dispute over roles. There should be a sense of organisation, but it does not necessarily have to be institutionalised. In saying this, my own coven does not even have a high priest/ess; we have a priesthood, which anyone can aspire towards as long as they are dedicated Witches, competent within the Craft, and have a genuine desire to serve the Old Ones and the community at large.

### 5. Should I be wary of Pagans who like to stir trouble and who I do not like personally?

Yes! Anyone who intends to slander someone, compromise others, or who simply thrives off heated conflict is a candidate for exclusion. Deception, arrogance, and egotism are not beneficial to a coven that is founded on perfect love and perfect trust.

Generally, anyone who denies the rights of another is someone who is most probably suffering from a power trip. You need to be straightforward and firm with anyone who matches the description above. It's as simple as telling them to stop what they're doing or refusing to tolerate their self-righteous nonsense and dismissing them from the group. If they continue to cause trouble externally, then you may need to contact established covens, either in your area or online, and ask for their advice. Most covens are aware of the "lunatic fringe," so they will most likely have a few words of wisdom to pass on to you.

As for people you don't like on a personal level, you will need to learn to justify these instinctual reactions so as not to destroy the morale of the individual. Perhaps you got off on the wrong foot or you misinterpreted something they did. Give yourself some time to understand where the person is coming from and discern whether they are going through problems of their own. Never judge a book by its cover. If the feelings of dislike still remain, then perhaps you need to discuss this privately with the other members. Perhaps others feel similarly. If so, then maybe your intuition was right in the first place, in which case let the person down softly.

## 6. What if the coven members turn on me?

This fear is a carry-on from our days of creating exclusive clubs in order to discriminate against someone in particular. There is that childish notion that filters through that convinces us that we will somehow end up the club scapegoat and be eternally ridiculed by the club members. A coven is much more serious than an informal coming-together of a few kids.

Do not give in to irrational fears, as this only conveys to others that you are uncertain of yourself and therefore unfit for a leading role. The only way the entirety of the coven will want to collectively gang up on you is if you are obnoxious, self-righteous, and arrogant. You need to make sure that you keep a balanced perspective at all times. You must also understand that a coven is not a one-person show. It represents the feelings, opinions, and attitudes of everyone involved. If there are any feelings of tension within your group, you need to approach the issue maturely and discuss things openly.

Generally, when an uprising occurs, it is because the people involved have become restless and desire quick change. To avoid attracting mistrust or dislike, you need to be flexible and adaptable.

Introduce new methods and techniques of ritual and raising energy. Go on coven outings or participate in community events that support the environment or are against social injustice, and just have fun! Cultivate the opportunities presented to you, and know that it is something you have all chosen independently to be a part of.

## 7. What if the coven members turn out to be superficial or are involved for reasons that are not aligned with the coven's purpose and that I do not personally feel comfortable with?

There is always the chance that your coven will attract the wrong sort of people—those who are into Witchcraft and Paganism because it is a popular trend. Don't invest too much time stressing over such people, as they quickly become disinterested and adopt a new guise of "social empowerment." These people are a minority, though they seem to have multiplied rapidly in recent years due to the resurgence of all things occult in the media, and we can blame the capitalist ventures of our century for that.

Those who disrespect the depth and seriousness of the Pagan path will meet their comeuppance soon enough and will most likely withdraw from anything associated with it ASAP! There's also the oddity that is the misguided "black" magician or the high, bleary-eyed moron from the next planet over, and we all know what type of things they're into. Such interests and recreational activities are evident in the occult underground of today but rarely surface unless provoked or invited. If such a crowd finds their way into your group, gently but firmly state that their presence is unwanted and their activities are considered distasteful.

### 8. Is sharing too much about myself straightaway a danger to my security and self-esteem?

Being involved in a coven requires a great deal of honesty and conviction. I can safely say that most Pagans are open, accepting individuals. If you fear that an aspect of yourself will be regarded as profane or immoral, then think again. Pagans are encouraged to speculate. Sexuality, political anarchism, gender equality, and food lifestyles are commonly regarded liberally within the Pagan community.

You will come to realise that Pagans as a whole uphold the individual's right to freedom of choice. A coven is a reflection of a greater entity and is composed of the same senses and responses. A coven should never be used to gratify the selfish and supremacist values of a misled individual.

## JOINING A COVEN: THINGS TO DO

You may have been personally invited to join a coven, or perhaps you actively sought one out. Whatever the case, if you desire to have a positive experience, then use the following as guidelines to fulfil that dream:

1. **Allow yourself a period of three months to get to know the people concerned.** This is not to say that you will be initiated at the culmination of this waiting period; in fact, it is highly unlikely! Most covens have this period in order to familiarise themselves with you and vice versa. In that time you will have been invited to a couple of circles and gatherings. You are now in the position to evaluate your feelings regarding ritual and structure, as well as build a rapport with the members. By the end of the period, you will have reached a conscious decision as to whether the coven is right for you.

2. **Find a group that suits your needs.** There's nothing to gain by compromising yourself in order to serve the standards of the first coven you make contact with. This issue arises when an individual who is unsure of what tradition they are inclined towards is invited to join a traditional coven. Of course, if you are not a traditionalist and wish to join an Eclectic Pagan group, you have much more choice. Each coven will allow you a period of time to familiarise yourself with their way of doing things. By the end of that period, you should realise whether the group is right for you or not.

3. **Understand that if there is any serious in-fighting within the group, then it will most likely disband.** If the members of a coven are not actively supporting each other or appropriately addressing problems, then the group will most likely collapse under pressure.

   Infighting is a sign that the coven is sitting on the edge of a knife. If the fighting develops into malicious sabotage and wilful desecration of one's vows, the blade will strike. You need to be sure that you are joining a group that deals with problems maturely and that regards each member's input as essential to resolving the situation. The leaders should stress the importance of cooperation and consider each candidate carefully before allowing them entry into the coven.

4. **If you feel negatively about the group or mistrust the central man/woman, take heed of your intuition.** Our intuition is one of our most precious gifts. When we receive an inspired burst, we need to pay close attention to the details. If the central person is, after close inspection, someone whom you could never trust, then step back from the group and cut all ties with the leader. Trust your instincts on this one.

5. **Make sure that you are comfortable with how the coven is organised and that you connect with the members on a deep level.** It's good to enjoy the rituals of your coven whole-heartedly. You need to be sure that you feel comfortable in whatever organisational structure the coven has. You should also feel connected to the members, as you will be developing strong magickal ties with them. Be yourself, and never allow your voice to be censored or compromised.

   Within the inner court of my coven, if one of us is feeling an intense emotion, the rest of us will generally be affected by it. We share strong psychic connections and often key into things around the same time. This is what happens when you work with Magick together in a group. It is inevitable that the Witches within the coven will become empathetic with each other.

6. **If you begin to feel romantically for anyone in the coven, don't hide it shamefully, but do not make your love interest the central theme of your involvement with the coven.** Romance and sexual attraction are inevitable in such intimate conditions. It is not taboo to pursue a covener; however, it needs to be done maturely. Sneaking around behind the coven's back in order to protect the secrecy of your relationship will not score you any brownie points in the trust factor. Be open, passionate, and express your love, but make sure that this is done in perfect love and perfect trust.

7. **Know that sometimes things can go wrong and for various reasons your coven could disband, leaving you feeling lost and confused.** It's common for groups to crumble under the

weight of disorder. Unfortunately, in most cases, this leads to the members feeling contempt for each other. If a coven is not built on loyalty, honour, and unity, then there is a great chance that it will dissolve because of the lack of positive ties a successful group engenders.

8. **A coven is a serious commitment and is not something you leave as an accessory on the side. However, a coven should not consume your life to the point where it becomes your life.** Paganism stresses balance in all aspects of life. You are not expected to devote the entirety of your free time to the study of Pagan spirituality; rather, it is encouraged that you integrate its principles into your life so that it becomes the underlying nature of your attitude. However, it should also be said that the individual is not expected to adapt to a Pagan's precepts; instead, you should have the freedom to creatively inhabit the spirituality and explore its dynamic traditions.

Working with a coven involves dedication, faith, and cooperation. It is not a periodic stop-off for you to attain the level of ecstasy that raising energy in a group provides. Covens are strongholds of power, and with power comes responsibility.

Covencraft opens us up to the nurturing serenity of community and the provocative challenges of the spiritual path. Maintain the delicate balance between coven and self, and the benefits will far outweigh the negatives.

## PERFECT LOVE AND PERFECT TRUST

*"How do you enter?"*
*"With perfect love and perfect trust."*

Perfection is not a standardised quality revered in the Pagan spirituality. To be perfect does not necessarily refer to contrasts or comparisons. It is not the stressed frame of an anorexic figure, nor is it the money-accumulating enterprise attached to the successful businessperson. To be perfect, at least in the Pagan traditions, is to live in integrity and in complete peace with the Self (the centre of being; all of it).

Nature is perfection. It is not a guilt-ridden entity suffering from trivial dramas; it simply is and flows accordingly. Each aspect relates to another in honourable coexistence. Nature is not merely composed of trees and rocks; it is the manifestation that is an expression of the divine. By extension, *it* is divine.

When I hear the word *perfect* used to describe "God" or the feeling of a moment, I do not associate the word with morality or a persistence that embraces all expectations and lives up to every ideal. When I hear of something being perfect, I know in my heart that it simply *is* the natural and purposeful being of a thing that evokes such strong emotional responses.

"Perfect love and perfect trust" is not a creed that orders us to banish all doubt and mindlessly agree with everything that comes to pass in coven decision-making. It is an active mantra continuously reminding each of us of the vows to remain diligent and earnest, and to do so in respect for each covener in turn.

During Wicca's early years, there was still a great deal of prejudice and fear concerning its cult status. The sensationalist media reports, which often made use of photographs of Witches performing rituals skyclad, did not help the matter. In fact, Gerald Gardner and Doreen Valiente had a falling-out over the issue of publicity and eventually parted to pursue their own paths because of this. As a result of this initial coven dispute, Gardner conjured up the Laws of Witchcraft, which lay down strict codes of conduct within a coven. The origins of the Laws remain unknown.

Many of the laws are specific to the organisation and structure of a coven and, of course, its secrecy. The passwords that accompany a Witch's initiation into a coven—*perfect love and perfect trust*—are the summation of these precautionary laws. In essence, this sworn love and trust entails a great deal of discretion on the initiate's part and a respectful attention to service and oaths.

Early Wiccans (and many today, including the rest of us) had to endure an intolerable consistency of persecution as the revival of Witch-craft occurred in a conservative Christian environment where the word *Witch* was synonymous with Satanist. Many ardent churchgoers refused to accept this newly formed group of individuals and therefore punished them for their daring to come into the public eye. Belonging to a coven was much more than a means of joining with those of like mind; it was also sanctuary and support.

Secrecy was/is integral to the Wiccan faith, and the personal details of initiations were not offered willingly. The right to deny one's own Witchhood was even included in Gardner's Laws. Taking the vow of secrecy inferred an obligation to protect one's fellow coveners. It ensured that the coveners did not have to live in constant fear of return-ing home only to discover their house had been crudely vandalised or their car windows smashed. The mutual bonds of love and trust were a healthy expression of a coven's future success. Without them, many Wiccan covens may have crumbled.

To illustrate the simplicity and reality of perfect love and perfect trust and the effect it has on a particular group or situation, I will refer to a pond. This pond I speak of is healthy, and the ecosystem it sup-ports is thriving. All is in balance and harmony, a picture of perfection. How does this pond continue to exist in its state of well-being when it is in truth a greater entity (the egregore) comprised of many volatile aspects (the coveners), which at first glance may appear to contradict each other (personality)?

The newly hatched tadpoles are devoured eagerly by a passing fish, and that fish is then swiftly eaten by a larger specimen, and so on and so forth. It is the renowned food chain that is occurring—survival of the fittest. Or is it? Now, not every tadpole is eaten; otherwise, there would be a shortage of frogs, and since this pond is exactly as it should be, there is definitely not a shortage of frogs. If, however, the number of small fish increased, then an imbalance would occur, and the number of predators preying on the tadpoles would greatly outweigh the suc-cession of tadpole births, until the fish ate the tadpoles out of existence.

On and on it goes, similarly with predator and prey. It is seen that there needs to be a balanced or complementary number of both predator and prey to ensure the continued survival of each species in the pond.

The very framework of this food chain and the state of the pond is the result of perfect trust. The trust lies in the expectation of each species within the food chain that there will be enough food to satisfy their hunger while also sustaining a number of each species for regeneration. This truth is essential to the ecosystem, and without it, the pond and its inhabitants would soon disappear.

Perfect love and perfect trust is not an empty vow. It is a powerful and self-decisive commitment that evaluates the integrity of the initiate. You should not have to join a British Traditional coven in order to experience the intense undertaking of an oath regarding secrecy. In fact, the code should be integral to all initiations, no matter what tradition the group is working in. It is the essential creed of covencraft that each covener has the right to participate without fear of retribution.

The ties of perfection are not flawless in that they remain untouched by the dilemmas of emotional friction; rather, they are flawless in that they are completely human, vulnerable to destruction and yet wholly ingrained in the conscience. They exist beyond the immaturity of personal dispute. The ties become something of value, an eternal force that we feel we must live up to. It transforms its subtle impression into a grand honour—something we must pursue in order to feel spiritually fulfilled. It touches the heart and plays with the mind, enthusing the body and exciting the soul. These are the bonds of the coven, and they resonate a profound depth of being, instilled in the essence of the group's collective unconscious in perfect love and perfect trust.

# 11: A CRAFT OF SOLITUDE

Witchcraft, Wicca, and Paganism are among the fastest-growing spiritualities in the Western world. Australia, the United Kingdom, and the United States have all experienced a rapid percentage growth in people identifying as Wiccans, Witches, Pagans, etc., as accounted by census records. In fact, between the years 1996 and 2001, the Australian Bureau of Statistics reported a 373.5 percent growth in individuals identifying as Witches within Australia (excluding Wiccans and other Pagans). Other Western countries have reported similar results. With such interest in Nature-based faiths in this modern world, how could the existing groups and covens possibly cater to each individual? Thus the new generation of Pagans embraces a new (and probably older) experience of living the Pagan spirituality.

The Craft of Solitude, promoted by the works of Scott Cunningham, Marian Green, and Rae Beth, is a wild path, one in which the dangers of literalism, passivity, and misinformation flourish. However, there is a great deal of self-evaluation, spiritual growth, and character development that stems from celebrating the Pagan paths independently. Many are dissatisfied with the traditional hierarchical structures of the various covens around. Others are simply happy on their own, self-educating and learning from texts, social contacts, and websites, as well as from communion with Nature and the gods.

Whether you are solitary by circumstance or by nature, this chapter will help you to reflect on the path before you, on the simple truths of wandering, and on the methods of learning and teaching oneself.

## Tackling Theory: A Guide for the Solitary

One of the most common pitfalls the solitary encounters is that of self-education. The most obvious of methods for learning is reading, and there is no shortage of texts out there to assist you. However, there is often a tendency to accept what books say as gospel rather than critically analyse and interpret the information in order to apply what is factual and practical to one's path. For instance, let's say you picked up a book which claimed that Wicca is a survival of the old folk religion of Spain and that Gerald Gardner was simply a masochistic charlatan who professed to inherit the Craft from a made-up coven. Imagine that you believe everything that the author of this book has said, and you begin to preach the word on every Pagan forum you are on. Immediately, there will be a catastrophic backlash and no doubt several obscenities thrown at you along the way. You, in your innocence, are berated and belittled by people who have a greater understanding of the history and lineage of Wicca. They will say "I have read this book" and explain to you that they concluded, from historical inaccuracies and a lack of bibliographical detail, that the author is simply a misled conspiracy theorist. You, in response, humbly state your shock and step down from your soapbox while simultaneously cancelling your membership with the forum and losing all confidence in yourself.

In the past, I have frequented several Pagan online forums, and I can tell you that there are certainly debates concerning such issues, and there are usually one or two persistent individuals who will simply not relent to fact and instead seek to uphold a defunct mythology.

Learning from books is not without its dangers; unfortunately, there is not much we can do to stop the flow of published texts whose authors pass on prepackaged crap. More and more, however, there is an interest in uncovering the truth and pursuing fact. But rather than setting yourself up, why not be willing to learn the truth and to develop your own ability at sorting wheat from chaff?

Paganism has become a deeply theoretical study for some. No longer are things simple; there is now so much variation and scholarly integrity that finding what you want is a complicated task in itself.

So why is theory important to Paganism? Obviously, with all this talk of emotions, psychology, metaphysics, and the deeply attuned celebration of Nature, the significance of theory in our community should be of little concern. But it is not, and the belief that it should be is simply a hangover from a society that relishes playing God to the point where more harm is done than good.

For Pagans, connections are vital and divine. Theory and practice are interwoven and support each other. What use is there in a spirituality in which the customs and practices have no theoretical basis, no practical application? This is why Paganism and science are mutually compatible. The nature of Paganism is that of exploration, evolving, and opening up.

As young people, we are all sick of having to live through the theory of what could potentially be a fun subject. I wish I could have danced and painted all day without having had to resort to thick texts about artists and choreographers I have no care for. But after a moment of contemplation, I am grateful that I had the opportunity to learn about dance and art (and whatever else!) in a theoretical way, because it enriches the experience of doing those things in a practical sense and opens my mind to a very interesting and stimulating world of facts, history, and culture.

What type of theory should a Pagan seek to study? What is seen as vital in securing a sound foundation of knowledge in Paganism? The extensive scope of topics that Paganism underlies today is far too vast to delve into; therefore, it is essential for us to break things up and direct our focus on different aspects at different times.

As this book is designed to cater to Pagans who are beyond the basics and who live their Magick, it is up to you to embrace areas of personal interest and deepen your understanding of each. Paganism is an undulating interplay of energy and expertise that shapes the mind and sings to the heart.

It is important to have a firm knowledge of our:

**History:** Observe the scientific methods of archaeology, anthropology, sociology, and psychology in order to deepen your understanding of our past and where we have come from. Honour ancestry, and remember.

**Magickal Theory:** This includes studying various occult sciences, including gnosis, the Qabalah, Ceremonial and Chaos Magick, Hermetic Magick, etc. It is also essential to be familiar with the simple practicality of Folk Magick and the rich tapestry of tradition involved in the Craft of the Witch.

**Society and Community:** Become aware of interfaith issues, governmental policy (past and present), political and social activism, feminism, and environmental issues.

**Traditions:** Delve into the diversity of tradition—Wiccan initiatory traditions, solitary practitioners, reconstructionism, and literary-inspired groups (e.g., The Church of All Worlds).

**Theology and Philosophy:** Ditheism, polytheism, pantheism, animism, archetypes, the Universal Spirit, consciousness, the Self, "Thou art God/dess," life and death, Nature, neutrality, yin and yang, polarity.

**Ethics and Morality:** Karma, cause and effect, the Golden Rule, "Harm none," respect, pro-circumstance/choice, labelled ethical inclinations (e.g., White Witch/Black Witch).

There is so much diversity and individuality that it seems dangerous to categorise all of the above as Pagan; however, through consensual association, personal identification, and principle commonalities, there is a unity that joins us.

If you are having trouble accessing information or fathoming anything from it, then social networking is a rewarding way to open yourself up to greater learning. By collaborating with others of like mind and similar experience, you have ground to develop your theory. Gradually, you will find that you will have grown accustomed to criticising almost every bit of information you absorb, but remember not to become bitter or rampantly destructive in your analysis. Authors and scholars are people, too, and they can make mistakes.

You must also be able to identify the degree of professionalism and integrity that goes into a work. A lack of reference notation and bibliographical support leads many readers to suspect foul play. However, it all depends on the text and the author's ability to use reason to support their purposes. For example, the bibliography in the back of this book is concise, and this is because this book is purely a spiritual and philosophical exploration of Pagan living. But in a book of a more academic nature, it is generally anticipated that there will be a thorough bibliography. When we absorb information, we must be objective but also passionately sympathetic and receptive, or whatever the case may be.

Authors and their books also fulfil another lesser-known role. Books are wellsprings of knowledge and reflection. They are speculative bondages of paper and ink that speak of ideas, concepts, and patterns in the fabric of our reality. In this, they are the perpetrators of ideas that already sit comfortably inside of us. For instance, many of my instinctive ideas concerning the nature of the elements were answered in books before I had the ability to articulate such matters. It is to such insights that many Pagans pay their respects. Paganism runs through the spirit like blood.

The vast majority of Pagans nowadays are successfully able to separate the wheat from the chaff when it comes to information. Our personal contributions to global discussions on web forums and mailing lists, and even on a more regional scale, are helping to develop a solid foundation of knowledge and wisdom for those to come.

The Pagan community will truly benefit from what has become a unique trait among us: we are priests, we are divine, and now we are scholars. It is up to the individual to make diligent use of their research skills and to apply the mental and emotional faculties to a wealth of wisdom.

Wisdom is not the fool's handmaiden, nor does it belong to those who are careless and negligent. Wisdom is on equal terms with those who respect its depth and honour the principles upon which it is based. With that in mind, I hope I have at least motivated you to reread some of the classics and regard them in a new light.

## NOSTALGIC RITES: MEMOIRS FROM THE UNCONSCIOUS

Nostalgia opens doors to the senses at random. It can come upon us at any time it chooses, even in the darkest hour of night while you quietly await the dawn. It crashes through the conclaves of denial and self-pity, releasing anxiety and self-loathing to the winds. Nostalgia is the guide of the hidden memoirs we all store in our personal libraries.

Paganism emphasises the importance of living in the present and rejects dwelling in the past and fatalism. We are encouraged, as Pagans, to embrace the moment and to fully awaken to life—its powerful continuity and paradoxes. As solitaries, the Nostalgic Rite is the threshold of personal and intimate initiation—the catalyst for great change. It is the slightest glimmer that enchants the mind and possesses the senses, ultimately stimulating the unfolding of overwhelming memories, feelings, and experiences.

The following is simply a pondering, a meaningful reflection and attempt at capturing, distilling, and suspending the Nostalgic Rite. Through it, perhaps, you may discover the essence and song of my soul.

Laughter. Soft, timeless, and utterly entrenched in the archaic elegance of the wind's currents. It floated to his ears as if by an intent sharper than any conceived by mortal minds. Simple and pure, a sacred rendering of the essence Spirit itself comprised.

*What is it that plays so persistently at me ... that removes the gauze of the woven dreaming from my shadow-pooled soul?* He pondered as his thoughts began to rearrange and submit to the scrutiny of consciousness. *Neither of this world or the other, and yet shall it remain just beyond, in the periphery of darkness, within the magnificent stitchwork of the light.* Perhaps it was another speaking. An elfin figure; regal, pretentious, lawfully arrogant? The cunning, stealthy gnomes of the reclusive caverns? *No ... the guardians do not beckon me at this hour ... This is the gods that stir me.*

The rusting metal grated and squandered in protest as a stream issued forth from the tap. Gradually, as courage stormed his heart, he proudly lifted his head. Startled by the reflection, the youth stumbled, reaching for the sink. Even and finely textured, an ancient face stared back. Hair so naturally delicate; eyes of diligence and marked passion; full lips curved to the rhythm of his dry wit. Features so exquisitely engraved that in that moment of untainted freedom there had been the truth of beauty framed in mortal skin. Egocentricity was unimagined and a cloak of humility woven from the threads of an unconscious landscape had settled around his broad shoulders. Moving from the bathroom, he gazed through a hallway window and reprimanded himself for remaining inside.

A chorus of serenity filtered through the indigo sky, bejewelled and glorious in its heavenly attire. His ears remained receptive, willing away the sirenlike piercing of the silence. He did not know quite where his feet were taking him. The draping willow by the stream gently dabbled at his forehead as he passed through its forest of twine. Overhead, a pearly gibbous moon peered down at the youth, restlessly singing of the sweet darkness that had enclosed her. Watching the ancient mirror, he began to cry. His tears comforted his racing mind and drew all thoughts away from the darting, wolfish shadows slipping between realms. There was nothing to fear when the moon herself illuminated his path.

Still following the stream, he came upon a slate of rock jutting out from the sloping bank. Running his hand across the coarse surface of the rock, he smiled, remembering the many times he had sat on the edge of it as a child, swinging his legs back and forth to disturb the soft sheen of water. There was no malice or will to interfere; it was the childish evocation of the dreaming that had kept him swinging his legs.

Thinking back to the innocence that once so voluntarily infused his world, other memories began to reappear. He remembered the undulating curves of the ever-mirthful water maids as they slid in between his toes and happily mocked his clumsy limbs. He had forged bets with them in order to win a fragment of pride as he playfully pulled his feet from the water every time he saw them coming. Laughter echoed throughout the endless night; the calm displacement and mythic landscape of the interweaving shadows nagging at him. Was it merely the memories of childhood that had stirred him this night, or was it something more, beyond such playful intrigue?

Standing, he reached into his pocket to find a single silver coin, which he placed reverently on the edge of the rock. In a flash of mist and light, a sinewy hand burst forth from the quiet stream and snatched up the offering, disappearing just as quickly as it had come. The youth smiled and left the stream, turning his attention to the stretch of forest that bordered the path. Beyond the row of oak and pine was a sharp ravine that twisted its way through the foliage and roots as if it had once been an enraged serpent flailing hysterically. The youth knew this land well and so readied himself for the leap he would have to make in order to pass into the forest. A test of worth, for only the feet of the prepared had felt the moist soil of the forest foundation.

Drifting against the short incline, he centred his mind and felt as the light of the earth entwined about his limbs, strengthening their reflexes. *One ... two ... three!* An exhilarating rush of adrenaline ignited in his body and urged him forth. Bounding off the edge, he felt the lift of flight as his mind forsook all thought and embraced the void. He landed, feet yearning for the earth to be beneath them. Before him lay an expanse of mystery, territory whose heir had long ago realised that wilderness warranted no ownership.

A cool breeze trickled through the canopy, fresh air upon his skin. Despite the cold, the youth surrendered his body to a warm, tingling sensation that trailed gently across him like sparks of electricity. His body became a sacred vessel charged within the embrace of shadow. He was not sure if he had anticipated this during his journey to the forest. Time had no refuge within the forest's hallowed depths, and the fleeting seconds each became their own eternity.

A sharp crunch to his right startled him from his trance as the scythe-like talons of a hawk pierced the brittle bark of an oak's bough. Stopping for a moment, their two eyes met; one pair innocent and reverent, the other beyond the strain of a translucent glow. What lay within the ember coals of the bird of prey who perched upon a limb? *What was it that enchanted him to revolt against the incessant need to blink his eyes?* Curiosity for the clumsy figure whose feet were merely an excessive nuisance? Or perhaps, as the hawk spread its wings to fly, it was a deeper understanding, a rhythmic and instinctive knowing that coursed between two souls of the same source.

The wilderness bred fatigue and loneliness, and yet in this moment all had come to rest in a mild calm, for there was a wholeness between the two. Once the feathered one had taken to the rippled stretch above and the youth below her drew into the comfortable embrace of self-awareness, the forest returned from its silent yearning and continued to coax forth the mysterious figure that had so successfully wandered upon the path that only few had taken before.

Emerging from a row of battered trees, the youth felt the soft pressure of pure air against his skin and gazed upward at the silken mirror of concave contentment. *What is it that pulls me here?* His abrupt return to consciousness stirred the serenity that infused the fabric of his mind. Once again, he had stumbled upon the unknown—vulnerable and exposed to the gaping jaws of the veiled mystery before him.

Timidly, his feet slid between the dry foliage and the fresh, green stalks of a curious grass as he made his way to the centre of the grove. Planting his feet firmly in the moist soil, he raised his arms and breathed in deeply, feeling as his heart took heed and began to work faster, pushing the blood. There he stood, a conduit for the power that swept through the sacred ring. The trees shifted, and the earth beneath him craved the sensation. It sang to be fulfilled, and at once the ancient spiral paths began to expand and flow, spilling intoxicating waves of power through Gaia's veins. The youth drew in a sharp breath as he felt a warmth enter through his soles and wash through his body, enlivening his cells and cleansing the breath he drew in. As energy infused his body, his unconscious drew him further and deeper into the void. The darkness was palpable, and fine tendrils carved from its interior wound about the youth's mind.

Fragments of keen voices and shallow wisps of something more sailed through the currents of air. The world was internalising, drawing into itself, and it seemed the youth stood at its centre, for the seed of creation lay within the fertile womb of his soul. The constant pulse of its potential throbbed erratically through him.

*What is it that fills my soul and sates the yearning I had not known* ... It is that which is beneath you, around you, above you and within you ... *What is it that knows the deepest of my secrets and plays my heart as if it were the glorious crest of a flaming harp* ... It is that which you have always known ...

Power surged through him. Peripheral flashes of white heat rippled against his body. In an abrupt shift of momentum, silence reigned, and all had fallen into oblivion. The world split at its seams, and a sweet light echoing the vibrant songs of the gods shone through, pooling at his feet. In swift succession, a familiar voice wove its song through the ancient bloodlines pulsing beneath his skin...

*Know me, for all that live breathe in my essence. Hear me, for all that do rejoice in the path of the unknown. Love me, for all that passion embraces swim with the current of my blood. Be me, for separation is illusion, and I am at your feet, one to the other upon this sacred night...*

The laughter rang brightly, soothing his dream's raw landscape. It nurtured his soul and brought forth a cradle of mirth and abandon— the legendary grail. All things must begin in darkness, where the distant flicker of flame and winding light knows no territory. For all must meet with their inner shadow in order to see what truth and what light casts it. Or so he pondered as his arms adjusted to his weight. *Perhaps,* he thought, *I shall write of this tomorrow.* I know, however, that if he decides not to, or simply forgets, that such a rich memory shall never really disappear, and who is to say that his vision was ever truly meant for paper?

## LIVING PAGANISM:
## A SPIRITUAL INTEGRATION

Most of us by now are familiar with Scott Cunningham and his phenomenal contribution to the Pagan community. His celebrated book *Wicca: A Guide for the Solitary Practitioner* is one of the most popular beginner's texts for Wiccan seekers. This book gave many people the confidence they needed to stand up for their spiritual rights. It was the sequel to this book that outlined the finer details of Wiccan spirituality and offered a system of personalising the faith. *Living Wicca* provided an interesting concept to the community with its sectioned parts dealing with particular aspects of Wicca and encouraging the individual to establish a new tradition by means of recording their own path on paper and recognising it as such.

This section offers a unique perspective on living one's spirituality, as well as highlighting advice that has worked for me and those I know in the past and to this day.

Living Paganism is not about creating a fresh and new tradition, it is a test of the individual's conviction to their path and the simple truths they choose to live by.

### The Path of Perspective Philosophy

It all begins with perspective. We cultivate, ponder, and act in accordance with how we perceive the world to be. There's no denying that our views, our presumptions, and our accepted form of logic shape the way in which we live our lives.

Consider the predicament of a troubled, impressionable adolescent. Now, this particular adolescent (let's name him George) was raised by fundamentalist Protestant parents who just so happen to be active committee members of a large organisation based on condemning social and religious minorities. They regard *Sailor Moon*[1] as a threat to the post-mortem fate of their children. How would George see the world? Most probably as a breeding ground for evil. Every moment of his conscious life is spent on discerning good from evil based on his faith. George's definition of good and evil is decidedly more defined than the moderate Catholic's. There's one thing that George has succeeded in doing, however, that I want to make especially clear: George has integrated his perspective philosophy into his everyday life, and this is something we as Pagans need to achieve.

The difference between a fundamentalist person and a free-thinking individual is that we know our perspective philosophies are merely some of the many paths that fulfil the nature of Truth. However, a Pagan's perspective is not bound to dogma. Our perspective is emphasised by the simple truths of everyday life and most importantly by our experience.

Paganism does not make any absurd claims that negate science or common sense. We are sometimes average human beings who live in a not-so-average world. We acknowledge and honour the creation, including ourselves, as sacred, and we attune ourselves to the sacred through ritual and myth. There is no delusion in our worldviews; we

---

1 *Sailor Moon* is a Japanese anime cartoon that is highly popular throughout the United States and Australia. It involves a young girl named Serena who is the reincarnation of the moon princess and who fights the Megaforce that tries to steal life-energy from innocents. She does this with a band of friends named the Sailor Scouts. Many fundamentalist Christian groups are vehemently anti–*Sailor Moon*, when really it's quite innocent. Of course, they are also against *Pokémon*.

are not led astray by the fleeting promises of the occasional New Age fancy. As Pagans, we seek to live in virtue and honour within codes that are essentially universal. These things and more form the basis of our perspective. It is then up to the individual to walk the path of Truth according to personal encounters with divinity.

Imagine being imprisoned within a tall, cold tower, in which your only view of the outside world is through a small window. You have no idea what is going on around you, and you become accustomed to your minimized perception of life remaining unchanged. Suddenly, a wild storm blankets the skies, and a deep sigh of thunder cleaves the peace in two. Inside your tower, you tremble with fear, uncertain of the fate that will befall you. In marvellous synchronicity, just as these thoughts form on the verge of your mind, a daggerlike flash of light makes contact with the ancient stones of the roof above you and shakes the tower to its core. A momentous blast resounds, and you are thrown from the tower. Your body does not react; it becomes numb with fear. Your limp figure falls, and suddenly the world's torrent of darkness engulfs you.

It's profound imagery, when you think about it. There can be no truth to perspective unless you have experienced the chaos of our world. There can be no light without darkness and no shadow cast without an intercessor to break the path of light. We form the delicate balance between polarities. We provide the channel for the powers of the universe to flow through. It is our perspective that shapes the way we deal with reality. This may be difficult for the hardcore rationalist to comprehend. After all, isn't there only one reality, one truth, and one method of attaining knowledge of both? Maybe and maybe not. While we are on this earth, the path and the perspective we walk it with should only serve one purpose: to fulfil the law of limitless possibility. There is no end to this spiritual odyssey we call the soul.

### Daily Devotion

Part of being Pagan is to live one's spirituality wholly and in each moment of every day. It is essential for us to celebrate the continuum by sharing in the exchange of Life, and this is the art of devotion.

Devotion comes in many forms and is expressed in many ways. There is devotion to one's gods, devotion to one's cause, devotion to one's destiny, devotion to one's kith and kin, and of course there is always honour, for without it we are speaking soulless words.

I cannot say to whom or to what to devote to, or how, why, when, and where you should do so; that is for you to discover. Paganism has no authorities; it has nothing of the tyranny that the monotheistic traditions systematically condone. We are each unto ourselves, and despite our connections, in the end we decide independent of external forces (but remember the tower).

We Pagans have a priesthood, but it is not one that undermines the strength at the centre of each of us. We do not submit to anybody who claims power-over; we are all about the power from within and the power that is shared with other beings and forces. To devote oneself to any form of politico-authoritarian institute would be to spit on the graves of all those who have suffered at the hands of oppression, ignorance, and the stricken ego-consciousness.

As Pagans, our devotion is marked. We form alliances and connections coloured by experience and which greatly exceed the generic definition of what an ally can provide for us. For instance, the animist in me is often allying itself with various entities around the place—traffic lights, for instance! I know that they will help to create the path of least resistance when our paths cross. Devotion can be about that sense of the spirit of things and places. We devote ourselves to the continuum that stems from a source that lies both within and beyond.

I devote myself every day to my gods, to my path, to my destiny, and to the All and all of Them. I contain within myself the very seed of the Mystery, and I know it intimately. I kneel and stand before my altar and devote my entire being to my unfolding cycle. I do not cling to an illusion of what is to come and see no reason to map out a course; I simply state that I am willing to walk the path I find myself on with purpose and clarity. With devotion comes understanding, knowledge, power, and wisdom.

As a last note, a wise goddess once told me that nothing can be truly gone, for something will always be there to replace what has been lost or taken. What this means is that, in the cycle of things, there is a flow—a continuum transforming, shifting, and fulfilling all that has been, is, and will be. The past, present, and future are simply faces of an intrinsic Truth exposed with cheek in the most obvious places. There is no central origin; instead, we exist as the chop and change of a chaotic underbelly of fusion.

Devotion is not about a stringent adherence to order or hierarchy. In devotion, we work to cleanse ourselves and to centre the channel so that we may rise and fall up and down the World Tree. Remember: the gods care not so much how you see them, only that you do.

### Establishing Ethics: The Golden Rule

Pagan ethics has been given its own chapter; however, I find it necessary to readdress this topic here.

We are taught from an early age to avoid danger implicitly. But what good is avoidance when the things that we avoid are, in fact, inevitable? A child will never lose their curiosity, and anything new presents a kind of revelatory encounter. Morals are therefore redundant, as the learning process is stimulated through experience. We have all been the boy to cry wolf. The concept of morality is foreign to Paganism, as we are experiential folk. Ethics, then, are our foundation.

To live ethically is to abide by a code, and this code is tailored to the individual and their voyage. We all have different priorities and values. Sometimes these are influenced by tradition, environment and law/lore. For instance within the growing reconstructionist communities various virtues come together to create codes of ethics. These codes of ethics (derived from ancient cultures) provide inspiration for many Pagans today. Within Hellenic reconstruction groups, some of these values include hospitality (*xenia*), moderation (*sophrosune*), piety (*eusebia*), justice (*dike*), modesty (*aidos*), and excellence (*arete*). These principles form ethical strongholds that empower us and demonstrate the beauty and sincerity of our philosophies.

In a neutral light, we, as a community, represent principles that uphold equality, diversity, evolutionary change, and pragmatism. However, this has nothing to do with the spiritual instinct ethics is based upon, especially for solitaries.

Along the journey towards deeper knowledge, towards the mirror, we each seek to abide by the common good. This can be expressed through ritual work and spellcraft at the "clincher" when some choose to say "For the highest good of all," or something to that effect. The word "involved" ("for the highest good of all [involved]") is not used, which demonstrates that this statement is really about all, not just the obvious factors/individuals related to the working. This statement wills that no harm come to anyone or anything in the process of the unfolding/manifestation.

Nothing should falter or cease to be (that is impossible!); it should strive for its highest good, which is the destiny of the centred and purified will. If the highest good becomes the common goal, then it is no longer a selfish thing. Good is not a predecessor of or an adversary to evil. *Good* is more often a verb than it is a noun. We are never good or evil—it is the acts themselves that colour our true natures or arise from them. Plato believed in a deity that ultimately is good and that is all. So too is the creation, as Qabbalistic lore can vouch. The solitary sees that good things done represent the good that is. This brings me to another piece of wise advice that is commonly quoted in Pagan circles: "Perform random acts of kindness and senseless beauty."

This is more often than not touted by the Erisians and Discordians (same thing!) who dwell in caves singing hymns to the Great Goddess of the Golden Apple (and of chaos/discord), Eris. She is seen by her followers as a lovely younger-than-middle-aged woman who whips around shopping malls causing children to scream and kick at their parents (and cats to sneeze fur balls). But I am losing my train of thought here, so back to the point! This promotion of random acts performed for others and in anyone's name is at the core of a profound ethic, one that calls for love and joy.

Laughter is the greatest music to the gods' ears and a smile the perfect picture, as corny as that sounds. But let's face it: living life positively and with great joy is a gift greater than any sacrifice. Eris and Discordia represent an energy that is essential to the solitary. This is the spark of chaos that ultimately fuses all things and in return causes division simply for the sake of more union. To go about the world picking up litter, topping up parking meters, or simply smiling at every passerby really does make the world a better place.

One of my teachers once told me (in the format of "do this as your homework") to wish everyone whom I came in contact with peace and happiness. It sounds very white-lighter, but I took up the challenge, and the more I wished it upon people, the more happy and peaceful I became! In the end, it all comes down to the Golden Rule. Wholly and soulfully treat others the way you would wish to be treated.

## ASPECTING THE CUNNING ONE: SERVING YOUR COMMUNITY

The cunning folk are those who spend their time resolving the mundane inadequacies of the common people. These are the clients who implore the cunning folk to produce a desired result or to look into a particular situation in exchange for a practical service, material goods, or money. Historically, the majority of cunning folk were not necessarily Pagan. They were simply those who by training or natural predisposition were able to manipulate the guise of reality and to effectively change or conjure certain things by certain means. In fact, many cunning folk define what they do as a job.

During the eighteenth and nineteenth centuries, Europe's fixation on heresy had receded, and the elitist classes of the era were more inclined to the rationality of an ordered universe and god.[2] The practice of Witchcraft persisted, however, and was carried on by the cunning folk and rural charmers whose business it was to serve their community magickally. The cunning folk (also known as wise wo/men) did not

---

2 M. Streeter, *Witchcraft: A Secret History*, 134.

owe their continuity to the legacy of an organised Pagan sect; in fact, many cunning folk drew on Judaic-Christian mythology and literature in their rites and spells.

They were also considered to be highly intelligent and literate people. They relied on a variety of magickal techniques, and the traditional Wiccan arsenal of tools often accompanied their practice. Interestingly, there was a great percentage of men involved in cunningcraft who also retained a primary income-based job. Due to the patriarchy of the time, women were bound to hearth and home. If a woman was involved in cunningcraft, she was generally restricted to it.

Historically and culturally, the terms *Witch* and *cunning wo/man* were not synonymous. In folklore, a Witch practised malevolent Magick and consciously sought to destroy the morale of victims. A cunning wo/man would do good and provide a means of battling the curses of Witches. There is a theory that suggests the cunning folk were instrumental during the Witch hunts in helping to convict accused Witches.

A BBC production entitled *Witch Craze* follows the story of Agnes Sampson, a Scottish folk healer who was accused of Witchcraft, imprisoned and tortured, and finally sentenced to be strangled and then burnt. Before Agnes was officially accused, a band of crazed followers provoked by Betty Akenhead, a woman who professed to be able to identify a Witch simply by looking into their eyes, sought her out to make the charge. Whether or not Betty was considered a traditional wise woman cannot be known; in fact, Agnes seems more the type. Of course, in my mind, Witchcraft and cunningcraft are of the same vein.

A solitary Witch should not be required to fulfil a service to others. In fact, a solitary often owes their solitude to the inclination to privacy. However, there are many practising Witches and Pagans who find themselves targeted by friends and family and who are asked to perform spells, make charms, and divine the future. Many find this kind of work satisfying and offer their services willingly. You may apply the following advice to your own practice in order to empower your cunning nature.

If someone who in ordinary circumstances would not ask for magickal assistance has done just that, then you will need to address their apprehensions. First of all, discuss the nature of your spirituality with the individual and reassure them that Magick is simply the essence of life, the power that resonates within us all. Perhaps the person is sceptical but knows you well enough to be able to trust you. Encourage them to suspend disbelief to help the process. If the client already acknowledges Magick in their lives, you won't need to do much in the way of assuring them of your capabilities.

Then there's the issue of money. Obviously, it depends on your situation. If you already have a job and steady income, then charging for your magickal services is a tad unethical; however, if you have devoted yourself to the cunning charge, then why not? Your payment could be in kind or it could be cash, whatever you prefer. Magick can be a highly spiritual matter and it can also be a simply practical one, though what's the difference?

If you wish to help someone in need who hasn't directly asked you, then you will need to seek their permission. A passing comment such as "I will pray for you" should be enough. You will most likely receive a curt nod or thank-you in reply. Once permission is secured, you can begin your work.

Part of the cunning charge is bonding with your clients in order to alleviate the pain periodically and to open the doors so as to ease in the energy. In fact, you don't even have to commit yourself to any intense magickal work, you could simply pray. Pray to your gods, the spirits of your ancestors, or whomever you feel comfortable addressing that your client (family member/friend) is healed, or whatever the case may be. When my grandmother went to hospital for a knee operation, I entered into a meditative state and visited her in spirit. I took her hand, and we flew through the skies. I wanted her to flow and heal naturally, quickly, without torment and other medical impediments. I recall feeling particularly peaceful after the meditation, and my grandmother was out of hospital as quickly as she had gone in.

## Signing and Divining

Another facet of cunningcraft is divination, the interpretation of omens and the foretelling of someone's future.

In reality, divination is simply another form of channelling the timeless energy of life, and Witches are often experts in the field. For that reason, if you wish to fulfil the traditional cunning charge, then you may find yourself targeted for readings.

If you already read the Tarot or interpret the lines on palms, then you are set, but if not and you find yourself oddly drawn to a form of divination, then go study it. Ask around at the forums you frequent, read books on the topic, and learn to apply the skills practically, with insight and intuition.

One of my old bosses comes to see me regularly to get her palm and her cards read, and I do so out of a sense of duty, as I know that she returns because she is fulfilled by what I tell her. If she pays me, she pays me; if she doesn't, I honestly don't care. If I help her, then that is the only reward I am interested in.

If your parents are open to your abilities, they might start inviting their friends along, and you may find yourself with a steady flow of clientele. If so, you probably won't want to invite the middle-aged woman from down the street into your room (your personal space); instead, dedicating a particular room to consultations might be a good idea.

Read with honesty but tone down the brutality. Speak with truth and conviction, adding words of wisdom and advice when your intuition speaks for you to do so. Try to remain neutral. Bias is never a good thing, especially when you don't know the half of what has happened. If, at the end of the consultation, you are asked how much the readings cost, don't shout "fifty dollars!" abruptly, simply shake your head and deny the money. The customer obviously wants to give you something for your services and will of their own accord leave you money or a gift in kind, no matter what you say. It is tradition in Balinese culture to always refuse money for aiding someone; however, you may feel differently. As they say, "Cross the gypsy's palm with silver."

You may also like to create an affirmation or charm to recite over your divining instrument/s to reinforce that your services arise from your gifts. Something like the following is ideal:

*By fortune's plot and fate's good way*
*I now perform my task this day*
*For cunning is the path I walk*
*Its name ablaze in all my talk*
*Guide my words and visions fair*
*To know, keep silent, to will, and to dare.*

## SHRINE OF THE ANCIENTS

A shrine is a place of reverence. It is a peaceful and strategically positioned expression of one's faith. The shrine I speak of is one that may also be called a hearth—the spiritual heart of the home.

In this section, I will outline the benefits of creating your own Shrine of the Ancients—an expression of your devotion to your own ancestral line. It is essential for anyone interested in fulfilling the cunning charge to acknowledge that which has given us life, purpose, and direction.

Before building the shrine, you need to research. Look into your family's past, into their history. Dig up old records and photo albums, and unlock your mind to the dusty cabinets of memories long forgotten. You may be surprised at what you find. Ask your parents about their parents, and if your grandparents are still alive, ask them about their lives. Open up to each perspective and cultivate the experience.

Prod your relatives about family traditions and look into the reasons of why they are and what they mean. Study up on the culture, geography, and customs of the country or ethnic group your family descends from. For instance, the cultural heritage of my Balinese family is so rich in folklore, mythology, healing, and spirituality that it's hard to ignore the beauty and divine energy that inhabits my father's legacy.

It's important to take a healthy interest in your parents' lives and their own beliefs. Ask about it, and you'll soon find yourself entrenched in an unfolding tapestry of experience. Delve deep and untwine the threads of the past so that you become more aware of how and why you, the culmination of everything that has happened in your family line, came to be. It could be the awakening you're looking for.

You should now have an intuitive understanding of the ancestral energies that watch over your family. Enter your sacred space and focus on this energy, channelling it and expressing it in the form of inspired prose, a poem, a picture, or a photograph (anything that has a material body). Bless and cleanse the product of your channelling, and keep it on your altar for a few days. This time should be used to design and construct your physical shrine. My parents have a small box with the foundation of 30 cm by 25 cm and 15 cm in depth. This basic design can be applied to any shrine.

After you have finished making the shrine, find a suitable place to position it on the wall, perhaps above your altar or next to your bed. If you parents aren't averse to the idea, you could even put it up in the main living area.

The following is a ritual designed specifically for the blessing and consecrating of your Shrine of the Ancients.

You will need:

> The physical shrine
> Frankincense incense (stick variety)
> Moon or holy water
> Rock salt
> 1 white votive candle
> Several items of significance representing both sides
>> of the family

Ground and centre. Establish your space by formally addressing your ancestors by name (if possible) and calling upon the guidance and protection of the ancients. Now focus your attention on the physical shrine before you. To the south of it should be placed a dish of rock salt, to the west a chalice of moon water, to the north a white candle, and to the east a stick of frankincense. Light the stick of incense, and place your hands a few inches above the tip of the incense, allowing the smoke to waft through your fingers. Recite the following:

*Air of fire, purifying smoke, I call on thee to dispel all negativity from this Shrine of the Ancients. So mote it be.*

In a sunwise manner, trace a ring of smoke around the shrine, and visualise white light circulating and cleansing with the air.

Pick up the dish of salt, and hold it in your palms to the south/north in an offering gesture. Focus on earth, and speak the following:

*Crystals of the earth, vibrating with power, I call on thee to cleanse and charge this Shrine of the Ancients. So mote it be.*

Sprinkle the grains of salt in a sunwise manner around the shrine and once again visualise white light cleansing it.

Pick up the chalice of moon water, and repeat the following while concentrating on water:

*Blessed water, tears of the sea's shining face, I call on thee to bless and consecrate this Shrine of the Ancients. So mote it be.*

Use your fingertips to flick the water in a sunwise manner, visualising as before.

Light the white votive candle, and focusing on fire, say:

*Bright and humble flame that burns within the temple, I call on thee to illumine and burn away the darkness that harbours past wounds. I hereby call on the powers of healing and the mighty force of the ancients and of the ancestors who share my blood. May you feel and be drawn to the warmth of this flame, and may it forever burn as a token of my love for you. Dwell within this shrine and guard us, your family. Within and without, blessed be.*

Pick up the candle and circle it once around the shrine deosil, envisioning the flame expanding into a wave of pulsating white light.

Make the sign of the pentagram over the shrine and declare it as consecrated.

Position the shrine in the chosen location, and decorate it with the items of significance to your families.

To complete the ritual, leave the white votive burning in the centre of the shrine. Whenever you wish to invoke the presence of your ancestors or if you wish to consult the ancients, light the candle, and open your awareness to their guidance. Continue to replace the candle whenever it burns out, and honour your ancestors daily. Compose a short prayer that you can say before going to bed. You will have created for yourself and your family a portal of love and a reflection of eternity. This is the heart and hearth of your being.

May your path be blessed, cunning one.

# 12: EVALUATING TRADITION

What is it about tradition that makes people feel so self-assured? Humans are not known for their cultivation of change. The possibility of change often scares people so much that they cling to the only thing that appears to offer permanence, which tends to be tradition.

Within Witchcraft, there still remain traditional aspects. Fasting, casting the circle, going skyclad, and pinching out the candles are examples of these. There is something archaic and beautiful about the old-time customs and practices. In Witchcraft, these traditions offer a sense of history and continuity.

Fasting, abstaining from sexual activity, and ritual bathing are all traditional aspects of Ceremonial Magick and have been absorbed into contemporary Witchcraft practices over time. These activities are part of the "preliminary energy-raising," as discussed in previous chapters, and are believed to aid in the releasing of specific energies that help to focus the mind on the task ahead.

As Paganism grows in popularity, its diversity flourishes. New traditions, concepts, and movements are introduced in order to cater to the vast interests of all. Tradition still remains a strong influence, and for that reason, this chapter is dedicated to its place in our spirituality.

## PRE-SPELL JITTERS

Preliminary energy-raising, which refers to prior energy work before the actual spell or ritual is begun, is comprised of various techniques aimed at heightening psychic awareness and initiating the flow of energy. Fasting, bathing, meditation, and periodic celibacy are the most common methods used, and all owe their efficacy to the transformation of consciousness initiated by the omittance of habitual activities. Preliminary activities are divided into two categories—subliminal and active.

Subliminal methods derive from the idea that abstaining from human routine/activity (e.g., eating, sex) causes the individual to crave. They are then constantly made aware of why they aren't eating or having sex, etc. Thinking about the working to come and honouring a periodic vow to emphasise the power of the working is a tried and true method.

Simply refraining from any routine activity will produce the desired effects; however, if you are devoted to your cause, you need to take this further. Fasting can go on for a period of days or even weeks if the individual is capable of it—think of the Hindu holy man, the Sadhu, and how he keeps from eating and drinking for years on end. Obviously, it's not plausible for a growing youth to commit to such extreme lengths, but a day or two should suffice. Always make sure you are physically capable beforehand and consult your doctor or healer.

If you want to be specific, you could stop eating a particular food, such as bread, eggs, or a type of fruit. Each type of food has traditional associations, and therefore when one is not consumed for a period of time, the body begins to crave it, and you are left thinking about the absence of this food in relation to your working. If, for example, you were going to cast a love spell, you could stop eating apples for a month in order to link your preliminary activities with the Witch's code and therefore with the working.

Active methods are extensions of subliminal techniques. These methods consist of therapeutic physical relaxations, such as meditation and bathing, in order to stimulate the mind into a peaceful state.

Through preliminary work, we are focused before we enter the circle. We have built up a reservoir of power for the working.

Whichever route you decide to take is up to you. Make sure that you are fully aware of what you are doing and how it will affect the working. Once you have achieved a considerable release of preliminary energy, you should be fit for the working. Good luck to you, and may the gods be with you!

## TOOLS OF THE TRADE

### The Altar

The defining feature of many Pagan traditions today is the use, symbolism, and placement of the altar and tools. Often the difference in a tool's lore can be the catalyst for the founding of a new tradition.

Ancient Paganism in its various traditions may not have used an altar as a focal point. Depending on the technology of the culture, the altar could be as simple as a tree stump or as complex as a marble sarcophagus. The Wiccan religion draws much of its inspiration from the cultures of Western Europe. Though many Wiccans will go to extraordinary lengths to prove the historical accuracy of their practices, many of the trappings of ritual descend from the ceremonial and occult groups of the nineteenth and twentieth centuries. The modern Pagan altar could be said to represent the remnants of the romanticised stone slabs of the Celtic Druids or the shrines to the *lare* and *lasa* of the ancient Roman households.

The altar is a personal shrine and expression of devotion to the gods. It can be any height, shape, or material, as long as it is still practical. Whether it be designed and constructed from scratch or bought brandnew from your local Pagan speciality store, the effect is the same: a physical manifestation of the universe within your home.

An altar is usually made of wood. Some traditions believe the altar must be crafted from a nonconductive material. This is said to heighten the effect of the conductive tools (the athame in particular) used to direct the energy within magickal work. Ultimately, the will of the Witch is the overriding factor of any ritual's success.

The main argument concerning altars is the positioning of them. Many Pagans (me included) place their altars in the east, the place of the rising sun. Other Pagans prefer to position their altars in the north, representative of the realm of the gods and of manifestation (in the Northern Hemisphere). Others will place their altar in the centre of the circle as a focal point to direct the raised energy.

Below, I have provided meanings for each cardinal direction, including centre, so you may make the informed choice of where to place your altar. (*Note:* I have given the Eurocentric elemental correspondences for symbolism's sake.)

East: Ruled by air, it is the birthplace of creativity, inspiration, wisdom, and eloquence. Home of the sylphs, the east is the beginning of new life. Place your altar in the east to receive the flowing gift of communication and to open the doors to the spiritual realms.

North: Ruled by earth, north is the home of the gods and assists in both the grounding and manifestation of your energy. To place your altar here is to link your energy to the physical world and to ensure a smoother transition of energy from the metaphysical worlds to the earthly planes. This is the realm of the gnomes. The gnomes are the humble warriors of your circle and will guard you well. North is the place of silence and secrecy.

West: Ruled by water, west is the realm of emotion, compassion, healing, and love. The west honours the cycles of life, death, and rebirth, and concentrates on the ancient, primal home of many of the world's goddesses. This is the kingdom of the merpeople, or undines, and to place the altar in the west is to honour the depths and darkness of the mystery.

South: Ruled by fire, this is the home of passion, integrity, courage, and power. Place your altar in the south to invoke determination, pride, and spontaneity. The south is the realm of the salamanders, amphibious creatures that can withstand fire, and is a place of change.

**Centre:** Ruled by Spirit, the centre of your circle is the apex of your cone of power. The centre is the pinnacle of focus within your sacred space and represents the creative energies of the universe. Place your altar in the centre to make the best of the natural channel within your circle and to honour the great unity of Spirit.

Altars are generally placed in your sacred space. However, if your sacred space is in a public park or garden, it would be best to keep your altar at home, in your room. If you are still in the broom closet, it is a good idea to have a portable makeshift altar. Store your materials and tools somewhere private. Otherwise, you can display your altar openly within your room.

Ultimately, the altar is the focal point of ritual and represents the physical qualities of Magick. The altar is the stage of the "play" of Magick, so to speak. All gestures, words, and physical symbolism enacted on its surface further intensify the link between the material world and the spiritual planes. The altar is the anchor of the ship of Magick, giving substance to the energy raised within the circle and supplying fertile land for the seeds of Magick to be sown. Your altar is the home of Magick in action. It is the filter of your intent and the translator of your symbolism; honour it well.

## Tools

The tools of Witchcraft are varied and can be extensive. No one Witch will have the same assortment of tools as the next.

Many Witches in restrictive situations do not own ritual tools, as this would compromise their security. This is fine, as one makes do with what they have. The very reasons we use things like candles, bells, and wands is to connect with the unconscious self. It is essential to remember that tools are not mere foci; they are our allies.

### Tool Etiquette

Tools are personal to each Witch. They are the physical representations of the Witch's Craft. Tools may be bought (newly or at second-hand stores), given as gifts, or found. However, each tool brings something new to the Witch's Craft. Each tool has specific correspondences, qualities and energies that help to inspire new feelings and experiences in our spirituality. Many Pagans form very close bonds with their tools (even physically) and will prefer not to go ahead with magickal work if the tool isn't present. However, these attachments to material objects are at times spiritually dangerous, instigating a psychological need. As such, there are a number of mores governing the handling of tools by others. The two main arguments constituting tool etiquette are (1) no one but the owner of the tool should be permitted to handle the tool, and (2) the handling and usage of the tool performed by trusted individuals further intensifies the energy of the tool.

The former stems from the more Ceremonially inclined folk who think of purity as energy bound unto itself, and the latter has links with the Eclectic and Kitchen Witch movements. I shall deal with both arguments respectively below.

The belief that if another person touches a tool it somehow contaminates the energy stems from the esoteric teachings of Ceremonialist orders. It is based on the idea that as each person has an energy imprint, a foreign touch may disrupt the flow of pure energy. This is because tools are ritually empowered and imbued with the personal energy of the Witch/magician. It is also a breach of trust to handle another's tools without asking permission beforehand. If you desire to make contact with another's tools, make sure you approach the person beforehand to ensure it is okay. Trust is deeply valued within Paganism, and to break these bounds is disrespectful at best.

The second argument is based on the idea that the handling of tools (by trusted individuals) increases the power and therefore its effectiveness. This seems to stem from the Eclectic-styled Kitchen Witch practices.

Kitchen Witchery is a tradition of the hearth and home and is centred on the family and practicality of Magick. I believe that this form of Witchcraft has the most historical credibility. As such, it can be assumed that children born into the homes of Kitchen Witches are encouraged to learn the Craft firsthand. They would be given permission to handle tools. A Pagan friend of mine who attended an open ritual I organised several years ago kindly allowed me to use her athame. I hesitated before taking it, but she simply said that the more power in it, the better.

Personally, I have no qualms with either argument. Basically it comes down to circumstance and feeling. Don't go chaining yourself to any particular school of thought unless you are completely confident in your choice. Allow yourself room for a flowing and less rigid philosophy. Ensure that you listen to your intuition when it decides to chime in.

Pagans honour respect, and while that definitely entails respect for others and respect for belongings, remember to save a little of that respect for yourself. Generally, tools should only be touched by folk with open minds.

## When in Circle...

The four main tools of Witchcraft constitute and mark the boundaries of the circle during ritual. Traditionally, each tool is ruled by a specific element.

There are generally three ways to mark the boundaries of the circle using tools. The first entails a traditional approach, the second is far more natural, and the third is practical. For simplicity's sake, I shall refer once again to the Eurocentric elemental orientation.

### TRADITIONAL APPROACH
- At north, place the pentacle
- At west, place the chalice or cauldron
- At south, place the athame
- At east, place the wand

NATURAL APPROACH
- At north, place a stone, dish of sand or soil, or crystal
- At west, place a shell or dish of water
  (preferably sea, spring, or rain water)
- At south, place a candle
- At east, place a stick of incense or a feather

PRACTICAL APPROACH
- At north, place a green candle
- At west, place a blue candle
- At south, place a red candle
- At east, place a yellow candle

You may also like to place a cauldron in the centre of your circle to symbolise the universal womb of creativity.

# THE TOOLS

Many of us have no use for tools. For some Pagans, it is easier to connect with the energies of the world through direct communion. Whatever your persuasion in terms of tools or lack thereof, it is important to know, understand, and appreciate the tools present in the Craft today.

## The Athame

The athame is traditionally (as dictated by the Wiccan traditions) a black-handled, double-edged, dull knife used to focus and direct energy. The preferable material for the blade is generally iron or steel, as these are said to conduct energy effectively. However, if you are planning on working with the Fey, then I suggest for both your sakes that you don't go anywhere near iron.

When I blessed my athame, I made sure that I communicated with the Fey that I was aware of their general dislike of human-forged metals. To honour them, I psychically removed the etheric charge from the metal that they would identify as being harmful. In doing this, I now feel comfortable using my athame in ritual with the Fey.

Many people have argued whether or not the athame does deserve the title of "the Witch's traditional tool" because of the historical implications. However, metal has been known and used for thousands of years now, and many peasants and farmers owned their own daggers, knives, sickles, and pitchforks, which were all made from metal.

In terms of symbolism, the athame is a phallic, or masculine, tool ruled by fire or air, depending on which tradition or logic you are using. Personally, I link the athame with fire, as the blade's physical appearance is striking and potentially dangerous, much like the flame. Also, fire was the primary tool of the blacksmith.

The athame is known for its part in the symbolic Great Rite, in which the athame (representing the God) is inserted into the chalice (representing the Goddess).

The sword, which features prominently in Ceremonial Magick, is aligned to the athame. The sword acts as a definer of the doors and boundaries of the circle, and the athame is suited to personalised, practical uses.

### The Besom

The besom (broomstick) has suffered the most from the literature and media of the modern day. The link of the broomstick with the Witch in popular culture has come from the Burning Times. Many of the accused "Witches" admitted to such acts as anointing broomsticks and staffs with "flying ointment," which then allowed the Witch to fly to the sabbat. This would lead many of us to wonder whether the broomstick was ever actually used in Witch rites.

The besom was first and foremost a tool of the peasantry. As Witchcraft was said to be more common among the agricultural communities, the besom became linked with it.

Primarily, the besom is a tool of fertility. The staff, which is phallic in nature, enters the bristles, representing the vagina. In modern Pagan handfasting rituals, the broomstick is leapt over at the end of the ceremony to ensure future happiness and even conception. As such, the besom is also used to signify a threshold.

One Beltaine, a close friend and I worked a ritual to aid her in conceiving. A storm was brewing over us, and I held my besom up high to the spirits of cloud and thunder and called on their power. I then placed the broomstick lovingly on the ground and I proclaimed the Great Rite through symbolism. It was then that my friend stepped across the besom, thus stepping across the threshold into a new reality. She was once told by doctors that she had little chance of becoming pregnant; today, her daughter Rhiannon is proof of the power of that night.

Another use of the besom is to exorcise, or sweep away, negative energy. In many cultures, it is taboo to sweep on certain auspicious days (e.g., Chinese New Year) as you will be sweeping away the good luck. This is akin to the idea that through clear intention, one can remove a place of negative vibes through the simple act of sweeping.

Throughout history, Witches have been rumoured to have the ability to fly, either with the help of a tool or psychotropic substance, on an animal, or on their own. This lingering belief probably comes from the fact that the original Witches could transcend the earthly plane and enter different, "higher" worlds. This may have filtered into medieval Witchcraft as astral projection or what the Witch may have thought of as physical flying. The recipe for the flying ointment is said to be full of hallucinogens, which can bring on varying levels of nonordinary reality and give the recipient the sensation of flying.

It could also be possible, as has been recounted constantly as means of explaining the history of the broomstick, that brooms were connected to the act of flying because of the discovery that Pagans would run across fields and leap through the air with brooms, pitchforks, and hobbyhorses between their legs to encourage the crops to grow higher.

### The Book of Shadows

The Book of Shadows derives from Gerald Gardner's book of the same name. The tome was used to record the rituals and lore of what came to be known as the Gardnerian tradition. The history and relevance of the Book of Shadows to Witches is obscured by several assumptions that tend to spark more debate than answer questions. It is believed that

Witchcraft was passed down orally through the generations. It has been claimed that the oral traditions are remnants of the Druidic belief that recording the sacred knowledge would dissipate its power and weaken the ability of one's memory.

The early recording of Witch lore on paper is very unlikely as the majority of Europe could not read or write, and in times of persecution any personal records of Witchcraft could be successfully used against the accused. However, there are documented instances in history where individuals accused of Witchcraft have been found with books containing magickal material.

The very term *Book of Shadows* has been likened to suggest that when Paganism went underground to survive, people began to record the lore and were forced to hide their books in darkness, hence "shadows." Others say that our entries into our books are shadows of truth and reflections of experiences that cannot possibly be captured by words.

In modern times, the fear of persecution and the threat of fatality are reduced, as each individual is protected by the law of their country and has free will. Today, Witches record their knowledge and understanding of Witchcraft and Paganism without fear of being discovered.

Many young Witches and Pagans today dismiss the term and embrace personalised descriptions. Some that I have heard in the past include Book of Light, Book of Mirrors, and Book of Illumination.

### The Candle

Candles offer a pinnacle of focus, and the flame is often described as the embodiment of the Witch's power and intent. They help to still the inner chatter of the mind. Through colours and scents, candles help to set the mood and to exude peace.

In terms of ritual, candles can be used to illuminate the space and to represent certain energies. If you haven't the time or money to buy the specific elemental tools used to mark the cardinal directions, then candles can be substituted (i.e., red for fire, yellow for air, green for earth, and blue for water). They can also be used to represent the God, Goddess, and Spirit energies in ritual, for those of Wiccan backgrounds.

In terms of symbolism, the candle can be equated with the rod of power, the cosmic phallus that connects the spiritual planes with our material one. Most occult spiritualities make use of a pillar-like object in their rituals to connect with the divine. In Voudoun and the Correllian Nativist Tradition it is the *poto mitan*, a grounded pole or pillar. Think of Beltaine and undoubtedly the image of a pole decorated with greenery and ribbons will come to mind. Towers are also symbols of earth power connecting to the heavens and have been considered in the past to be phallic symbols relating to the dragon energies of earth. Even Catholicism makes use of this metaphysical law in the construct of its cathedrals, specifically the spire. The spire concentrates the collective power of the prayers within the cathedral and sends them out to God. The spire is also known as the finger of God. As it is impossible to erect tall, polelike structures at every ritual or spell, we can make use of candles instead.

Candles are most often employed in spells, as they are a very simple yet effective technique of Magick. It is generally the colour of the candle that is harnessed to evoke specific emotions and feelings. Also, candles are sold in most stores and are comfortably cheap.

There are a few intriguing superstitions that modern Witches hold regarding candles and their flames that I would like to mention here. The belief that blowing a candle out will anger the fire elementals (as air is being used to dominate them) or blow away the Magick is one particular custom with origins that are obscure. I have been told by a Hedge Witch that the actual origins of this tradition hearken back to British folklore. She warned that blowing out a candle might also cause the wax to spurt onto the facing wall; the shape it took would be a portent of one's death. Therefore, Witches make a rule of not blowing out candle flames to avoid seeing into one's own death.

I personally do not blow out candles, I pinch the flames out. Scott Cunningham wrote that this was locking in one's power, ensuring the efficacy of the spell cast. I think of it merely as being reverent.

## The Cauldron

The cauldron has been transformed from a harmless cooking pot into the birthplace of the Witch's malice. Originally, the cauldron was a universal cooking vessel. It was also used to boil the water for bathing and washing. Coincidentally, the cauldron had its place in the hearth. Therefore, it can be assumed that through these practical applications, a secondary use for the cauldron as a tool of Magick evolved.

The cauldron wins its place in myth from the story of Cerridwen and the birth of Taliesin. In the Welsh myth, Cerridwen, who is later deified[1] as a Mother Goddess of wisdom and Magick, brews an elixir for her dumb son in her cauldron to bless him with deftness and skill. The complete process took a year and a day, and Cerridwen ordered a young servant boy, Gwion Bach, to watch over and stir the brew. As the last day arrived and Gwion looked over the brim of the cauldron, three potent drops of potion landed on his thumb. Immediately, Gwion Bach sucked on his burnt thumb to cool the affliction and became imbued with great power and wisdom. In an attempt to thwart his mistress, he shapeshifted and escaped. However, Cerridwen was alerted, and thus begins a great chase, where both Gwion and Cerridwen change into several different forms until Gwion becomes a grain and Cerridwen, in the form of a hen, eats him. Unbeknownst to Cerridwen, she becomes impregnated with the seed of Gwion Bach, and after nine months a babe is born with the same powers and wisdom Gwion had acquired. Cerridwen, who is wooed by the beauty of the child but wishes to be rid of him, throws the babe into a river, wrapped in a leather bag. The child is later discovered by a man called Elphin. The child is named Taliesin, meaning "radiant brow," and he later became the great bard of Celtic lore.

Along with this myth, there are many other stories and films that convey the cauldron as a tool of sorcery. There are several medieval woodcuttings portraying haggard women surrounding cauldrons and

---

1 It is believed that the characters in Celtic myths (as recorded by Christian scribes) are actually older Pagan divinities who were stripped of this identity so as not to conflict with the premise of an almighty God.

throwing various pieces of animals into the brew. Today, we use cauldrons mainly for the aesthetic theatrics and spiritual symbolism.

The cauldron is a vessel of the Cosmic Goddess and of water, symbolising the universal womb of transformation. It is a place of potential and creativity. Often, the cauldron is used in substitution for the chalice in the symbolic Great Rite.

The cauldron represents all that is feminine and receptive in this universe and is often the focal point of ritual in which written petitions to the gods are burnt and fires are made to concentrate the energy raised. The bowl of the cauldron is often said to be the place where wisdom is born, and as such cauldrons are often employed to assist in acts of divination.

The cauldron also features in many shamanic tales that speak of demonic forces tearing apart the spirit and body, which is then mended and made whole (within the cauldron) by the guardians of the cauldron and the sisters of Fate, who sing over the bones. This is a common mythic theme across Europe and Asia. It is an archetypal truth that speaks of facing the shadow to be reborn anew in the guise of the wounded healer.

### The Chalice

For centuries, it has been a gesture of peace and friendship to offer a cup or chalice of liquid to another. This ritual harks back to Pagan times, when hospitality was one of the greatest virtues.

The chalice is the ceremonial goblet used to hold the ritual wine (or whatever liquid you are using) and to act as the feminine tool in the symbolic Great Rite (see "The Athame," page 246). As the chalice is receptive in nature, it is linked with the womb and therefore the Cosmic Goddess. Often the chalice is placed in the western quarter to symbolise the element. A chalice may be made from a variety of materials, including stone, wood, and metal. They can be jewel-encrusted and carved with various occult symbols relating to either water or the Goddess.

In Christian mythology, it is linked with the holy grail, referring to the chalice Jesus drank from at the Last Supper and that which caught his blood at his crucifixion. In the Arthurian legends, the Knights of the Round Table are on an eternal journey to seek out the holy grail and to behold the sight of God.

Many feminist Witches today speak of the holy grail as being a metaphor for the attainment of that which is at the end of desire. It has also been suggested that as the knights seeking the grail were men, then the holy grail must symbolise the feminine spirit (the anima) they yearn for.

## The Pentacle

As an elemental tool, the pentacle is placed in the quarter representing earth and often takes the form of a flat stone or disc with a pentagram drawn or painted on it, among other symbols.

Perhaps the reason the pentagram represents the earthy qualities of existence is its association with the form of the human body. This was best demonstrated by Leonardo da Vinci in his drawing of the Vitruvian Man, in which a naked man is shown lying sprawled in the midst of geometric patterns. His arms are held at even length and his legs are apart. If a line was drawn from head to leg, leg to arm, and so on, the pentagram manifests.

The word *pentacle* itself is believed to descend from Ceremonial Magick and the old grimoires that attest to Qabalistic influence. High Magick is a very goal-orientated system and calls upon the aid (evocation) of various orders (both demonic and angelic, usually of Judaic origin) to assist in the obtaining of success. Pentacles are created by high magicians in order to promote particular planetary energies within their rituals; they are also worn on the person for various reasons, but largely to protect.

## The Wand

The wand has long been associated with Witches and Wizards in popular culture. The Harry Potter series features the wand prominently as a tool of "wizardry" and sorcery. Generally, the wand is very similar to the athame in its functions, e.g., the channelling and projecting of energy. The wand, however, has often been given a far more passive role in ritual despite its long history and association with the Craft.

In almost all ancient civilisations, the staff (simply a larger wand) has been seen as a symbol of authority and power. The Egyptian pharaohs are often depicted in their mummified form with a shepherd's crook and whip crossed over their chests. This is believed to have symbolised the influence of pharaoh as both law enforcer and king in the afterlife—the shepherd's crook symbolizing love and guidance, and the whip his authority and dominion.

In ancient Greece, the kerykeion (or caduceus), the rod of Hermes, was an instrument of healing and balance. The familiar insignia of two serpents entwining a winged rod is now a well-known symbol of the modern medical profession. In fact, the staff of Asklepios (also associated with medicine) also consists of a serpent and a staff. Biblical tales in the Old Testament tell of Moses' staff, which was given to him by God as a channel for his divine power. With the staff, Moses bloodied the Nile River and parted the Red Sea to deliver the Jews to freedom.

There are countless literary references to the wand and staff as an instrument of the divine and of Magick. In Wiccan covens today, the wand is often secondary to the athame, which is odd, as the athame's intimate association with Witches seems to have sprung out of nowhere, whereas the wand has always traditionally accompanied the Witch.

In my coven, we have both a wand and an athame. We generally cast a circle with our athame; however, if we are invoking the elements with a tool, then we work with the wand, because we feel that the elementals are far more receptive to wood than to metal (which to them would be regarded as an implement of careless human destruction).

As a phallic symbol associated with the Wiccan fertility god (think of the thyrsus-carrying maenads who dance for Dionysos), the wand is seen as corresponding to either fire or air. It is my personal opinion that somewhere along the way, the traditional lore relating to the wand and athame became interchanged due to their phallic symbolism and similar functions. I tend to connect the wand with air, as traditionally, wood was used to fashion the tool, which in its original form of a tree bends to the winds, whereas the athame's blade is forged in the fire.

Traditionally, the length of the wand should span from the crook of the elbow to the tip of the index finger. In terms of width and size, you should be able to comfortably hold the wand in between your thumb and index finger. Most wands are straight in nature to aid in focus, but I know for a fact that a slightly curved or bent wand will not hinder the flow of energy, as my first wand was a bent piece of wood and worked spectacularly. Also, there are certain types of woods that are favoured. For example, rowan, apple, oak, and willow are said to produce the best wands, but ultimately the tree your wand comes from shouldn't matter at all, as long as the wand suits your purpose.

However you find (or buy) your wand, the experience and initial power lies in the connection felt between the wand and yourself. There must always be an element of familiarity between you and your tools.

## ECLECTIC TRENDS

Eclecticism has always existed within the Pagan community. Wicca is itself a healthy fusion of a collection of metaphysical and spiritual traditions. However, because of its early place in NeoPagan history, it has become what is "traditional." Then again, Norse Heathens would argue vehemently against the suggestion that Wicca is traditional, as Heathens have a particularly strong link to their history and their ancestral lands. It is clear that tradition, history, and culture form the foundation for NeoPaganism.

Over time, the exclusivity of Wiccan covens and their scarcity spurred a silent revolution in the community. Publications such as Rae Beth's *Hedge Witch* and Scott Cunningham's *Wicca: A Guide for the Solitary Practitioner* have given ample reason and support for both the solitary path and self-initiation. Prior to this, both were perceived as being of lesser value than membership in a traditional coven and were considered to invalidate the individual's experience. Nowadays, the number of solitary practitioners is presumed to outnumber coven-bound Witches, and the concept of self-initiation (or no ceremonial initiation at all) is completely valid, at least in the eyes of the majority. The overwhelming embrace of the solitary life has led to the discovery of Eclecticism and its positive aspects. Despite the somewhat flimsy New Age hue of the Eclectic approach, there is certainly a sense of cohesion, personality, and creativity that is primary in all Eclectic styles. The prevailing reluctance against Eclectics among the minority may be understood as an insecurity or unwillingness to breach cultural and religious boundaries. Or perhaps it is a case of superiority based on the belief that a specific tradition is the be-all and end-all. Whatever it is, there arises a question of respect whenever the topic of Eclectic Paganism crops up.

As Pagans, respect is high on our priority list, and to intend harm is a crime of great measure. The belief that Eclectics relish the chance to steal from another's belief system or cultural practice is absurd! The very reason for Eclecticism is the impersonality within the current traditions, which then inspires the individual to focus on their own needs, desires, and preferences and develop a spirituality that draws on the rhythm of the heart. In both practice and theory, Eclectics are particularly astute in focusing on their own growth and reconnecting with the primal patterns of their soul. Intent is not a matter of incision or cunning but rather the subtle channelling of what the inner self already knows as truth. To illustrate this, I shall introduce a fictional character by the name of Rachael and tell her story.

Rachael has been studying with an Alexandrian high priestess for the past four months and is working towards her first-degree initiation; however, the more she learns about the Alexandrian tradition, the more she realises that its Ceremonial elements will not serve the unfurling pace of her own magickal journey. When Rachael discusses this with her teacher, the high priestess smiles knowingly and congratulates Rachael on listening to the beat of her own drum. Before they part, the high priestess recommends a few books and individuals whom Rachael might find helpful in her journey to spiritual fulfilment.

The next morning, Rachael travels into the city and heads for the local occult bookstore. There she purchases Scott Cunningham's *Wicca: A Guide for the Solitary Practitioner* and *Living Wicca: A Further Guide for the Solitary Practitioner,* as well as Phyllis Currot's *Book of Shadows*. On talking with the store clerk, she is drawn into an in-depth conversation about the intricacies of spirituality and the beauty and vibrancy of Paganism. The store clerk, who is fascinated by Rachael, suddenly mentions a new book entitled *The Dancing Shaman,* which he believes Rachael will find interesting. After perusing the contents and the blurb, Rachael agrees and collects her purchases before leaving.

In the next three days, Rachael devours book after book, discovering a mystical world steeped in the symbolism and dreaming of the unconscious mind. Working with the practical structure of *Living Wicca,* Rachael begins to flesh out her core principles and practices while forming a greater understanding of herself. Finally she reaches her last book, *The Dancing Shaman.* Upon opening the book, Rachael is suddenly struck by a strange sense of déjà vu, and the words seem to writhe and vibrate. That night, after having finished the book, she walks into her room and retrieves her athame and a torch from the kitchen.

Rachael stands beside a glistening stream and, breathing deeply, she centres herself, growing more and more aware of the blood that pulses within her veins. Spirals flutter along her periphery and the world slips away; there is nothing, and yet all of creation is within this concentration of being. Entranced, Rachael's body moves to the patterned lessons of Alexandrian Wicca. She casts the circle and invokes the quarters. Then, in accordance with the teachings of *The Dancing Shaman,* Rachael withdraws to the void and enters a world of rippling darkness and shattered light—a world that is strangely familiar to her.

Rachael journeys through the landscape of her mind, searching for what calls her. Then suddenly a flash of light illuminates the shroud of grey and a many-faceted diamond appears, wedged in the dark earth. Rachael hesitates and a sense of foreboding overtakes her body. But persistence, curiosity, and faith coax her forth, and her slender hand reaches for the diamond. Upon contact, the air around her begins to shake dangerously and blinding white light floods her vision. A voice, so pure, ignites in the fissure of silence, and a flowing meld of notes forms a distinct understanding inside of Rachael. *"All things are reflections of the other, and it can only be within that truth weaves a path of its own. Freedom is but a flame upon the torch of the divine, and choice is the hand that bears it."*

Rachael opens her eyes and finds herself lying down beside the stream, the fresh glimmer of dawn light dappling her pink skin. The inner journey that Rachael experienced the night before returns to her memory, and the soft lull of morning gently caresses her. Standing, Rachael is overflowing with an exuberance she has never felt before. A harmonic resonance of something special remains within her; an ancient wisdom courses through her being. She looks to the subtle sphere that surrounds her, the vague shimmer of something more, and sighs a note of release. Rachael farewells the elemental guardians and opens the circle in the Alexandrian fashion, for it is something that she has grown close to and feels is useful. She walks from the stream, never looking back, for she knows that she will spend many nights with the company of her Self and Nature.

At home later on, Rachael calls the high priestess and relays her experiences. The priestess listens patiently, absorbing Rachael's words.

"Last night, I was told that freedom is the key, that choice is my path. And now I understand that I should do what feels right to me."

The high priestess pauses and smiles before she speaks. "A path is three things. The foundation upon which it is laid—this is its strength, its security, the reason it exists in the first place. The second is its direction and movement—its turns, its surroundings, and its focus. And the third is the traveller, the Fool of the Tarot. This is you, and you are choice. For the mystery is that as you walk and as you make the decisions about which way to turn, what you want to see along your journey, what experiences you would like to encounter, you create your own path. For in truth, there is no foundation but you, and there is no direction but you."

After the phone call, Rachael turns and walks to her bedroom. Kneeling by her altar tools, Rachael pledges an oath.

"The path I walk is a mirror. It reflects that which I seek and yearn for. It is the cultivation of effort, energy, and spiritual union. The path I walk is mine and forever shall it be. Blessed by the gods and by Magick, so let it be."

Rachael's story is one of seeking. It is typical of those who desire metamorphosis—all those who are willing to break free from traditional moulds and embrace their divinity. This is the central truth of the Eclectic way. There is no disrespect, infringement, or flaky naïvety. Instead, there is contemplation, understanding, deepening, and honesty. For it is in the face of the Self that we must learn to be open and ultimately accepting. In fact, I often remark that Eclecticism is the best thing that has ever happened to the Pagan community. After all, the arrogance and exclusivity communicated by many tradition-obsessed individuals and groups does more harm to our spirituality than good.

Tradition marks intervals along our road of progression. It indicates what worked for a certain group of people and when it did. The Eclectic is timeless, forever changing with the tide and looking deeper into the mysteries of life, never feeling imposed on or restricted. Paganism was never meant to be dogmatic.

Eclecticism is natural. It is our innate curiosity and our willingness to participate upon observation. Tradition is our inheritance, not necessarily a stagnant remnant of the past but a romantic and subtle aspect of our own identities. At all times we should actively question what appears backward or useless while at the same time acknowledging what works.

Eclecticism and tradition are not adversaries. They are simply two different things that cross paths and seem to deny the other. Hopefully, the next time they meet, reconciliation will be first on the priority list.

# 13: INTO THE FUTURE

*We are an old people, we are a new people.*
*We are the same people, stronger than before.*
—Morning Feather and Will Shepardson

## AN ERA OF CHANGE

We are living in a time of social upheaval, environmental unrest, political folly, and spiritual ambiguity. Boundaries are blurred, dogma rejected, and systematic public liaisons are no longer fodder for the masses. The propagandist tricks of the government are passing into the tides of karma, and all seems to hang in the balance.

There is a cosmic shift occurring on a grand scale. The New Age, perhaps? The transition from Pisces into Aquarius (finally)? Or is it something else—deeper, primal, and grounded within the old mysteries of the earth? Being a Pagan, I am somewhat biased towards its terminology, and therefore I call this energy shift, this transition into a new era of change, the Greening.

### The Greening

*Deep beneath the shade and power*
*Of this Tree we call our Tower*
*Day is fleeting, shadows fall*
*Across the Path our feet touch all*

*End to end the Circle's Path*
*Blazing, shining, as we laugh*
*Dance the merry round with spark*
*As we Witches tread the dark*

*Wheel turning, eight-rayed sun*
*Spiral serpents birth the One*
*Crescent Moon lays down her claim*
*To her lover, hanging lame*

*And we the Witches of WildWood*
*Stand where ancient stones once stood*
*Now the Greening seeks the Grove*
*And that which rests in treasure trove.*

—*The Call to WildWood* used by the Coven of the WildWood
and written by Gede Parma, 2006

The Greening is a force of the primal wild. It is an etheric current of infinite possibility that drives into the very heart of the vessel and shakes the firmament of what we call creation, of what we know as the kingdom (the power-current wielded by sovereignty). Its garment is the splendour of a higher vibration. It is both celestial and terrestrial, deriving from the star-strung stellar regions and the pulse of Gaia herself. The earth dances and spirals as the cosmos contracts and expands, and wave after wave of the Greening is focussed into a finer and finer thread, and then into ivy that will cover the earth. So what is this Greening, anyway?

Whether by divine decree of the gods or because of the shameless desecration of this earth and her resources, the Greening has been conjured, and it has heard its charge. Like the serpent at the base of the World Tree, it is rising, and like fire, the energy is being felt. Soon it will merge with the boundaries of earth and become the ouroboros, symbol of eternity, the continuum. It will circle about the earth and then, at some point, all will break loose, the skin will be shed and swallowed, and the dance of chaos will ensue. A cleansing will eventuate and all will come to the scourge. Earth Mother will rid herself of all that stagnate and conserve outworn strictures. I have seen the gods gathering and taking their mounts, weapons in hand, to begin their Wild Hunt. A gathering of forces is at hand, and many are blissfully ignorant. To aid in rebalancing the earth and bringing peace to this paradise, we should aim to live our lives with honour and respect and do all we can to cherish, celebrate, and care for our Mother.

Before I was dedicated to the Coven of the WildWood, I lived my solitude in the Craft in earnest (and still do to this day). However, despite visions and sensations of the heightening Greening experienced by my coven, I sensed this oncoming power long before.

*"An old and ancient power is returning—opposites/enemies will blend— things will not appear as they are. A dark shroud clouds us to the deeper changes now—an old charge will be fulfilled."* This passage comes from one of my old Books of Shadows, and it came from a vision I had several years ago while gazing in my dark mirror. At the time, I thought it may have referred to my path, but as it stands, it seems to prophesy the Greening in perfection. Since then, I have received countless visions, and through my own self and my work with the coven, I/we have been witness to many wonders. But things are moving—and at a pace that defies any rationale on progression. For the Greening, most naturally, rides with the cyclic flow of Nature, and in doing so, the seed becomes the sprout, which becomes the tree, whose fruit then falls to sow the seed of itself and to begin the process anew. A forest will cover the world, and this is the charge the Old Ones decree.

What can this all mean to the Pagan youth who are uncertain of their place in the world and of their destinies? To those who are priest/ess born, it means devotion and service to the current as it unfurls. To the Witches, it can mean spirit flight to the astral sanctuaries to view the process of it all, and it also may entail magickal work to aid and empower the Greening tide. To the Pagans, it means pausing to listen and to open the senses to the amazing cacophony of voices that are chanting for the Greening to blossom.

We have an obligation to the future, but we must be ever diligent in the present moment, working for compassion, peace, love, and trust, and dispelling the ruthless tyranny that seeks to root out and destroy the beautiful anarchy that our spirits pertain to.

### The Age of Anarchy

*Each one of us is one alone*
*Upon the earthly, mortal throne*
*To live and die and be reborn*
*This is the making of our scorn*

*In service to the Gods most high*
*These men do murder, rape and lie*
*Sated innocence of flame*
*Lay siege to unwarranted acclaim*

*Danger darkens heaven's lustre*
*And Woman beckons those who trust her*
*Power over is power won*
*Until the debt is paid and done*

*For truth is greater than one stone*
*Though men scar Earth—pillaged and hewn*
*Radiate eternal skies*
*And sear the flesh of unseeing eyes*

*Looking upward, spiral down*
*Where is the path, the middle ground?*
*Temple pillars, strong and proud*
*About the sacred site they crowd*

*Solomon is seated near*
*The two who bide the blue-robed seer*
*Columns, black and white, do pierce*
*The fearful gaze of ignorance fierce*

*Love is love and love is fire*
*Come forth by true heartfelt desire*
*Flesh and body wither and wane*
*But pain inflicted will remain*

*Now rules the cruel, oppressive king*
*The tyrant dancing in his ring*
*A ring of malice, cruelty, greed*
*His sickness spawned within his seed*

*The Serpent stirs within her sleep*
*She battles for what she will keep*
*She swallows fools, destroying fear*
*The Age of Anarchy is here.*

—Gede Parma, 2005

## THE GREENING CREW

We must never forget that within the riddle of the prophecy, there is always a solution offered—a promise beseeched to the people from the divine. In this case, Gaia has made her message clear, and she declares that it will be the "bringer of peace" who will clear the debris after the destruction and once more ignite the flame of the sacred within the heartland of earth.

I have seen the great Earth Mother tower like a mountain cradling our planet, and her eyes are brimming with rage and despair. We have forsaken her and fallen into a routine of desecration. We have opted for transcendence over immanence; we have forgotten and dismissed the delicate balance between what is within and what is without, what is illusion and what is reality. We can no longer tell the difference. Our minds collectively grapple with the consumerist tendencies of this day and age, built upon a concrete slab of industrialisation. But we must re-member. We must restore the lost fragments of our souls if we are to champion the cause of the sovereign and invoke the Blessed One of Light, born from the darkest hour. This is our prophecy. The once and future king...how could we forget?

The "Greening crew" is the term my coven uses when referring to those involved directly with receiving messages from the gods concerning the Greening (oracles, signs, omens, and indeed their own literal words) and who also battle on the astral with destructive thoughtforms[1] seeking to implant notions of separation and subjugation within our psyches. Across the globe there has been an awakening, and Pagan or not, there are myriad individuals who feel within their core that there is something to be done (now)! They feel restless, useless if left idle, as if they need to be doing something, but they are unsure of what that something is. The physical laws of our universe seem to impinge on the forces that are peaking within them as latent realities stir. I know all of this because I have felt it. I have imparted the message, and now I must teach and work with those who are to come. We of this experience are the messengers and the teachers.

A messenger is one who feels and lives the reality that I have described above, though words cannot do justice to the frustration that ensues when self-doubt and uncertainty seek to blot out the broader possibilities. The teachers are those who are drawn into roles of responsibility and leadership, and who often find themselves offering support, advice, and words of wisdom. A teacher can be intolerably harsh, but this is necessary in the grand scheme of things. We can also be bright, loving, and merciful. We embody she who is most enraged at this current time: the Sovereign Queen herself—the indwelling dragon-fuelled vital flow of power that is land, that is earth. She is more than Mother. She is Creatrix, Celestial, Scourge, Destroyer, Dancer of Life, Preserver, and Decay. She is the matrix of Nature, the spiral pattern that connects us to what was once, and still is, the WildWood of the Witches. May it flourish in our hearts and minds forever.

Interestingly, my coven seems to attract these folk, and we have received intuitions of the whereabouts of several other messengers globally. I have received glimpses and psychic flashes of teachers who have sought me out simply to say *we are here, you are not alone in your task.*

---

1 These negative thoughtforms are both products of the corrupt dealings that are occurring daily between politicians and world leaders, and parasiticlike entities that seek to influence through psychic contact (thereby connecting with the desired host). Psychically they appear to be black, oozing sluglike creatures, though there are several variations. I have had an octopuslike thoughtform attempt to intercept during my magickal work.

The Great Mystery does not seek to obscure or confuse, nor does she toy. By the sky, the land, and the sea, she has wrought her message, and it is up to us to convince humanity of the rest. This is not a crusade of conversion; this is a wake-up call to those who slumber, tucked away beneath their own ignorance.

My coven, in one of its many facets, is a Greening crew. I teach the messengers what I know of psychic self-defence, of working with energy, of drawing down the gods, of sight and the divine. Magick is of utmost importance in our endeavour; it is at once one of our most sacred principles and also the life force with which we shift and shape the folds of Wyrd to attain necessity or desire. We gather together to aid the Greening forces. This is not a task reserved for specially assigned individuals; this is something we can all participate in. In fact, at the Pagan Summer Gathering 2007 (a Church of All Worlds event), a fellow priest and I led a cone of power ritual to aid the Greening, and we received only glowing response from the participants. It really hit hard with all of them.

If you feel as if this all has something to do with you, feel free to contact me, and I will gladly discuss with you what I know—what the Great Ones have decided to tip me on this week (divine updates, if you will). Let's embrace the change; after all, it is the Law. Remember, however, that the Greening is a reality; it will come (is here), and its tide will be felt by all. Like the Christian vision of an apocalypse, the ending of the Kali Yuga, the Ragnarok of Norse legend, the Mayan year of great change and upheaval (2012), the Arthurian mythos played out—it is all myth suggesting a convergence and therefore a death of the old and rebirth of the new. Order or (and) chaos, who knows?

## OBLIGATIONS: TOMORROW'S LEADERS

Who holds the light of the way into the future? Who will remain when our elders depart to the fair realms and bid us farewell? It is the youth, and we are the Hidden Children—the leaders of tomorrow.

## The Hidden Children

*Hidden Children by the fire*
*Dancing, singing of desire*
*Cloaked in secrets, shadow dwelt*
*Ancient power seen and felt*
*Here we stand between the worlds*
*Circle marked and light unfurled*
*Air and Fire, Water, Earth*
*Bless our spells and give them birth!*
—from "Invocation of the Two" by Gede Parma, 2006

The Pagan youth of today are a spirited bunch! From what I have seen of late, we are also diverse. In the Coven of the WildWood, our circles often consist of both experienced and inexperienced practitioners. There are those who have been at it for most of their current incarnations (and most certainly their previous ones) and those who come as the neophyte to the sword. We are an ecstasy-driven, earth-based Pagan group that upholds perfect love and perfect trust as best we can.

The majority of Pagans are "hidden," and any division in the community because of age, race, gender, or sexuality is perceived as sheer prejudice. Films such as *The Craft* have damaged our reputation in that some choose to identify us with power-obsessed fantasists. My coven's focus is on spiritual awakening, celebration of Nature's rhythms, and homage paid to the Old Ones. We leave power-over to the politicians and power-with to the Pagans.

The Hidden Children are those who feel at home within the beauty, peace, and rhythm of the natural world and who are inspired by its chaos and power. We live in a time of conflict and uncertainty. A Pagan friend of mine once told me that uncertainty leads to doubt, and therein lies the truth. With all the doubt that infests this world, that corrupts the purity of the heart and denies the passionate embrace shared between the seeker and Life, there is little room for one to wonder at the raw power of Nature and the cosmos. The Hidden Children, however, rebel against that which wrests free consciousness from the soul and immerse themselves entirely in the now.

We are cloaked by the shadows of secrets long lost to the shifting sands of time. We work with the power (Magick), and this is no tomfoolery; it is a serious undertaking, crossing over the boundary of no return. What is there but the power we know through our work and spirituality, and how shall we wield this power? What kind of individual does it take to genuinely and respectfully represent our communities, values, and wisdom to the world? Is this a path reserved solely for the priesthood? What does it mean to be a priest/ess? What does it mean to be a Witch? What does it mean to be Pagan? What does it mean to be youth?

## As a Priest/ess...

Does the Paganism of the twenty-first century and the future require a priesthood? Are there lay Pagans and those of us who are called to service? In my experience, there is little difference that exists, at least in the Witch traditions, between those who are the priests and priestesses and those who integrate the principles of Magick into their lives as a tool for self-empowerment.

We are each our own priest/ess; there is no middleman. However, within my own coven there are those who are working toward priesthood via their initiation and those who simply await initiation as a gateway into further knowledge and insight. This may demonstrate the varying levels of readiness in terms of taking on the vows of service to the gods from person to person; however, I can attest to the concept of being priest-born.

In past Pagan civilisations, there was a thin line between the priesthood and the laity. Throughout the Fertile Crescent in the Mediterranean, the state religions employed officiating priests whose job it was to oversee ritual sacrifices, ceremonies, and festivals. There were both male and female priests, and they were either born into the role or chosen for it by key political figures and also by the families of the nobility.

Being a priest or priestess in these societies was in sharp contrast to the concept of the clergy nowadays within the Abrahamic faiths. For instance, the minister, vicar, imam, and rabbi are all trained and consecrated figureheads representing the power and authority (not necessarily the persona) of the divinity (the supreme Godhead) of the church, mosque, or synagogue they serve, respectively. They are human and mortal, of course, but they are endowed with unequivocal wisdom (at least in the eyes of their laity). They are the appointed officials of their faith and therefore are elevated in that they are also the ones who reprimand sin and preach doctrine and dogma to the masses. A Pagan priest/ess was not one to preach or to lay down law and order; their service was to celebrate the divine through ritual and consecration and act as a spiritual vessel. They propitiated the gods, but it was not their will or power alone that secured a response, it was the collective energy raised by the congregation that gave power to the gathering. This is mirrored in the covencraft of Witches and the large gatherings common to Paganism.

In the Greek and Roman religious traditions, there existed the priests of the state temples that enshrined the cults of various deities, and the celebrants, who worshipped within their own homes in what is known to historical scholars as private religion, or faith of the hearth. Interestingly, it was generally the hearth (the sacred spiritual centre/heart of the home) that was largely the focus of offerings, prayers, and blessings made by the residing family.

In Roman tradition there was an altar made to the *lare*, who represented the ancestral spirits, and in Greek culture there was the *agathos daimon*, who was the "good spirit" that protected the family and was often symbolised by a serpent. It is therefore clear that within the privacy of the home, each individual was able to communicate with the gods and with the spirits of place simply by willing it and offering an appropriate libation whilst reciting a prayer of praise. While this is sometimes reflected in today's Christian culture through charismatic worship and prayer, there still remains no notion of offering or of a sacred interchange indicative of an honourable relationship with the divine. It seems that many of these charismatic Christians nowadays (in Dionysian style) abandon ego and allow themselves to be absorbed into the collective energy body that is their church. While this is a valid pathway to enlightenment, they often forget to allow themselves to step back, reclaim their individuality, and then once more assert their unity with God. Grounding is a technique for everyone!

What, then, of the priest/esses of the Paganism of today? Within the various Witch traditions, all who are brought to the sword and initiated are consecrated priest/esses and serve the gods in perfect love and perfect trust. In this endeavour, they are often supported by their coven. Solitary Witches often find themselves yearning for a similar experience or else stylise their own practice into a spiritual tradition that embodies the principles of covencraft.

The idea of a high priest or high priestess descends from the British Traditional groups, and while these two can sometimes be volunteers (in the case of open rituals), they are generally individuals who have been through the third degree and therefore claim the right to hive off from their coven and start a group of their own. In some traditions, the titles of "Witch Queen" and "Magus" are bestowed upon the initiated females and males respectively. At the worst of times I find this to be all a grand ceremonial wank, and at the best simply grand.

In its purity, the concept of a Pagan priesthood is not about ascending through the ranks to claim certain titles. Things like "Witch Queen" and "Magus" are not conducive to the transcendence of ego that is a necessary prerequisite to becoming a high priest/ess to begin with. Ceremonies and rites of passage that mark specific phases of the human journey through growth and decline, such as croning and saging rituals, are a much better idea.

The idea of a priest/ess holding leadership rights over a congregation in the name of ascension through degrees is not one that remains popular with the vast amount of Pagans today, many of whom are not necessarily interested in being initiated at all. So where does this leave those who aren't Witches? What does it truly mean to be a Pagan priest/ess today?

There are various skills and qualities that are generally associated with the Pagan priesthood. They are to be adept at various magickal techniques or otherwise ritualistic skills (if they are not Witches), have patience, be trustworthy, and be good teachers and even greater listeners. They are counsellors and comforters, oracles and vessels for the gods. They are able to transcend their ego and draw down into themselves (invoke) a deity or spirit for the purpose of insight, divination, and perhaps even as a symbol of a coven/group mystery. In my time with the Coven of the WildWood, I have done all of the above and more, and without having to publicise or cheapen myself, I have become exactly what I have wished to be for my brothers and sisters, and of course my gods. I am both priest and Witch. As I stand, so do I kneel.

### As a Witch ...

Many who know me know that I view my Craft as non-religious, meaning I do not acquiesce to dogma and doctrine. I am a Witch, pure and simple. I capitalise it because it has spiritual meaning for me and because I honour the word and its spirit by doing so. What does it mean to be a Witch in the twenty-first century?

When Wicca was first brought to the attention of the Western world in the mid-twentieth century, there was plenty of heated argument concerning its authenticity as an unbroken, intact Pagan Nature-based tradition that honoured the old gods of England, as this is what Gardner professed it be. Gerald Gardner, who came to be Wicca's (*Wica's*) main propounder and is now considered to be the father of modern Witchcraft by many in the community, is remembered today as a fraud, a charlatan, a man of many titles, and above all as a great Witch. The term *Wicca* was never considered to be a variation of Witchcraft, it was used synonymously with Witchcraft. As Eclectic trends grew more popular among magickal practitioners, a distinction was made between the traditions that were thought to represent the "truth" and the "heresies" that were diverging from them. There is also some conflict between those belonging to "pre-Gardnerian" family traditions or covens, who do not ally themselves with the word *Wicca*.

For there to be a Pagan heresy is an oxymoron in itself; therefore, for one to condemn another of it is to diminish the wild current underlying our power and vision. As Witches, we cultivate this rich vibrancy as a necessity; it is part of our charge, what we breathe in daily. To ignore the divine current, its continuum and cycle, is to deny the truth and beauty instilled within the heart.

Witchcraft is a spiritual tradition of Life, which embraces the heart and draws forth all its yearnings and innermost desires so that they may blossom and bear fruit.

Witchcraft has been described by many, historically and even in recent times, as a (sub)culture of parody and desecration. We do parody and desecrate, but this is limited to what the normative feels is opposite to the principles of social conservation. Witches work to fight against the separation of matter and spirit; we seek to unite the "profane" with the "sacred" and to bring forth and reveal the Shining. One of our most holy rites is, of course, the Great Rite (*Hieros Gamos*, the High Marriage), which unites apparent polar opposites (personified generally by the masculine and the feminine) and then celebrates the oneness between the two that is, in truth, innate. It is the illusion of separation that enhances this perception for the majority of people.

Witchcraft bears no message or hope of salvation from earth, nor does it preach dogma. Witches lead lives of empowerment and celebration, of connection and sacred realities. We are journeyers, artists, crafters, and Nature folk. We share in a blessing that has been viciously torn from us time and time again and flung into a burning bush to become the ash of an age-old era of superstition; but we know better. No one can defeat or suppress what is innate within the soul, for it would simply find other portals of expression, and it has done so countless times before.

We are magickal and spiritual creatures; once we learn to accept this reality, we become the better for it. Magick is not so much a process or technique of changing consciousness and fulfilling desires, it is a sacred principle that defies the rigid logic imposed on our society by the patriarchal, unfeeling, nonreceptive paradigm.

Witchcraft is intuitive, experiential, transformative, and evolutionary. Though its heart will remain eternally timeless, we Witches know that through any age and at any time we are able to connect, to destroy the illusion of separation, and to achieve enlightenment. We come to the Great Mystery, and here it is that we are initiated.

## As a Pagan ...

In my graduating year of high school, my ancient history class was studying a unit on religion, and during one class we mapped out a chronology from the earliest signs of "religious" instinct to the present day. When my teacher asked us what was generally considered to be the oldest religion by history scholars, I raised my hand in earnest. When chosen, I replied, "Paganism." My teacher nodded, adding that it could also be called animism. The majority of people today dismiss things like animism and Paganism as relics of the past; however, they are extremely relevant to this day and age.

NeoPaganism, which has been the focus of this book, is a conflicting term for many people. Many believe that it is a useless and contradictory word that merely brings confusion to an already confused set of spiritual traditions. Those who hold this opinion generally have well-rounded and articulated reasons for their argument, something along the lines of, "Paganism has never been and is not today an unchanging, conservative fossil; it is on the frontier of change! There is no reason to suggest that what we do today differs in any essential sense from what was happening thousands of years ago when our ancestors lived." I think, however, that the correct reasoning behind adopting the term NeoPaganism for our community today lies in the simple truth that many things about our spirituality, its exoteric forms and symbols, have been resurrected and revived in a new light.

Many of us are not attached to any intact Pagan survival or lineage other than through successive past lives and inborn spiritual predispositions. For instance, in my coven we all share common past-life experiences (of having been involved in spiritual communities as priests and priestesses, shamans and seers, etc.), and we are also connected through our work with the Greening, which we believe to be a sacred charge. The majority of us come from either nominally Christian or agnostic backgrounds (atheism and Hinduism seem to be the exceptions). There are simply too many fey souls nowadays waiting for an incarnation and not enough Pagan families to be born into.

NeoPaganism is a global phenomenon; Paganism is a global reality and certainty. We have come forth from the shadows into something new and bright, but we have not quit the night for the day, for we hold both to be sacred and necessary. Paganism's popularity is nothing new, for it is pre-Christian and was once ubiquitous; we have simply fused the old with the new, producing something dynamic that resonates with countless people the world over.

As Pagans, we have much to offer the global community. We are, generally speaking, eco-conscious, politically liberated, spiritually empowered, and integral thinkers with streaks of individuality and social flair. What does this say about the reality of our spirituality in a modern context—about its power and its privilege? Are we set apart because we are privy to an underlying flow and rhythm that infuses all of life? Are we special; are we different? How does one distinguish oneself as Pagan, and what does that truly mean?

### As a Youth...

Of the three spoken above, I can attest to belonging to each. I am priest to my gods and to my coven, I am a Witch in all I know, and I am Pagan-born, a wild child of Nature. I can then also admit to being of the youth, a delicate yet stringent category that demands from its adherents devotion to a strange paradox of work and whimsy, of passion and profession. With one foot firmly placed in the lucid land of misadventure and another dangling in the realm of rudimentary rites of passage and responsibility, we are neither bound nor free. We stand at the threshold of initiation; however, it is our choice to accept the status quo or to walk away unheard of, unseen beyond the perfectly trimmed hedges surrounding suburbia.

As the youth, there is no denying that we possess an edge—a clarity by which we glisten in the light of the new day. We are highly opinionated, with zealous cries abounding in righteousness and temperamental fervour. Youth is a moment captured; a fleeting procession of memories against a grey horizon. But instilled within its depths hides potent energy, prepared to rise to the occasion and imbue the individual with power and confidence. This, of course, is of utmost importance in the raising of power that is customary to many, if not all, Pagan rites. After all, we are an ecstatic and transformative group of people!

As the current incarnation of youth, we are also the emissaries for the future, and we must begin to make our mark if we are to create the change we wish to see in the world. We must champion the earth and work for peace among the tribes. The prophecies of many will come to pass, and we must prepare for the tremendous field of potential we will encounter. It is here we will reap what we sow.

The Wyrd Web is vibrating higher, keening tones each day, and like blue fire it strikes at the heartwaves, causing intuitive palpitations. Where are we going? Who are we? What are we? What is this power that we can and must raise?

## Power & Privilege

One of the most highly regarded members of the global Pagan community is undoubtedly Starhawk. With the publication of *The Spiral Dance* in 1979, she displayed such poetic flair and warmth of spirit that it was hard not to fall in love with her and her writings immediately. In saying this, I was born after 1979, and *The Spiral Dance* was not one of the first books I read on Paganism. However, when I did finally manage to get my hands on it, any expectations I had were dashed by the immense beauty and grace that arose from the words. Every sentence was a thread of pure Magick woven by a priestess who was not only well-versed in her Craft but also had depth of insight, passion, and integrity. Starhawk also articulated the concept of power and how we relate to it best of all through power-over, power-from-within, and power-with. The former is, of course, the paradigm that produced the rigid, logos-loving, authoritarian culture of society today. The latter two are essentially Pagan in that they speak of the power that stems from the autonomy of the individual and our harmonious connections with other beings in the cosmos. As the Pagan traditions are earth-based and pluralistic, the concept of wielding one's power over another aspect of the divine whole is a foreign one.

Earlier on in this chapter is one of my poems, "The Age of Anarchy." I wrote it at a time in my life when I was extremely antagonistic towards any form of authority. During this time I was also collaborating with a Pagan friend living in Italy concerning something we called "The Revival," which represented to us the very essence of Paganism and, more specifically, Witchcraft. The ideas of freedom and empowerment and turning back the tide of tyranny and oppression were central. Much of the inspiration seemed to stem subconsciously from the Stregheria teachings concerning their prophetess Aradia and her mother, Diana. The famous Charge of the Goddess reveals to us (as is done in the way of drawing down) that we are to be free, and as a sign of our freedom we are to be naked in our rites. Interestingly, at my coven's pre-Lughnasadh circle in '07 (falling on a full moon night), our crescent-crowned Goddess was drawn down into my body, and as usually happens I was moved to speak and move by the deity. The Goddess seemed to speak a semblance of the Charge through me, giving especial emphasis to the nakedness as a symbol of freedom. None of us thought much of it after the circle, however at Lughnasadh, without even realising, we began to slowly strip until we were completely naked with each other, something we had never done before.

Once liberated from the shackles of a life-rejecting philosophy, we are free to embrace life as it is, in all its power and privilege. Life is a gift, one that we cannot return without dire consequences. We must not forsake the charge to fulfil our individual destinies and to add to the myriad colours that are the wellspring of our unconscious. Perhaps when old Gerald spoke of clothes as being inhibitors of the natural life force that flows from the body, he was also alluding to the concept that the power within each of us will only come forth when we have dispensed with the illusions of a society that seeks to mask our inner realities and truths from the megalomaniac macrocosm that is Western civilisation. Therefore, power-from-within is a journey from isolation to connection, and in so doing we reveal the divinity within and choose to embrace it for the betterment of oneself, the community, and the cosmos. Power-with is something else altogether.

In an animistic culture such as ours, there is no denying that the interconnection of life is one of our most sacred principles. As Pagans, we are each intimately aware of the relationships between ourselves and other beings.

Totemism in indigenous cultures is one example of animistic spirituality, and this has filtered down into the modern traditions of the Craft as the relationship between the Witch and her familiar. Shamanistic influences have, of course, revived the practice of seeking out one's totem, or power, animal, though whether this has become the substitute for the Witch's familiar is a question of choice, varying from person to person.

Many Pagans today are also fans of the Standing Ones, the tree folk and the plethora of plant spirits that co-inhabit this world. Some choose to focus solely on the plant kingdom and weave connections infused with the green power of the earth. Darkness, moisture, contraction, and feminine mystery punctuated by the dance of the Lord of Life—this is the truth of all that dies only to rise again; the sun that goes into the seed.

Power-with is the term Starhawk uses to describe the Pagan affinity with the natural world and the strands of power that are woven between us all. In the Craft, we draw on these strands to send vibrations out into the cosmos so that we may sow our own seeds and prosper from their yield. We also reflect on the internal microcosmic reality in which the essence of the macrocosm also dwells. It is here we face our Shadow, the repressed Self that has sought refuge in our darkest corner. The Shadow contains within itself all that we as individuals seek to be rid of—all that the ego detests as abominable to the persona.

It was Carl Jung who articulated this psychological process and called the journey of attaining to the ideal wholeness *individuation*. As we work towards integrated, spiritual wholeness, it is possible to forge connections between all the essential fragments that comprise the sum and create a synergy to empower and balance the parts. Ultimately we are enlightened to the inherent unity infusing the Self, and that this unity is of the same essence that underlies all things. The substance of this essence is known as Magick to Witches, and it is a secret that we hold dear and close to our hearts. The secret is by its nature sacred, and if abused there is much to answer for. This is our power, and this is our privilege.

## SONG OF THE YOUTH / WEAVING THE WEB

*We are the flow, we are the ebb*
*We are the weavers, we are the web;*
*She is the needle, we are the thread*
*She is the Weaver, we are the web.*
—Shekhinah Mountainwater

In the Coven of the WildWood, one of our principle deities is the Weaver, and she is the first invoked. She is the gossamer thread of the Otherworld that weaves its way into the heartstrings of all those of the old ways. She is the flow, she is the ebb; she is the Weaver, she is the web!

When we invoke her—when we call her forth and honour her paradox of transcendence and immanence—we come to the core, the spiral, the origin. We see not a spot to be marked and remembered but a threshold into a mystery, and the spiral path goes on. A graceful unfolding of shining power, the light is hidden within the shadow; the sun is but a fleeting flash over the sea of darkness.

The womb is eternal, and yet she knows not to keep us within her sanctuary for too long at a time, underdeveloped and yearning for selfhood. We are released with the ancient Charge in our veins. It is this desire to be free that is called the Dance of the Lord of Life. It is he who is born with the ancient sun at the dawn. It is he who frolics wildly across the ashes of the dead, beating the bounds and calling up the old spiral-ways so that the great Earth Mother may be revitalised and re-membered. His dance is spirited, and as he dances, he sings to add power, to aid rhythm, to keep the beat; this is his Song of the Youth.

Sent forth from the womb, given strong new bodies to complete our earth "walk" ... I'd much rather dance—dance through death into rebirth.

## DANCE OF LIFE, SONG OF YOUTH RITUAL

This ritual is designed to be performed not only by the youth (in terms of the conventional age categories) but by all of those who are spirited and who yearn to be free.

We were given these bodies to honour and celebrate, not to desecrate and destroy. We all fall under the shroud of age, but we can choose to dance on or to be dragged kicking and screaming by the gleaming scythe of Death. Invoke the Spirit, the Quintessence, the Heart and Truth, and take it in completely. Let it infuse your every fibre with vibrating power. Become as you are. Become your divinity. Dance life and sing youth. Blessed be!

You will need:

> A coven / grove / circle / temple / group of
>   like-minded individuals
> A representation of the axis mundi (e.g.,
>   a maypole, tree, or besom)
> Blessing oil (a combination of sandalwood,
>   rose and frankincense)
> Personal offerings
> A drum, rattle, or other rhythm-keeper
> A chalice filled with fruit juice or water

The space is demarcated and made sacred in the eyes of the participants. You may choose to cast a circle, acknowledge the ancient Celtic trinity (land, sky, and sea), smudge, or whatever you prefer. The participants should then link hands, if this has not already been done, and the connection between everyone should be reaffirmed through the opening of both inner and outer senses.

The representation of the axis mundi is placed in the centre of the circle, and beginning in the east, one by one deosil, each participant will go forth and kneel before the axis mundi to receive the universal blessing, followed by the giving up of personal offerings. As this is happening, a preappointed individual should be drumming a simple beat to maintain a level of energy and to enhance focus. After all have received their blessings and given their offerings at the axis mundi, the blessing with oil will begin (once again deosil and beginning in the east).

With the blessing oil, anoint the person next to you with the index finger of your power hand. It is best to anoint on the forehead, just below the crown. You may choose to use the spiral or wheel of life motif. You may also recite the following whilst doing so:

> *Thou art blessed by the inner and the outer, by the spiral and the sun-wheel of Life, in the name of the axis mundi, our centre and continuum. By the light of the divine, before these, your friends and family, I bless you with this pure oil. Spirited, blessed be.*

Once this cycle of blessing has been completed, hands are linked again to begin the raising of power. The circle should begin to move slowly deosil. The feet should follow the general pattern of the circle-dance, with the leading foot stepping first (either to the right or the left, depending on the hemisphere and using the respective foot). For example, in the Southern Hemisphere where our deosil is anticlockwise, we begin with our right foot, followed by the left foot stepping behind it, and then the right foot moves to the side again and the left foot steps in front of it. The pattern is repeated. Once you have been around the circle at least once, you should be familiar enough with the pattern to speed it up. As you dance, you may choose to sing the following:

> *Dance the rhythm, dance the beat*
> *Tread the circle, pound the feet*
> *Sing the song of youth around*
> *Feel our power, hear our sound!*

As the power begins to peak, the dancers should send out astral ribbons to the axis mundi and imagine ascending up the World Tree into a sky of pure white light. Faster and higher the circle goes until there is a peaceful vibration felt by all. At this point, the energy should be released and the word "Spirited!" shouted by the group to seal the rite.

To ground, the participants should sit down and share the chalice of juice or water, offering words of wisdom and encouraging anecdotes, whimsical adventures, or renewed vigour and promise for the future. This should be a time to share the Spirit with each other, to connect intimately in sacred space and to truly evoke the passion and power of Paganism in ritual. This is the Song of the Youth.

## Last Words: An Open Letter to the Global Pagan Community

For a while, I was disillusioned with the somewhat misleading concept of "Pagan community." In my time as an actively interactive Pagan in my area, I have been witness to both miracle and madness. There seems to be an underlying fear that unity implies dogmatic structure that we must all yield to or else! But we must learn, as have many inherent subcultures that exist within the greater matrix known simply as "society," to uphold one's personal convictions no matter how adverse the mainstream current is. We must realise that "community" in Paganism is an innately tribal concept arising from the first stirrings of human consciousness. We come together to celebrate the ancient mysteries rather than perpetuate an egocentricity centred on gratifying one another all in the name of sensationalist glamour.

We are a spirited culture; one full of youthful flair and age-old wisdom. We are a paradox and tread the holy way between light and dark. We are the crafters and the Nature folk, never forgetting that divine powers exist within the world, permeating every layer. We are no more important than the single-celled amoeba and no less important than the farthest star. Our thoughts and feelings are focussed on rhythm, pattern, insight, evolution, and transformation. We are inclined to deepening awareness through the medium of myth, seeking balance and wholeness through ritual and sacred action. We are Pagan.

As the earth stirs beneath us and as the ancient trinity of land, sky, and sea make their warnings clear, the power of the Greening grows. In my coven, we have a blessing: "May the WildWood flourish in our hearts and minds forever." The WildWood is our sacred heartland, the realm we are tied to, though it definitely does not exclusively belong to our coven.

The WildWood is an ancient place of sovereignty and power. It is of no fixed morality, meaning that it is not a paradise reached through salvation like the Christian heaven, nor is it a hellish region. It is beautiful, striking, raw, and mysterious. It is the primal reality underlying what once was, or rather the state of earth before the cancerous wave of a corrupted humanity destroyed Gaia's green carpet.

Just as the WildWood flourishes in our hearts and minds, so does the youth. It is forever instilled within the nostalgia of all who have lived and all who will come. We often forget that experience and wisdom (and the physical process of aging itself) do not necessarily connote barrenness of spirit or the fertility of the mind. Youth is eternal. It is the spiral inward and the flourish outward. It is celebration of Life. It is the cycle, the change, and the circle.

I sometimes wonder how, in years to come, the inhabitants of this earth will experience and embrace Life, and I somehow think that maybe Life will be taken to mean any one of many things. These many things, all being simultaneously valid, will arise from freedom of (the) Spirit and freedom to do as thou wilt. The world will not constrict the voyage of the soul, and it will not divert or deplete the flow of vitality, effervescence, and inspiration in the name of authority, power-over, and tyranny. The Greening will flourish, and all will herald its coming. Nature will be honoured, and those who choose to will know the great intimacies of its purpose. The gods will be united not as "One" under a single banner but as expressions of and denizens of Life. Those of the future will understand and accept the passages of Life, the sacred rites that come to pass, and death will not be feared but revered. The elders will know the youths, and they in turn will know the elders, and a stronghold of wisdom, initiation, experience, and energy will be forged in the heartland of the world. But if this vision does not come to pass, it will be the fault of those who stood aside passively, allowing the world's destruction to spread like wildfire and consume all that is sacred, all that is as it is because it is meant to be.

My words of wisdom? My advice? All that I can offer from my experience as a priest and Witch in this incarnation is this: Know your truth. Walk it. Never run from your Shadow. Do not refuse an experience that will ultimately enrich and empower your Self. Grow inward, outward, upward, downward, and in any direction you can conceive of. Magick is power; power is neutral. An ye harm none, do what ye will. Never say believe, simply experience and feel. Do not submit to ways of thinking that are against the way of your heart. Love and be loved; you are worthy of it. Celebrate Life; never stop. Give and receive, in equal measure. Know the consequences of your actions and accept responsibility for them. Rise above evil, for there is no such thing. Pray unto the gods; they are listening, and they will answer. Cherish your friends and family; they are each a part of the Great Mystery's yearning to remember, know, and love again. Sing and dance the rhythm of Life; perpetuate it and nourish it wherever you go. Share with others who would wish to share with you. Make mistakes, and do it with honesty. Question always; it will only expand your consciousness. Lie down on the earth and let your heartbeats be at one. Pour a libation upon her breast and know you have just quenched your own thirst. Know all is connected; not one thing is separate from the whole. Be kind, be well, be wise. You are divine. You are spirited.

Blessed be, my brothers and sisters.

## Charge of the Power of Youth

Begin at the centre, the core and the heart
Inside the Earth and never apart
Nourish the mind, enflame the soul
Whisper the secrets, the body is whole

Feel the power growing, the serpent aroused
She is now feeding on all that allows
Her to strike rhythm and dance out the beat
Of force that is vigour and vigour is sweet

Elixir of Life, Fountain of Youth
Lead the veiled seeker to the Book of Truth
Turn each page ancient, gnarled oaken bark
Draw down the Gods, reveal the mark

Magick in climax, peaking in light
Twin pillars flank the black and the white
Children are laughing, worry not is their cry
Ascend into realms of azure blue skies

Walk the round circle, call up the power
Feel the World Tree, the trembling Tower
It shakes and is struck by the dagger of fire
Blue shards ignite the spheres upon higher

Spiral-dance deeper, into the dark womb
Bright-Silver Weaver is spinning her loom
Chaos complete, undying abyss
Comes to the charge of the fivefold kiss

Thou art divine, comes the Old Ones' call
Throbbing pulse enraptures the All
Stillness is fleeting and silence is here
Banish the blackened bruises of fear

Live to let live, perish in naught
But the light of the flame after which has been sought;
Tide turning inward, tide waxing near
The Power of Youth! The power is here!

Khaire, sláinte & blessed be,
Eilan/Gede

APPENDIX

## Recommended Resources

*Books*

**Deity**

Beth, R. *Lamp of the Goddess*. USA: Weiser, 1995.

Harrow, J. *Devoted to You*. USA: Citadel Press, 2003.

Pollack, R. *The Body of the Goddess*. UK: Vega, 2003.

Stein, C. *Persephone Unveiled: Seeing the Goddess & Freeing Your Soul*. USA: North Atlantic Books, 2006.

**Fiction**

Bird, I. *Circle of Three* Series. USA: Avon Books, 2001, 2002.

Bradley, M. *The Firebrand*. USA: Roc, 2003.

———. *The Forest House*. UK: Penguin Group, 1995.

———. *Lady of Avalon*. UK: Penguin Group, 1997.

———. *The Mists of Avalon*. England, Penguin Group, 1993.

————. *Priestess of Avalon*. USA: Roc, 2002.

Coelho, P. *The Witch of Portobello*. USA: Harper Perrenial, 2007.

de Angeles, L. *The Quickening*. USA: Llewellyn, 2005.

————. *The Shining Isle*. USA: Llewellyn, 2006.

de Lint, C. *Forests of the Heart*. USA: Tor Books, 2000.

Gardner, G. *High Magic's Aid*. UK: Michael Houghton, 1993.

Lamb, C. *Brigid's Charge*. USA: Bay Island Books, 1997.

Pennicott, J. *Circle of Nine* Trilogy. Australia: Simon & Schuster, 2001, 2004.

Santer, L. *Professor Midnight*. Australia: Zeus Publications, 2005.

Starhawk. *The Fifth Sacred Thing*. USA: Bantam, 1994.

## Paganism

Adler, M. *Drawing Down the Moon*. USA: Penguin Group, 2006.

Bates, B. *The Way of Wyrd*. USA: Hay House, 2005.

Bonewits, I. *The Pagan Man: Priests, Warriors, Hunters, and Drummers*. USA: Citadel Press, 2005.

Day, J. *Patchwork of Magic*. UK: Capall Bann, 1995.

de Angeles, L. *Pagan Visions for a Sustainable Future*. USA: Llewellyn, 2005.

Digitalis, R. *Goth Craft: The Magickal Side of Dark Culture*. USA: Llewellyn, 2007.

Godwin, D. *Light in Extension: Greek Magic from Homer to Modern Times*. USA: Llewellyn, 1992.

Jones, P. *Voices from the Circle*. UK: Aquarian Press, 1990.

Kalder, R., and T. Schwartzstein. *The Urban Primitive*. USA: Llewellyn, 2002.

Orr, E. R. *Spirits of the Sacred Grove*. UK: Thorsons, 1998.

Roads, M. J. *Journey into Nature: A Spiritual Adventure*. USA: H. J. Kramer Inc., 1990.

Starhawk. *The Earth Path*. USA: HarperSanFrancisco, 2005.

————. *Truth or Dare*. USA: HarperOne, 1989.

Telesco, P. *Cakes and Ale for the Pagan Soul*. USA: The Crossing Press, 2005.

Wildman, L. *Celebrating the Pagan Soul*. USA: Citadel Press, 2005.

Wood, R. *The Great Work*. Australia: Conjunction Press, 2006.

## Witchcraft & Wicca

Beth, R. *Hedge Witch*. UK: Hale, 1990.

Bourne, L. *Witch Amongst Us: The Autobiography of a Witch*. UK: Robert Hale, 1995.

Coombes, M., and D. Ganchingco. *Feelin' Witchy*. Australia: CG Publishing, 2004.

Crowley, V. *Wicca: The Old Religion in the New Millennium*. UK: Element Books Ltd., 1996.

Cunningham, S. *Living Wicca*. USA: Llewellyn, 2002.

———. *Wicca: A Guide for the Solitary Practitioner*. USA: Llewellyn, 1988.

Curott, P. *Book of Shadows*. USA: Broadway, 1999.

———. *Witch Crafting*. USA: Broadway, 2002.

de Angeles, L. *When I See the Wild God*. USA: Llewellyn, 2004.

———. *Witchcraft: Theory and Practice*. USA: Llewellyn, 2000.

Dugan, E. *Elements of Witchcraft*. USA: Llewellyn, 2003.

Farrar, J., S. Farrar, and G. Bone. *The Healing Craft: Healing Practices for Witches and Pagans*. USA: Phoenix Publishing, 1999.

Farrar, J. and G. Bone. *Progressive Witchcraft*. USA: New Page Books, 2003.

Farrar, J. and S. Farrar. *A Witches' Bible*. USA: Phoenix Publishing, 1996.

Farrar, S. *What Witches Do*. USA: Phoenix Publishing, 1983.

Gardner, G. *The Meaning of Witchcraft*. Canada: Weiser, 2004.

Geddes-Ward, A. & N. *Faeriecraft: Treading the Path of Faerie Magic*. USA: Hay House, 2005.

Grimassi, R. *The Wiccan Mysteries*. USA: Llewellyn, 2002.

———. *Italian Witchcraft*. USA: Llewellyn, 2000.

Gwyn. *Light from the Shadows: A Mythos of Modern Traditional Witchcraft*. UK: Capall Bann, 1999.

Heselton, P. *Gerald Gardner and the Cauldron of Inspiration*. UK: Capall Bann, 2003.

Hutton, R. *The Triumph of the Moon*. UK: Oxford University Press, 2001.

Johnson, K. *Witchcraft and the Shamanic Journey*. USA: Llewellyn, 1998.

Lamond, F. *Fifty Years of Wicca*. UK: Green Magic, 2004.

Leland, C. *Aradia: Gospel of the Witches*. Hong Kong: Phoenix Publishing, 1996.

Palin, P. *Craft of the Wild Witch*. USA: Llewellyn, 2004.

Penczak, C. *The Temple of Shamanic Witchcraft*. USA: Llewellyn, 2006.

———. *The Witch's Shield: Protection Magick and Psychic Self-Defense*. USA: Llewellyn, 2004.

Polson, W. *The Veil's Edge: Exploring the Boundaries of Magic*. USA: Citadel Press, 2003.

Rain, G. *Confessions of a Teenage Witch: Celebrating the Wiccan Life*. USA: Perigee, Penguin Group, 2005.

Starhawk. *The Spiral Dance*. USA: HarperOne, 1999.

Valiente, D. *The Rebirth of Witchcraft*. UK: Robert Hale, 2008.

———. *Witchcraft for Tomorrow*. USA: Phoenix Publishing, 1978.

*Internet*

**Church of All Worlds (CAW)**—www.caw.org (The official website for the international Church of All Worlds. CAW was founded in the 1960s by Oberon Zell-Ravenheart [then Tim Zell] and Lance Christie. Much of its philosophy was inspired by Robert Heinlein's novel *Stranger in a Strange Land*, which is to this day read and recommended by CAW members globally. I am a member and seeker of the Church of All Worlds Australia, and we can be reached at www.caw.org.au.)

**Copper Moon E-zine**—www.copper-moon.com (Copper Moon E-zine is a "Witch's publication for teens and early twenties." It was created by Gwinevere Rain, the author of *Confessions of a Teenage Witch* and *Spellcraft for Teens*. It is regularly updated with articles, rituals, reviews, and other Pagan miscellany and has a gifted team of writers.)

**Coven of the WildWood**—www.members.optusnet.com.au/wildwoodcoven (My coven's website. It has information about who we are, what we do, our upcoming open events and circles, members of the coven (Children of the WildWood, Aspirants, Dedicants, Initiates/Priesthood), and ritual photographs. For more photos and

online interaction, add us on myspace: www.myspace.com/coven
ofthewildwood.)

**Esoterica Bichaunt**—http://esoterica.bichaunt.org/ (Eran, the author
of the website, is a knowledgeable and level-headed Gardnerian
Witch, and his arguments for Witchcraft history are both alluring
and convincing.)

**Gede Parma**—www.gedeparma.com (My website! Enough said.)

**Magick TV (Living the Wiccan Life)**—www.magicktv.com (A side-
project of the Correllian Nativist Tradition. Rev. Don Lewis is the
host of the show and conducts many fascinating interviews with not
only Pagan authors, but Pagans in general!)

**Pagan Awareness Network (Australia)**—www.paganawareness.net
.au (An amazing network of Australian Pagans. PAN, as it is known
in Australia, is one of the largest Pagan organisations in Australia
and was founded by David Garland, the current president. They run
several events each year and publish and circulate the *Small Tapestry*. Various state-committees also hold open full moon circles each
month, which are vigorously attended.)

**Sannion's Sanctuary**—www.winterscapes.com/sannion/ (Sannion is a
proud, outspoken Hellenic reconstructionist and delivers interesting
and insightful essays and articles on various Pagan topics.)

**Spellcraft Magazine**—www.spellcraft.com.au (*Spellcraft* is Australia's
leading Pagan magazine and has a readership of over 15,000 people.
It comes out quarterly with the seasons and is host to a vast array of
information on Magick, Witchcraft, and Paganism.)

**Wicca: For the Rest of Us**—www.wicca.timerift.net (For thinking Wiccans who are serious about their religion. However, I do not fully
endorse the entire site's content, especially what is targeted at certain
authors.)

**The Wiccan/Pagan Times**—www.twpt.com (The Wiccan/Pagan
Times is an online community resource that provides Pagan stories
and articles, insightful interviews, and news/reviews of upcoming
books and authors.)

**Witchvox**—www.witchvox.com (An extensive global resource that allows Pagans worldwide to come together and pool our energies.)

**Young Tree Grove**—www.youngtreegrove.org (An amazing American Pagan activist organisation that helps Pagan teens and their families to become more acquainted with the Pagan community at large.)

SELECTED
BIBLIOGRAPHY

## Books

Adler, M. *Drawing Down the Moon*. USA: Penguin, 2006.

Altman, J. *1001 Dreams: An Illustrated Guide to Dreams and Their Meanings*. UK: Duncan Baird Publishers, 2002.

Armstrong, K. *A History of God*. UK: Vintage, 1993.

Bird, I. *Making the Saint* (Circle of Three). USA: HarperCollins, 2001.

———. *Written in the Stars* (Circle of Three). USA: HarperCollins, 2001.

Buxton, R. *The Complete World of Greek Mythology*. UK: Thames & Hudson, 2004.

Cunningham, S. *Wicca: A Guide for the Solitary Practitioner*. USA: Llewellyn, 1988.

Drew, A. J. *Wicca for Couples: Making Magick Together*. USA: New Page Books, 2002.

Gardner, G. *The Meaning of Witchcraft*. USA: Weiser, 2004.

Garret, D. *The Cambridge Companion to Spinoza*. USA: University of Cambridge, 1996.

Glover, E. *Freud or Jung*. UK: George Allen and Unwin Ltd., 1950.

Hinnels, J. *Dictionary of Religion (Expanded New Edition)*. UK: Penguin Books, 1997.

K, Amber. *Covencraft: Witchcraft for Three or More*. USA: LLewellyn, 2002.

Leland, Charles G. *Aradia: Gospel of the Witches*. USA: Phoenix Publishing, Inc., 1996.

McLynn, F. *Carl Gustav Jung: A Biography*. UK: Black Swan Books, 1997.

Odier, D. *Tantric Quest: An Encounter with Absolute Love*. USA: Bantam, 1997.

Pearson, C. *The Hero Within: Six Archetypes We Live By (Expanded Edition)*. USA: HarperCollins, 1989.

Schroeder, Gerald L. *The Hidden Face of God: Science Reveals the Ultimate Truth*. USA: Free Press, 2001.

Streeter, M. *Witchcraft: A Secret History*. USA: Fair Winds Press, 2002.

Winston, D. *Wide Awake: A Buddhist Guide for Teens*. USA: Perigee Trade, 2003.

## INTERNET

Coughlin, John. J. "The Wiccan Rede: A Historical Journey, Part 3: Eight Words." <http://www.waningmoon.com/ethics/rede3.shtml> (accessed May 7, 2008).

Hefner, A. and V. Guimaraes. "Animism." <http://www.themystica .com/mystica/articles/a/animism/htm> (accessed October 23, 2007).

Meaden, T. "Elements of Pagan Belief in the Megalithic Age: Was Tara the Earth Goddess at Avebury?" <http://news.megalithic.co.uk/ article.php?sid=2146411660> (accessed October 14, 2007).

"Pantheism: The World Pantheist Movement." <http://www.pantheism .net/> (accessed May 7, 2008).

# INDEX

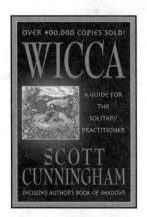

## WICCA
### *A Guide for the Solitary Practitioner*
### SCOTT CUNNINGHAM
*(Updated edition)*

Cunningham's classic introduction to Wicca is about how to live life magically, spiritually, and wholly attuned with nature. It is a book of sense and common sense, not only about magick, but about religion and one of the most critical issues of today: how to achieve the much needed and wholesome relationship with our Earth. Cunningham presents Wicca as it is today: a gentle, Earth-oriented religion dedicated to the goddess and god. *Wicca* also includes Scott Cunningham's own Book of Shadows and updated appendices of periodicals and occult suppliers.

978-0-9754-2118-6
6 x 9, 264 pp., illustrations          $12.95

## LIVING WICCA
*A Further Guide for the Solitary Practitioner*
### SCOTT CUNNINGHAM

*Living Wicca* is for those who have made the conscious decision to bring their Wiccan spirituality into their everyday lives. It provides solitary practitioners with the tools and added insights that will help them blaze their own spiritual paths—to become their own high priests and priestesses.

*Living Wicca* takes a philosophical look at the questions, practices, and differences within Witchcraft. It covers the various tools of learning available to the practitioner, the importance of secrecy in one's practice, guidelines to performing ritual when ill, magical names, initiation, and the Mysteries. It discusses the benefits of daily prayer and meditation, making offerings to the gods, how to develop a prayerful attitude, and how to perform Wiccan rites when away from home or in emergency situations.

Unlike any other book on the subject, *Living Wicca* is a step-by-step guide to creating your own Wiccan tradition and personal vision of the gods, designing your personal ritual and symbols, developing your own book of shadows, and truly living your Craft.

**978-0-8754-2184-1**
**6 x 9, 208 pp., illustrations**      **$12.95**

## Beyond 2012
### *A Shaman's Call to Personal Change and the Transformation of Global Consciousness*
#### James Endredy

War, catastrophic geologic events, Armageddon . . . The prophecies surrounding 2012—the end of the Mayan calendar—aren't pretty. James Endredy pierces the doom and gloom with hope and a positive, hopeful message for humankind.

For wisdom and guidance concerning this significant date, Endredy consults Tataiwari (Grandfather Fire) and Nakawe (Grandmother Growth)—the "First Shamans." Recorded here is their fascinating dialog. They reveal how the evolution of human consciousness, sustaining the earth, and our personal happiness are all interconnected.

Discover what you can do to spur the transformation of human consciousness. See how connecting with our true selves, daily acts of compassion and love, focusing personal energy, and even gardening can make a difference. Endredy also shares shamanistic techniques to revive the health of our planet . . . and ourselves.

978-0-7387-1158-4
7½ x 9⅛, 240 pp.          $16.95

TO ORDER, CALL 1-877-NEW-WRLD
*Prices subject to change without notice*
Order at Llewellyn.com 24 hours a day, 7 days a week!

## SOLITARY WITCH
*The Ultimate Book of Shadows*
*for the New Generation*
### SILVER RAVENWOLF

This book has everything a teen Witch could want and need between two covers: a magickal cookbook, encyclopedia, dictionary, and grimoire. It relates specifically to today's young adults and their concerns, yet is grounded in the magickal work of centuries past.

Information is arranged alphabetically and divided into five distinct categories: (1) Shadows of Religion and Mystery, (2) Shadows of Objects, (3) Shadows of Expertise and Proficiency, (4) Shadows of Magick and Enchantment, and (5) Shadows of Daily Life. It is organized so readers can skip over the parts they already know or read each section in alphabetical order.

978-0-7387-0319-0

8 x 10, 608 pp., 53 illustrations, appendices, index          $21.95

TO ORDER, CALL 1-877-NEW-WRLD
*Prices subject to change without notice*
Order at Llewellyn.com 24 hours a day, 7 days a week!

## ELEMENTS OF WITCHCRAFT
### Natural Magick for Teens
### ELLEN DUGAN

This is a teen primer on the theory, techniques, and tools of natural magick. Being a witch is not just about casting spells. It's also about magick—the magick of nature and of life. This book, by a veteran witch and mother of three teenagers, shows teens how natural magick is both quietly beautiful and unstoppably powerful, and how they can harness that energy to better their own lives.

The young seeker will be introduced to the theory of witchcraft, the God and the Goddess, and ethical considerations. There are elemental meditations, correspondence charts, nature spirit information, magickal herbalism, spells, and charms. Teens will also learn how to create their own magickal tools and altars with natural supplies, cast a circle, avoid magickal mistakes, and live a magickal life.

978-0-7387-0393-0
6 x 9, 288 pp., illustrations          $14.95

## SPELLCRAFT FOR TEENS
*A Magical Guide to Writing & Casting Spells*
GWINEVERE RAIN

Wiccan magick for teens written by a real teen witch!

Empower, bewitch, and enchant. Written by a teen witch with her own popular website, *SpellCraft for Teens* contains fifty-five chants and incantations. In addition, it provides a twelve-step guide to casting a magick circle, an in-depth look at the moon phases, and the magical properties of colors, herbs, and charms. From finding a craft name to performing the three types of love spells, *SpellCraft for Teens* addresses issues specific to young adults, including telling parents about their interest in Wicca and dealing with gossiping classmates.

978-0-7387-0225-4

7½ x 7½, 160 pp., illustrations, bibliography, glossary          $12.95

## COVEN CRAFT
*Witchcraft for Three or More*
### AMBER K

Here is the complete guidebook for anyone who desires to practice Witchcraft in a caring, challenging, well-organized spiritual support group: a coven. Whether you hope to learn more about this ancient spiritual path . . . are a coven member wanting more rewarding experiences in your group . . . are looking for a coven to join, or are thinking of starting one . . . or are a Wiccan elder gathering proven techniques and fresh ideas . . . this book is for you.

Amber K shares what she as learned about beginning and maintaining healthy covens in her twenty years as a Wiccan priestess. Learn what a coven is, how it works, and how you can make your coven experience more effective, enjoyable, and rewarding. Plus, get practical hands-on guidance in the form of sample articles of incorporation, Internet resources, sample by-laws, and sample budgets. Seventeen ritual scripts are also provided.

978-1-5671-8018-3
7 x 10, 480 pp., illustrations          $19.95

## True Magick
### *A Beginner's Guide*
#### Amber K

For fifteen years, Amber K's "little green book" has guided thousands down the life-changing path of magick. Selling more than 200,000 copies, *True Magick* has truly struck a chord with Witches, Pagans, and magicians around the world.

Presented here for the first time is the revised and expanded anniversary edition of *True Magick*. It features the same delightful introduction to the history and lore of magick, in addition to several varieties of magick, ranging from shamanism and Norse Magick to Voudun and Qabala. Amber K explains the basics, such as how to find or create ritual tools, establish a temple, plan a ritual, and cast spells safely and ethically. New material includes six more chapters, recommending reading for each chapter, and more than 100 added exercises.

978-0-7387-0823-2
6 x 9, 360 pp., glossary, suggested reading, appendices     $12.95

## To Write to the Author

If you wish to contact the author or would like more information about this book, please write to the author in care of Llewellyn Worldwide and we will forward your request. Both the author and publisher appreciate hearing from you and learning of your enjoyment of this book and how it has helped you. Llewellyn Worldwide cannot guarantee that every letter written to the author can be answered, but all will be forwarded. Please write to:

Gede Parma
℅ Llewellyn Worldwide
2143 Wooddale Drive, Dept. 978-0-7387-1507-0
Woodbury, MN 55125-2989, U.S.A.

Please enclose a self-addressed stamped envelope for reply,
or $1.00 to cover costs. If outside U.S.A., enclose
international postal reply coupon.

Many of Llewellyn's authors have websites with additional information and resources. For more information, please visit our website at http://www.llewellyn.com.